PRAISE FOR THE SETH BOOKS

"The Seth books present an alternate map of reality with a new diagram of the psyche . . . useful to all explorers of consciousness."

— Deepak Chopra, M.D.
author of *The Seven Spiritual Laws of Success* and *Creating Affluence*

"Seth was one of my first metaphysical teachers. He remains a constant source of knowledge and inspiration in my life."

— Marianne Williamson
author of *A Return to Love*

"I would like to see the Seth books as required reading for anyone on their spiritual pathway. The amazing in-depth information in the Seth books is as relevant today as it was in the early '70s when Jane Roberts first channeled this material."

— Louise Hay
author of *You Can Heal Your Life*

"As you read Seth's words, you will gain more than just new ideas. Seth's energy comes through every page, energy that expands your consciousness and changes your thoughts about the nature of reality."

— Sanaya Roman
author of *Living with Joy*

"The Seth books were of great benefit to me on my spiritual journey and helped me to see another way of looking at the world."

— Gerald G. Jampolsky, M.D.
author of *Love is Letting Go of Fear*

"To my great surprise — and slight annoyance — I f
eloquently and lucidly articulated   at
only after great effort and an exte
phenomena and quantum physics.

— Mi
aut   *Universe* and
Beyond the Quantum

BOOKS BY JANE ROBERTS

The Bundu. A short novel in *The Magazine of Fantasy and Science Fiction* (March, 1958)

The Rebellers (1963)

How to Develop Your ESP Power (1966) (Also published as *The Coming of Seth*)

The Seth Material (1970)

Seth Speaks: The Eternal Validity of the Soul (1972)*

The Education of Oversoul Seven (1973)**

The Nature of Personal Reality. A Seth Book (1974)*

Adventures in Consciousness: An Introduction to Aspect Psychology (1975)

Dialogues of The Soul and Mortal Self in Time (1975)

Psychic Politics: An Aspect Psychology Book (1976)

The "Unknown" Reality. A Seth Book in two volumes (1977-1979)**

The World View of Paul Cézanne: A Psychic Interpretation (1977)

The Afterdeath Journal of an American Philosopher: The World View of William James (1978)

The Further Education of Oversoul Seven (1979)**

Emir's Education in the Proper Use of Magical Powers (1979)

The Nature of the Psyche: Its Human Expression. A Seth Book (1979)**

The Individual and the Nature of Mass Events. A Seth Book (1981)**

The God of Jane: A Psychic Manifesto (1981)

If We Live Again: Or, Public Magic and Private Love (1982)

Oversoul Seven and the Museum of Time (1984)

Dreams, "Evolution," and Value Fulfillment. A Seth Book in two volumes (1986)**

Seth, Dreams, and Projection of Consciousness (1986)

The Magical Approach: Seth Speaks About the Art of Creative Living (1995)

The Way Toward Health. A Seth Book (1997)

* New editions co-published by Amber-Allen / New World Library, 1994 and 1995.
** New editions published by Amber-Allen Publishing, 1995, 1996, and 1997.

Handwritten inscription:
6/22/97
To Tom —
Many Many
Thanks —
Rob

A
Seth
BOOK

DREAMS, "EVOLUTION," *and* VALUE FULFILLMENT

VOLUME ONE

Jane Roberts

NOTES AND COVER ART BY ROBERT F. BUTTS

AMBER-ALLEN PUBLISHING
SAN RAFAEL, CALIFORNIA

This book is dedicated to my husband, Robert F. Butts, for his love and devotion.

Published by Amber-Allen Publishing, Inc.
Post Office Box 6657
San Rafael, CA 94903

Cover Art: Robert F. Butts
Cover Design: Beth Hansen
Editorial: Janet Mills

Library of Congress Cataloging-in-Publication Data

Seth (Spirit)
    Dreams, "evolution," and value fulfillment / [channeled by] Jane
Roberts : notes and cover art by Robert F. Butts.
       p. cm. — (A Seth book)
    Originally published: New York : Prentice Hall, 1988, c1986.
    Includes index.
    ISBN 1-878424-27-0 (v. 1 : alk. paper). — ISBN 1-878424-28-9 (v. 2 : alk.
paper)
    1. Spirit writings. 2. Reincarnation — Miscellanea. I. Roberts, Jane,
1929–1984 II. Title. III. Series: Seth (Spirit). Seth book.
[BF1301.S374 1997]
133.9'3 — dc21   97-11965
                                                     CIP

ISBN 1-878424-27-0
Printed in U.S.A. on acid-free paper
Distributed by Publishers Group West

10 9 8 7 6 5 4 3 2 1

CONTENTS

QUOTATIONS FROM SETH

(A note by R.F.B.: The following quotations are from sessions Jane delivered for her trance personality, Seth, just before and during the time she worked with him on Dreams, "Evolution," and Value Fulfillment. One is from a private session, two are from "nonbook" regular sessions, and one is from Dreams itself.)

"Science has unfortunately bound up the minds of its own even most original thinkers, for they dare not stray from certain scientific principles. All energy contains consciousness (underlined). That one sentence is basically scientific heresy, and in many circles it is religious heresy as well. A recognition of that simple statement would indeed change your world."

—From a private session, July 12, 1979

"I feel sometimes as if I am expected to justify life's conditions, when of course they do not need any such justification."

—From Session 896, January 16, 1980

". . . basically, consciousness has nothing to do with size. If that were the case, it would take more than a world-sized globe to contain the consciousness of simply one cell"

—From Session 917, May 21, 1980, in Chapter 8 of Dreams

"It is a gift, a boon, an exquisite pleasure, to become physically alive on your functioning planet, couched securely within your dusk and dawn, your existence supported by the seasons and by an overall operation of spontaneous order."

—From Session 929, November 26, 1980

A POEM AND COMMENTARY
BY JANE ROBERTS

(Jane experienced many painful physical and psychological delays while producing Dreams. *Finally, she had only six sessions to go for the book when she came through with this material for herself:)*

"On Friday, October 23, 1981, I received the following message from Seth: 'Attend to what is directly before you. You have no responsibility to save the world or find the solutions to all problems—but to attend to your particular personal corner of the universe. As each person does that, the world saves itself.'
"The same day I wrote:

> *Dawn is breaking.*
> *Why should I lie in bed*
> *worrying about my body or the world?*
> *Before time was recorded*
> *dawn has followed dusk*
> *and all the creatures of the earth*
> *have been couched*
> *in the loving context*
> *of their times.*

"After writing the above poem I felt a sense of faith—and realized that like many I'd become afraid of faith itself. It was a fear hidden in my deepest aspects. . . ."

INTRODUCTORY ESSAYS
BY ROBERT F. BUTTS

August 12, 1982. Originally I'd planned to write the standard kind of introduction for *Dreams, "Evolution," and Value Fulfillment*. However, as I became involved in describing the complicated, emotionally charged series of events surrounding the hospitalization earlier this year of my wife, Jane Roberts, the material automatically began organizing itself into a series of dated essays. I was more than happy to follow this intuition from my creative self, for it answered many questions I'd started to consciously worry about.

We could have presented *Dreams* as is, or at least have avoided mentioning certain less-than-advantageous circumstances surrounding its production by Jane and by Seth, the "energy personality essence" she speaks for while in a trance or dissociated state. The facts are, though, that Jane's already impaired physical condition grew steadily worse while she was working on the book. Shortly after finishing it, she went into the hospital. Since we've always wanted to make sure that our "psychic work" is given within the context of our daily living, I've undertaken to present in these essays intensely personal material relevant to the creation of *Dreams*. (The mechanics of Jane's still-fascinating trance phenomenon have been described in some detail in the six previous Seth books she's produced—with my help—and they'll also be referred to, if briefly, in *Dreams*.)

I worked on the essays in succession, just as they're given here, although I found myself adding to the earlier ones as I moved into the later ones. In terms of length alone, it soon became obviously impossible to write all of the material for any piece on the date given. Even by going back over them, however, I couldn't discuss everything I wanted to: The essays could have easily grown into a book of their own. This weaving things together to make them "fit" is only natural for one of my temperament, but I didn't alter any of my original copy—that I'd have refused to do—and I kept intact those first spontaneous descriptions of the events attendant to Jane's physical difficulties, as well as our deep-seated, sometimes wrenching feelings connected to them. I did not look at Seth–Jane's *Dreams* itself while writing the essays, in order to avoid having them overly influenced by work in the book. Instead, we want all of this preliminary material to show how we live daily—regardless of how well we may or may not do—with a generalized knowledge of, and belief in, the Seth material.

Seth, then, has finished his work on *Dreams*. I wrote the original version of the notes for each book session as he delivered it through Jane, and also began collecting other notes and reference material that might be used. Since I've completed the essays, all I have to do now is "refine" the session notes (and addenda) as I type the finished manuscript. Jane will help as much as she can. We expect to have the book ready for our editors, Tam Mossman and Lynne Lumsden, by the end of the year.

Jane appreciates that the dates I'm always giving merely furnish a convenient framework for our material, but she's hardly enamored of such precise methodology; she understands that it's my way of doing things, realizes it's very useful, and goes on from there. I use a similar system in presenting all of the published Seth material. It has the great attribute of allowing for quick reference timewise (if not always by subject matter) to any of the more than 1,500 regular, private or deleted, and "ESP class" sessions Jane has given over the past 19 years—until July 1982, that is, when I began work on these passages.

Moreover, the choice of presenting the material in essay form proved to have one virtue that was more valuable than all the others combined: It allowed us to delve into the events I describe, and "our deep-seated, sometimes wrenching feelings connected to them," a little bit at a time. Those situations might have been too devastating for us otherwise, too emotionally threatening, too *charged* for us to present them with at least the minimum amount of objectivity required by the written word. Many of the events and feelings evoked such deep implications of trial and challenge for Jane and me that we were often left with strong feelings of unreality: This can't be happening to us. At our ages (52 and 62, Jane and I, respectively), why have we created lives with such nightmarish connotations? Why do I have to leave my dear wife alone in the hospital each night, so that I feel like crying for her when I go to bed by myself in the hill house? Why can't we be left alone to live lives of peace and creativity? And how many millions and millions of times through the ages have other human beings on this planet felt the same way—and will yet? Why are our lives ending like this, when we feel that simply getting through each day is an accomplishment?

That basic impetus toward survival came to take precedence over everything else. Indeed, for several weeks following the initiation of the challenges I relate in the essays, supposedly creative activities like writing books and painting pictures often faded into insignificance by comparison. And for me, Jane's condition came to stand for everything we don't know in our particular joint, chosen, probable earthly reality.

Yet, Jane and I *were* being creative with it all—the whole time —and moving several stages closer to understanding All That Is in the process. If we were often badly frightened, we also felt surges of grim elation (when we allowed them to surface) that we were survivors. We'd *chosen* the entire experience, which is still continuing, of course. "You make your own reality," Seth has told us innumerable times. We agree—and that is where Jane and I diverge most sharply from the conventional establishment belief that events happen *to* people, instead of being created *by* them.

The essay form gave us chances for at least a minimal study of the various forms our creative learning experiences have taken to date. We quickly agreed that we'd been setting up the illness syndrome for years, yet the deep emotional shocks accompanying its physical developments seemed to come at us like attacking dark birds zooming in from another probable reality. We learned. We adjusted in ways that a few weeks previously would have seemed unbelievable to us—and, ironically, as must often happen in such situations, once we'd moved into our new joint reality, it appeared that those particular challenges had always been incipient for us.

The essays contain many insights into the meanings the whole experience with illness has had for us, and will continue to have for many years. Our lives have been irrevocably changed—by choice—and not for the worse, either. Jane and I used our wills to intensify our focuses in certain areas. And I'm sure that as the reader works his or her way through the essays, it will become quite apparent that I wrote them just as much for Jane and me as I did for others—all in our ceaseless attempts to better understand, to grasp a bit more firmly, those mental and physical adventures that we're trying to delve into "this time around."

ESSAY 1
THURSDAY, APRIL 1, 1982

"Let my soul find shelter elsewhere."

That evocative, prophetic line is from a Sumari song that Jane sang to herself a few days before she went into an Elmira, New York, hospital on February 26, 1982. Sumari is a "language" she can speak or sing while in trance, and which she can translate into English if and when she wants to. She recorded her brief song in a sad, low-pitched, quavering voice that was like none I'd heard her use before. Its indescribable depth of feeling was remarkably prescient in light of the events in our lives that preceded—and then followed—the hospital experience that affected us so much.

Indeed, I didn't learn that Jane had made the tape until five weeks later, after she'd returned to our hill house from the hospital: I found it on March 30, amid others in her writing room. She hadn't labeled it, and I began to play it out of curiosity. The song's mournful tones swam heavily in the room. It reminded me at once of a dirge or an elegy, and I felt chills as I began to intuitively understand just how meaningful it was, even without any translation at all.

"Let my soul find shelter elsewhere," Jane said, by way of a quick translation when I played the tape for her a few minutes later. It was midafternoon on a cold day. She sat bundled up in her chair in the living room, her head down as she listened. I asked her for more on the song's interpretation, but she just repeated that line. She roused herself enough to stubbornly maintain that she'd give me more later. I knew at once that the tape's contents were so revealing of her feelings about her illness, so disturbing and frightening, that she couldn't bring herself to explore those deep emotions at that time. I also knew that my wife feared the effect of the message upon me—for what could the phrase she'd already given me mean, except that her soul had at least considered the *possibility* of leaving her physical body, perhaps to find shelter in a *nonphysical* realm? I accepted her reactions, and could only wait in some frustration as I began work on other parts of this essay.

As the days passed Jane kept putting me off about doing the translation, until finally I grew resentful and despairing at her refusal to cooperate. I decided to write around that one great line as best I could. For by then I knew that she had no intention of producing an English version: Some childlike and naive, yet deeply stubborn portion of her psyche, some "perverse area," as Seth, her trance personality, jokingly characterized it long ago, had simply taken over and decided not to do any more on that subject. For its own reasons it didn't want to, and that was it. I'd seen Jane operate in that fashion before, and I knew she'd have her way.

Lest I give an inaccurate picture of my wife, however, let me add that she combines instances of that seeming intransigence with a profound intuitive innocence before nature (and thus All That Is), and with a great literal acceptance of nature's manifestations and of her own being and creations within that framework. Although she's not entirely in agreement with me on this point, I think that essentially Jane is a mystic—not an easy thing to be in our extroverted, materialistic society, for it represents a way of life that's little understood these days. It's a role she's chosen for many reasons. Mysticism is still overwhelmingly regarded as a profoundly religious expression, and one that's hardly practical, but in my opinion neither of those situations applies to Jane. Her "mystical way" is reinforced by a strongly secretive characteristic that's usually belied by her seemingly outgoing character and behavior. It took me a long time to realize this. I also had to learn that her literal cast of mind grows directly out of her mysticism, and that because it does, she can be quite impulsive. There's nothing halfway about Jane. She's intensely loyal. She's a very perceptive person with many abilities, a fine intelligence, and an excellent critical sense. Whatever reservations she shows—her conscious inhibition of impulses, for example—are learned devices that are literally protective in nature. I've certainly found her particular combination of attributes to be unique, and I don't think she'd be able to express the Seth material as she does without them. Throughout these essays I hope to add many insights into her character. For now, though, I present what I have to work with from the saddest, most mournful Sumari song she's ever created and sung. The tape goes into our files, although I'd love to know what she said on the rest of it. . . .

In the meantime, two days after I discovered the tape, I asked Jane, "Do you want to have a session tonight?"

At first she didn't know. The question followed the little talk we'd had after supper. My back hurt somewhat. I'd finally decided that the ache wasn't because I'd been lifting her physically —all 82 pounds of her—but because of the medical bills we'd received today. (That had been my somewhat amused speculation to begin with.) We've gotten a flurry—a small *blizzard*—of bills from doctors during the last few days.

Jane has been home from the hospital since last Sunday, March 28. She spent 31 days there, being treated for a severely *under*active thyroid gland (hypothyroidism), protruding eyes and double vision, an almost total hearing loss, a slight anemia, and budding bedsores, or decubitus ulcers. Several of the ulcers had been incipient for a number of months, although neither of us had realized what those circles of reddening flesh meant as they slowly blossomed on the "pressure points" of her buttocks, coccyx, and right shoulder blade. Decubitus ulcers: one of the first terms we'd added to our rapidly growing medical vocabulary—and one of the more stubborn afflictions for a human being to get rid of once they've become established. Even now not all of Jane's decubiti have fully healed, although several of them have closed up nicely.

I should note, by the way, that her bedsores weren't infected when she went into the hospital, but *were* less than a week later. How come? "It's staph," several of the nurses told us. A sign warning of infection was put on the door of 3B9, Jane's room, and stayed there until she went home. "If the infection in that ulcer on your coccyx reaches the bone, it means at least a six-week stay in the hospital," exclaimed Jane's principal doctor, Rita Mandali (not her real name). Twice-daily treatments with hydrogen peroxide and a sulfadiazine cream were started. And I began to read up on how many kinds of staphylococcus bacteria alone there are, and indeed how common infections are in hospitals, since by their very nature those institutions are far from being the cleanest in town. . . .

Jane's hearing is much improved after treatment with decongestants and a pair of minor operations in which tiny drainage tubes were inserted through her eardrums—the procedure is called surery—to relieve internal blockage. Jane's thyroid gland, Dr. Mandali finally told her, has simply ceased functioning, so the doctor has begun a program of cautiously rejuvenating my wife's endocrine system, and thus all of her bodily processes, with a synthetic thyroid hormone in pill form (a low 50 micrograms to start). Jane is to take these pills for the rest of her life. At least that's the current prognosis. Her double vision is not as severe and is supposed to keep improving as the hormone takes effect. Dr. Mandali has prescribed drops to keep Jane's eyes lubricated, and a liquid salicylate medication (as a substitute for aspirin) to control joint pain and inflammation. Both of these products are taken four times a day. The increased glandular activity is also expected to have some beneficial effects upon Jane's arthritis, and possibly upon her anemia (a condition that often accompanies arthritis). I asked that she be tested for food allergies, since I'd read that reactions to various foods and additives can trigger arthritis, but Dr. Mandali said that "if Jane is allergic she (Jane) would know it"—a position I came to most thoroughly disagree with. But usually, I thought, the trouble with having something diagnosed as rheumatoid arthritis is that not only do you have it when you go *into* the hospital, but when you *leave* it. Such is the state of the art of medicine in this case, unfortunately.

Because of her much-reduced thyroid activity, Jane often dozes or even sleeps in her chair. She'd very gradually started doing this before entering the hospital, but any physical causes behind her behavior had been unsuspected by us then. I only saw that she could use the rest, since she obviously didn't feel well generally—but I also thought she was waiting for one of her characteristic surges of creative energy before digging into her next book (of which she always has several going). Our agreement was that in the meantime she was to start checking the sessions and my notes for *Dreams;* then I was to type the final manuscript. Jane never reached her goal, however. Instead she napped or drifted—even as she does now—while intermittently reading and rereading our material for *Dreams* without ever doing anything with it.

She hadn't dozed quite as much in the hospital, for there she'd been roused by much more constant stimuli. And now, we just have to wait an unknown number of weeks or months for the thyroid treatment to rejuvenate her vitality. At the moment it seems that Jane uses her available energy for the main task at hand. If she's just eaten, for example, her body focuses its resources upon digestion, with perhaps conscious lapses resulting. During other longer periods, say, those resources may direct themselves toward healing or dreaming—or possibly both.

After some hesitation following my question about having a session this evening, Jane decided she wanted to contribute introductory material for *Dreams*. This was to be a new experience for us: Because of the arthritis she was having trouble even holding a pen, so she intended to dictate her material as though she were writing it herself in longhand. I was to take it down for her. This wasn't to be Seth speaking. For Jane's own work, however, I note times, occasional pauses, and any other information in italics, just as I do for Seth's dictation.

(7:10 P.M. Thursday, April 1, 1982. Once she began dictation, Jane's pace was good. In fact, I had to write very rapidly, for I didn't want to ask her to slow down during this initial experiment.)

Seth uses the term "value fulfillment," as in the title of this book, to imply life's greater values and characteristics—that is, we are alive not only to continue, to insure life's existence, but to add to the very quality of life itself.

We do not just receive the torch of life and pass it on as one Olympic runner does to another, but we each add to that living torch or flame a power, a meaning, a quality that is uniquely our own. We do this as individuals, as members of the family, the community, and members of the species. Whenever that flame shows signs of dimming, of losing rather than gaining potential energy and desire, then danger signals appear everywhere. They show up as wars and social disorders on national scales, and as household crises, as illnesses *(pause)*, as calamities on personal levels as well.

In *Dreams, "Evolution," and Value Fulfillment* Seth outlines the great cosmic and private energies that in our terms once brought into existence the reality of the universe and the birth of those private, cohesive realities in which our own individual daily lives are couched.

(7:20.) It is impossible in our time scheme to intellectually know our own potentials without trying them out, without testing them against the world's edges. We must activate our impulses and desires, try out our abilities, seek out our strengths by joyfully advancing into the given world of physical energy, physical time and space. In the development of each individual we act and reenact the startling events that brought our own universe into existence. The universe was *not* created in some dim past, but is newly *re*created by our own thoughts, dreams, and desires—so that reality happens at all possible levels at once. And in that living endeavor we each play our part.

When we hesitate, hold back, falter, when we hold back energy in the hopes of saving it, when we allow fear rather than trust to guide our activities, when the *quality* of our lives becomes less than we know it should be—then warnings flash. *(Long pause.)* One crisis after another may arise to gain our attention. This has happened in many people's lives— and so recently the same kind of warning recently appeared in my own life.

(7:35.) As I write this Introduction I am recovering from a group of illnesses, recuperating from a month's stay in the hospital, and now I'm trying to see where my personal situation fits into Seth's larger views. That is, the individual is not just a side issue in what people usually call the evolutionary process—but he or she *is* the entire issue, without which there would be no species, no survival, no exquisite *web* of genetic cooperation to produce living creatures of any kind whatsoever.

("Well, I need a cigarette," Jane abruptly said at 7:36.

"You did terrifically, hon," I exclaimed, patting her on a knee. "Terrific."

"Yeah, I knew I got it—thank God," she replied. Then we sat quietly side by side at the round card table we'd placed at one end of

our battered old couch in the living room. In a far corner a sitcom rerun played on the large-screen television set. I'd turned off the sound before the session began. The whole room was bathed in a friendly, subdued yellow light. A rather strong northerly wind periodically rattled the house's metal blinds. The whole creative intimacy of our hill house was one that we'd enjoyed many times; we desperately wanted to return to that same ambience many more times.

"Well, I don't know—maybe that's all I can do tonight," Jane finally said, with a bit of an embarrassed grin. "It's hard for me to get into the next part. . . ." But then at 7:45:)

In our other books I'd mentioned my physical symptoms now and then. By the time Seth finished dictating *Dreams* last month *(on February 8),* however, my physical condition had deteriorated. Two weeks later I could hardly get out of my chair onto the couch or the bed. After answering approximately 50 letters one weekend, the next weekend I could barely hold a pen to write my name. Soon afterward my hearing began to fade, then suddenly became blocked. A few days later I wound up in the emergency room of one of our local hospitals—and there, all too quickly I became familiar with the medical profession's battery of testing paraphernalia. *(Long pause.)* I was placed in a CAT scanner, my bare backside pressed painfully against a cold metal table, my head encircled by the strange doughnut, or globe, while bright white lights and numbers, it seemed, flashed everywhere. They only X-rayed my head.

(Jane meant, of course, a CT or computerized tomography scanner, a modern X-ray machine that shows the interior of the body in a series of brilliant cross-sectional images.)

(With a laugh at 7:51:) Later that same bare backside, thin and bony, was pressed against another metal table, while this time electrodes were attached to every available area of my head so that an electroencephalogram could be taken. No instructions were given to me except to close my eyes as the test progressed. *(Pause.)* Some kind of white gum, or glue, had been rubbed into my scalp through my hair to improve the electrical contacts, and when the test was finished the attendant simply grabbed one area of the equipment and pulled the entire mess off my head in one motion—which felt like my entire scalp was coming off. The obvious unconcern on the part of that middle-aged female attendant made me furious.

"Value fulfillment?" I thought. "What the hell am I letting myself in for? And how have the events of my life come to such a turn?" This was, of course, as anyone familiar with hospitals knows, only the beginning. There were numberless blood tests. I also had to be lifted onto and off the bed, onto and off the portable *commode*.

(Pause at 8:05.) My 82 pounds of flesh were hauled, dragged, pulled, and stretched by good-natured but often impatient strangers—nurses and orderlies and aides—and the most private of my physical processes became a matter of public record. What a shocker!

("See, I never know how much to put in these intros," Jane said. "So many different kinds of people read the books—"

"Just do it your own way," I said. "The hell with it. There's nothing else you can do.")

I remember when I had my first bowel movement at the hospital. Eyes closed to hold back tears of humiliation, I felt my arms lifted by an orderly *(long pause)*, my thin belly and ribs straining in the brightly lit room, my backside lifted and supported by two other strange arms, while a third person— I don't want to sound too vulgar—

(8:12. "Forget it," I said. "We'll fix it if necessary.")

—wiped away the results of the three strong doses of prune juice I'd been given. Yet there was, I knew, a fellowship even in those processes—one that I had perhaps too long ignored: the quality of fellowship, as a species or a family or a community comes together to help one of its own kind. And as I was to see, even for all of the pessimistic suggestions of medical science itself, in the very middle of crisis there was a certain indisputable sense of cooperation— a "vulgar" physical optimism, and a kind of humor that I had long forgotten existed.

(8:21.) In this book, Seth does discuss to some degree the nature of certain illnesses as they apply to individual life and genetic survival. And there I lay in the hospital for a full month, with physical survival uppermost in my mind— hardly a coincidence. They told me that my thyroid gland was very underactive, and that I had arthritis. They X-rayed my hands but not my knees. One of the blood tests showed that I was slightly anemic. But other tests and X-rays revealed that I had sound lungs—in spite of my smoking—a good heart and stomach and other organs. I laughed.

(Long pause at 8:22. I thought Jane was tiring. She might have added that she also laughed because neither did she have a brain tumor, cancer, vasculitis [an inflammation of the blood vessels], or any of several other diseases the doctors thought might be present. She felt she'd beaten a number of negative suggestions from medical personnel in connection with all of those afflictions.)

I liked practically all of the doctors and nurses and orderlies, and they liked me. Most of them didn't know or care "who I was." Very few were familiar with my work (although a few local fans—strangers—eventually found their way to my hospital room). I found I could hold my own in that environment that at first had seemed so alien. I learned to joke even as my backside swung perilously above the commode, while I hoped that its aim was true in the hands of the nurses and orderlies—and again I felt that long-forgotten camaraderie with people, and a growth within myself apart from my work, or what I did. I had a right to be on earth because I'd been born here like every other physical creature, and on that level alone I was part of a great framework of physical energy and cooperation.

(8:31 P.M. "Well, that's all for now," Jane said after a long pause. "I sure am surprised I did that much. I didn't know I could do it— especially that way. . . . I'd never have tried it if you hadn't suggested it."

Jane hadn't dictated this material while in a trance or a dissociated state, as she does when producing her Seth material. She hadn't felt particularly inspired, nor at all sure how to proceed. It was just that she's always used longhand or a typewriter for her own work, she said, and never dictated it, as many writers do these days. Just the same, her creative abilities had immediately come to her aid.)

This is a good place to explain that while Jane was in the hospital neither of us ever made any attempt to "convert" the people there—doctors, nurses, technicians, say—to a belief in the Seth material. Beyond saying that Jane was a writer and that I was an artist, we told no one of our interests in life. We weren't there to impose our beliefs upon anyone else. We'd made the conscious, joint decision during a time of crisis to seek certain kinds of help from skilled practitioners in the medical field, and we were willing to learn from them, even if those people were pretty certain to have belief systems very different from ours.

(Well, I should add with a touch of a smile, at least we were *more* willing to learn in the beginning!)

Jane and I didn't know whether the doctors we did business with even knew what a trance state was. I envisioned some hilarious episodes during which Seth, speaking through Jane, would try to explain to gatherings of medical people just who he was and what he believed. Next, he'd go into what Jane and I believed, and why. Then he'd add some very pungent remarks as to what those in his audiences believed, and why. . . .

Joking aside, though, after her month in the hospital Jane and I ended up with a collection of medical experiences that were mixed at best—positive and negative—and most expensive indeed.

ESSAY 2
MONDAY, APRIL 5, 1982

(7:15 P.M. Our next "Jane session" took place four days later, on the date shown above. Once again we sat at the card table in the living room. And once again Jane wavered at times between waking and dozing. When she did begin dictation, though, her pace was good.)

In later years it's become impossible for me to close my eyes to the multiple pressing differences that exist between Seth's explanation of the nature of reality, and of our own private experience of it. In this book, *Dreams, "Evolution," and Value Fulfillment,* for example, Seth portrays us as a vibrant, well-intended species—a physically attuned kind of consciousness beautifully *tailored* by our own cosmic ingredients to live lives of productivity, of spiritual and physical enjoyments, with each individual life in charge of its own fate and adding to the potentials of all other life as well.

Yet, I read all of those dire newspaper stories predicting disaster, and (oh yes, dear readers) I watched the daily tragic news events dramatized in living color on our television screen. But more than that, I've seen in my own life the steady accumulation of physical symptoms.

If life has such great potentials, as Seth maintains, if it

began—and begins (and *continues* to begin) at such rich creative and productive levels—then why did our experience so often make it seem that we struggled against unknowing or uncaring cosmic forces, or that we were at the most so ignorant of our own source and creativity that our hands were tied, or that we were forever shut off from our natural heritage?

There was no doubt that we'd been *reading* ourselves "wrong." There was no doubt as far as I was concerned that every one of our standard explanations for life *(pause)* were relatively useless now, regardless of how much they might have helped or hindered us in the past.

(Long pause at 7:51.) It began to strike me that even my own physical incapacities were indeed creative ventures that appeared in my experience as bad, or limiting, or even tragic. Perhaps they were instead efforts on the part of my own explorations of value fulfillment to reorganize my life's vast energies. But instead of facing up to a considerable change in life-style, I panicked and felt myself to be almost assaulted, forced into a life that offered less and less physical freedom. So again, how did that experience fit into Seth's *Dreams, "Evolution," and Value Fulfillment?*

As far as I can see, I've been living with two sets of "facts" for some years. The old established explanations had faltered, and finally seemed almost incomprehensible, while the new explanations of Seth seemed beyond my reach, at least in certain areas—areas that were vital to physical and psychic peace. The same processes appeared in my husband Rob's life, of course, as our lives seemed to impinge into the area of man's greatest hopes, and into the opposite area of his greatest fears.

(8:02 P.M. "Oh, that's all," Jane suddenly said. Her delivery this evening had been as fast as that of last time, yet more subdued. Her voiced had carried the same tremor. She was tired, and I was far from being at my best as I fought off a half-repressed cough—an affliction that seldom troubles me.)

Yesterday, Sunday, had marked the end of Jane's first week home from the hospital. We'd found it to be an exceedingly difficult one for a number of reasons. "The toughest week of our twenty-seven years together," I told a neighbor last night.

To see my wonderful, lovely wife so reduced to her present near-helpless state was almost more than I could bear. Jane herself was displaying a stoicism (I'm afraid to write "acceptance") regarding her condition that I'd have found unendurable were I the one experiencing it. I reacted very badly at times, I'm afraid, alternating profound moods of despair with those of great tenderness, love, and compassion. I wanted to cry and could not. With a more painful heart I yearned for my wife to *walk* to me, hips innocently and joyfully swaying, as she used to do years ago, when she'd meet me every day as I left the printing company where I worked as a commercial artist. That had been shortly after we married, in 1954. We were living in Sayre, Pennsylvania, a middle-class railroad town in which I'd grown up, which lies only 18 miles southeast of our present home in Elmira, New York. Not that I wanted Jane to be magically transformed into a 25-year-old again—just that I ached to see a resurgence of that uninhibited, unplanned *joy* of motion for its own sake. For now I understood that freedom of motion was at least one true reflection of an individual's creative potential.

Our week just past had been filled with a desperate energy as we struggled to get settled so that we could return to "work"—to our arts—on some sort of a regular basis. To our dismay, we discovered that Jane had lost much of the use of her legs while in the hospital, since during that month she'd been actively discouraged from using them in her accustomed way. This complicated enormously all of our efforts to help her move about the house as she used to in her office chair, which is on rollers, and nearly signaled the failure of our efforts to live by ourselves. We'd scheduled just a two-hour visit by a registered nurse five afternoons a week for Jane's physical therapy, and to change the dressings on her decubiti. Neither of us wanted live-in help on the premises 24 hours a day. I, for one, was afraid that such an arrangement would not only demonstrate our acceptance of the fact that Jane was really caught in a terrible, permanent situation, but that it would end up destroying us psychologically and creatively.

Jane struggled to regain strength in her legs. Without being aware of it, I'd begun to lose weight after she was admitted to the hospital, and by now my loss had reached the point where others began to notice it. Deliberately I began to eat more. I became extremely busy after my wife came home, making what seemed like endless calls and trips about getting prescriptions filled, about trying out various kinds of beds and mattresses and chairs and hospital gowns, about insurance, about a commode, about having a speaker phone hooked up to our regular phone so that Jane wouldn't have to hold the standard bulky handset to her ear. We even had a small remote-controlled television set installed in our bedroom so that she could watch it, say, when she was restless during the night. When I began sleeping on the couch in the living room, where it was quieter and darker, we bought a pair of wireless intercoms so that Jane could call me from her bed at any time. We also made some rather expensive mistakes, buying certain equipment that proved useless to us.

And amid all of this frenetic activity our painting and writing —those activities we'd always regarded as the creative hearts of our lives, the very reasons we'd chosen to live on earth this time around—had receded into a far distance, so that they'd become like dimly remembered dreams, or perhaps actions practiced in probable lives by "more fortunate" versions of ourselves.

We've had no Seth sessions yet, either regular or private. Jane's energy still isn't up to where it should be, although the synthetic hormone she's taking is helping her considerably. (Dr. Mandali told us that the hormone dosage has to be increased very slowly, over a period of months, in order to avoid strain upon the heart and the endocrine system.)

ESSAY 3
FRIDAY, APRIL 16, 1982

Our days and nights passed in such a kaleidoscope of activity, broken by such uneven periods of sleep, that we hardly noticed whether they were hot or cold, clear or rainy. The grass began to change color from brown to a pale yellow-green. Jane often dozed in her chair in the daytime, but woke up during the nights to watch old movies on television. During her first weeks home, I seldom slept more than two hours at a time: It seemed that I was always getting up to check the dressings on her decubiti, to adjust her pillows, to help make her more comfortable on the motor-driven, pulsating air mattress we'd finally settled upon as the best recommended support available. I'd give her a sip of something to drink, and massage her legs as she lay on her back with her knees drawn up. (She can't straighten out her legs.) I'd sit with her while she had "a few puffs" on a cigarette. The nighttime had a sublime sense of timelessness that I'd always admired. It surrounded our bedroom—but even as bleary as I often was, I became acutely aware of how that serenity could be jarringly compromised by the television set, showing programs that contained their own times of day and seasons.

Jane tried to write with her impaired right hand, frustrated again and again because she couldn't hold a pen well enough to put down the ideas stirring in her mind. At times she used her recorder in an effort to compensate for her lack of writing ability, but this left us with the prospect of finding the time to transcribe the tapes—and so far we haven't done so. (Much of that material is so personal that at this time we don't want others involved with it, by the way.)

(We finally held our first "new" Seth session last Monday evening, on April 12. It was short but, as I expected it would be, excellent. We were pleased to get it for, as I told Jane, if ever we're to understand all of the events in our lives that led to the hospital experience, we must call upon every ability at our service. And even though this is *a personal session, still I think it contains clues that apply to all of us. Jane went into trance as easily as ever, but her Seth voice contained the same underlying tremor I've noticed on a number of occasions since she's returned home. Remember that in the following excerpts Seth—who claims to be discarnate—calls Jane by her male "entity name," Ruburt, and thus "he" and "him.")*

For all of your complaining *(Seth told us with some humor at 8:56),* you understand in rather good measure the decisions and actions that motivate your lives, so that Ruburt is more than usually aware of the manipulations that psychologically and physically lie just beneath the material usually carried by what is ordinarily called the conscious mind. Therefore, a kind of momentary gap appeared between his life and his living of it—a pause and a hesitation became obvious between his life and what he should do with it, as his condition showed just before the hospital hiatus.

I will help you still further understand those

manipulations, for many people—most people—carry on
the same kind of procedures while making important
decisions as to whether or not they will continue life at any
given time. But they hide the issues from themselves far
more than Ruburt did.

(Long pause at 9:05.) Give us a moment. . . . The entire issue
had been going on for some time, and the argument—the
argument being somewhat in the nature of a soul facing its
own legislature, or perhaps standing as a jury before itself,
setting its own case in a kind of private yet public psychic
trial. Life decisions are often made in just such a fashion.
With Ruburt they carried a psychic and physical logic and
economy, being obvious at so many different levels of
actuality. In such a way buried issues were forced into the
light, feared weaknesses and inadequacies were actively
played out where they could be properly addressed,
assorted, and assessed. To whatever degree possible, given
your time requirements, I will try to explain such matters.

(9:10.) To such a degree, of course, the affair was, then,
therapeutic. Ruburt is now far more willing to make certain
changes in his life than he was earlier, and he sees himself
more as one of a living congregation of creatures—less
isolated than before, stripped down from the superperfect
(subconscious) model, and therefore no more under the
compulsion to live up to such a psychological bondage. *(All
delivered with considerable emphasis.)*

He *(Ruburt)* need not try to be the perfect self, then, the
superimage—and in fact to some extent he found himself
the supplicative [self], knocking upon creaturehood's earthly
door, as any creature who found himself wounded through
misadventure might ask aid from another. He found a
mixed world, one hardly black or white, one with some
considerable give-and-take, in which under even the most
regrettable of circumstances there was room for some action,
some improvement, for some . . . creative response. The
rules of the game have therefore been automatically altered.
The issues are clearer, dramatically etched.

(9:18.) The arthritis situation is as I gave it *(in a number of
private sessions),* but you are still faced with the medical
interpretation of that situation, so that it is up to Ruburt to
set it aside. He is returning to activity at his creative,

naturally therapeutic pace, no longer afraid that he is going too fast—or will—but shown only too clearly that activity and motion represent the only safe, sane, and creative response [to life's challenges].

We do not want long drawn-out discussions of why and what exactly happened, simply to understand the dynamics of the activity. Ruburt can work with the self-image he has now. It is imperfect, but it is pliable and willing to change.

There will be more. This is to give you a starter—and as always my heartiest regards to you both.

("Thank you very much, Seth. Good night.")

(9:25 P.M. Jane's pace had generally been okay, considering the circumstances. "I felt like when I got slow there a couple of times that it didn't have anything to do with dozing off," she said, referring to a few longer pauses. "They were just normal things. . . ." I told her she'd done well. "But I really got worried tonight, when I started drifting like that before the session," she added.

We were very pleased with the session. It contains a number of important clues. The arthritis diagnosis, Jane said, was the only one the medical profession could offer, given its insights and viewpoints —but after all those years would she be able "to set it aside"? Seth has insisted all along that she doesn't have arthritis per se. Instead, according to him, Jane adopted her physical immobility as a form of protection against going too far, too fast, with her unique abilities. Yet she also used her "symptoms" to intensify her focus upon those abilities, and to reinforce the strongly secretive aspects of both of our natures. I must add, however, that these three statements represent great simplifications of very complex psychological phenomena.

Equally important is Seth's suggestion that Jane no longer needs "to try to be the perfect self," even on an unconscious basis. And, frankly, I want a good amount of additional material—from Jane and from Seth—on her progress in resolving her deliberations on the merits of continuing physical life.

Actually, I was amazed at the opacity of my perception: It seemed that once again I was just beginning to understand that Jane had chosen to embark upon a journey in which she would explore herself and the world in intensely physical and emotional terms—in contrast to the more intellectual ways by which she and I have usually conducted our searches, through the Seth material and our own inquiring minds. . . . I was frightened by her resolve, and by my own acquiescent participation in such a plan. And why, I wondered, did most of us, most of the time, buy our new experience and knowledge at such high prices?)

(9:30 A.M. Friday, April 16, 1982. Seth-Jane came through with that little session five days ago. One might say that this morning Jane continued it in her own session, exploring especially Seth's opening material. At first she tried to do it as best she could through writing: Painfully, holding her pen awkwardly, she spent over an hour recording the first four paragraphs—even then, after checking our records, I added to her work material about dates and sequences.)

So, one thing I know: I'm a far different person now as I write this Introduction than I was when Seth dictated the book. And as he spoke of the beginnings of the world, I began to play with the idea of quietly ending my own private sphere of existence. Not through a violent suicide, but through a half-calculated general retreat.

Few overt hints of this appear in Rob's notes for *Dreams*. For one thing, the process of withdrawal was slow at the start. For another, when Seth was more than three-quarters of the way through *Dreams* he began devoting a series of private sessions to an in-depth discussion of "the magical approach"—material that was calculated to help me personally, and others like me, change our approach to experience and thus experience itself. Rob's detailed notes about my physical condition, then, appear in those pages.

All of that work—and more—accounts for the long delay in the completion of *Dreams, "Evolution," and Value Fulfillment*. Actually, with the exception of one session held in November 1980, I let my work on the book go for over 13 months, from early June 1980 to mid-July 1981.

We might have inserted some of this introductory material into that large gap in *Dreams*, since very important portions of it were acquired during that time, but we didn't want to interrupt the sessions for the book with different subject matter. We decided to outline our story here instead, and to carry it through the hospital experience, since that was its logical outcome. Rob also wants this material presented as a unit so that it can serve as a foundation for future books we're already discussing, and I agree with his decision.

(11:30. Finally I began writing down Jane's words as I'd done before. Very unusual, by the way—her coming through with dictation from whatever source this early in the day.)

Indeed, Seth's material on the magical approach was so fascinating that by the time he finished *Dreams* I'd already put together large portions of it in a separate book, even if much of it was personal. Not only that, but those "magical" sessions had naturally developed into *another* series, this time on a portion of the personality Seth called "the sinful self"— mine as well as that of others—and those sessions had in turn led me to produce many pages of material directly from my own sinful self. That great personal revelation took place in June 1981. Ironically, then, in the midst of my own half-conscious withdrawal I'd been giving birth to not only Seth's *Dreams*, but several other intriguing long-range concepts. And even if all of those sessions had been born out of my own psychic and psychological challenges and dilemmas, I knew they were excellent and deserved publication.

I could feel Rob hoping that my own efforts would help me. In a hundred ways he tried his best to help me on his own. Seth resumed work on *Dreams* during that July, but each day I seemed to work less and less. Summer turned into fall, then winter, and I hardly noticed. I began to doze in my chair as I sat at my desk. On occasion I was consciously aware of thinking how easy it might be on certain levels to let my desires drop one by one—there seemed to be few left in any case—and to let myself simply drift off into an unastonished death.

That is, I thought it could all happen so easily and naturally and painlessly that there would be no one point where you could say, "Now she lives and now she doesn't."

Maybe I'd produced all I was meant to. Maybe the fire of my life was coming to its own natural conclusion. Why try to fan it into life again, particularly if its initial *joy* had forever vanished? Maybe that course was better than the determination and painful discomforts that might be necessary to prolong lifely existence. So I was to some extent only half alarmed to hear from some strange inner existence my own voice slow down. Tremors appeared in it, as if the vowels and symbols had endless gaps—uneven edges—and some part of me was escaping like smoke even between my words.

(11:35. "Let me relax for a minute," Jane said. Her pace had been fast. Then more slowly:)

My hearing began to fail, at first gradually. Let people talk *around* me, I thought: I no longer cared. Then with bewildering impact I found myself one day almost entirely deaf. Here was no gentle lulling silence, for the absence of sound frightened me beyond anything I could remember. *(Long pause.)* Was Rob in the room? If I couldn't see him I couldn't tell. Did he stand protectively just behind my chair, ready to help me in my maneuvers into bed, or was he in the kitchen, rooms away? There were no sounds of footsteps upon the carpeted floors, no telltale hint of activity. The experience interrupted my retreat. I remember somehow equating all the silence about me with *a forbidding white wall.* And in parentheses: (I don't know why I felt that way, but I did.) I couldn't die deaf *(Jane said with a laugh at 11:45).* I think I had imagined that everything would shut down gradually. I certainly hadn't planned on one sense suddenly turning off.

The next few days, in mid-February 1982, found me determined to clear up the hearing problem—and on one level at least, it was that determination that led me finally to the hospital's emergency room. We had no family doctor to call upon, but through the invaluable help of a dear friend who was also a nurse, we set up an appointment with a doctor at the hospital.

(11:50 A.M. We stopped for lunch. Jane had dictated her material just as she had on April 1 and 5, without going into trance. And I told her I was almost certain that when I went back to finishing the notes for Dreams *itself, I'd be adding much personal material to them. She didn't object, although I'm sure she would have done so— and strenuously—in earlier years.)*

We didn't return to "work," however, until we'd enjoyed a covered-dish supper that a loving neighbor had prepared for us. By then our visiting nurse had come and gone. I'd run quick errands to the drugstore and the supermarket, and written two letters to correspondents explaining that we had no time for visitors. There was more than a little irony and humor connected with my efforts here, though, for no sooner had I sealed the second letter than there was a knock on the front door of the hill house. An unexpected visitor stood there: a young woman lawyer who had flown to Elmira from San Francisco to see Jane. Although Jane was hardly at her best, she discussed her caller's personal problems with her for an hour. I took a nap as soon as the lady left.

(This evening [on April 16] Jane suggested that we sit at our living-room table while I read her morning's dictation to her. But instead: "Well, I guess I'll do a Seth thing tonight," she announed, rather to my surprise, "but it won't be long at all. . . ." This is the second time she's spoken for Seth since leaving the hospital. When she went into trance at 7:39 her Seth voice had a distinct tremor—one decidedly more pronounced than on April 12—and a hard-to-define faraway quality. She spoke with many long pauses. I think that in the following excerpts Seth rather neatly encapsulates her past beliefs, her present condition, and how far she has yet to go in meeting her challenges. [Not that I'm the innocent bystander in all of this, of course. I'm deeply involved.]

Just as he's done at least a couple of thousand times before, Seth opened the session with a certain famous word:)

Now: The same process involving the thyroid gland has happened several times in his *(Ruburt's)* life, and in each of those cases it has repaired itself.

If earlier, however, Ruburt had the erroneous idea that he was going too fast—or would or could—and had to restrain himself and exert caution, now he received the medical prognosis, the "physical proof" that such was not the case, and in fact that the opposite was true: He was too slow. If our words could not convince him, or his own under-standing grasp the truth, then you had the "truth" uttered with all of the medical profession's authority. And if once a doctor had told him years ago how excellent was his hearing, the medical profession now told him that his slowness (his thyroid deficiency) had helped impair his hearing to an alarming degree.

Moreover, here is the medication necessary—the thyroid supplement—that will right that balance. And so it will.

(Long pause at 7:46.) If Ruburt once found himself imagining that he must be strong and perfect enough to help solve everyone else's problems, now he found himself relatively helpless and "undefended"—that is, his physical condition put him in [such a situation]. The superperfect, impractical self-image simply fell away. It could not survive such a situation.

(7:50.) So contrary to its own beliefs, and helpless or not, Ruburt was holding his own. . . .

(7:58.) There was a certain comradeship existing between himself and others [in the hospital]. Desires and impulses

became more immediate, clearer-cut, easier to identify. The discomforts of a physical nature led to instant responses. . . . His weaknesses were out in the open, dramatically presented, and from that point, unless he chose death he could only go forward—for suddenly he felt that there was after all some room to move, that achievements were possible, where before all accomplishments seemed beside the point in the face of his expected superhuman activity.

He will, then, continue to improve, because he has allowed himself some room for motion, for change of value fulfillment. Trust the body's rhythms as these changes occur, however. Going out in the yard (*as Jane did this afternoon in a wheelchair, accompanied by her nurse*) was an excellent case in point, important on practical and symbolic levels.

(*Long pause at 8:01.*) In a manner of speaking, the sinful self created the superhuman self-image that demanded so much, and it encased Ruburt's body as if in concrete. Well, that image cracked and crumbled in the hospital experience, leaving Ruburt with his more native, far more realistic image of himself. It is one he can work with. Do, when you can, look over my "magical approach" material. Ruburt kept turning down his thermostat, so to speak. Now his desires and intents have set it upon a healthy, reasonable setting, and the inner processes are automatically activated to bring about the normal quickening of his body, as before his intent led to the body's automatic slowness.

Enough for this evening. I bid you a fond good evening— and know that you have taken, both of you, important new strides.

("*Good night, Seth*," I said.)

(*8:10 P.M. Jane's Seth voice had grown a little stronger as she progressed with the session. We were very encouraged by two key points Seth had mentioned: that her thyroid gland had repaired itself before—such an event happening now would free her of dependence upon medication—and that her sinful self's superhuman image had "cracked and crumbled in the hospital experience." Those two developments could leave her body free to heal itself. [In the first essay I wrote that according to her doctor Jane's thyroid gland has ceased functioning, and that she has to take a substitute hormone daily for the rest of her life. But the doctor hadn't expressed any idea at all that a thyroid gland could regenerate itself.]*)

"I wonder what you'll be doing six months from now, if Seth's right?" I asked. "The body finally became so desperate to free itself from that rigid sinful-self superhuman image that it took itself into the hospital for a month—even if it did almost kill itself in order to get there. . . ." Jane concurred. And right away she described several occasions when she thought her thyroid gland had rather seriously misbehaved. I remembered two of them.)

After the session I began to wonder what Jane's "sinful self" would have to say now, in comparison to the material she'd received from it in June 1981. During that fervent bout of activity her sinful self had explained and defended its actions most eloquently throughout some 36 closely handwritten pages. Both of us had been appalled at the revelations coming through Jane's pen, even if we did grudgingly admit that we understood, intellectually at least, many of the points that self made. I'd grown very angry as the material unfolded—angry at that portion of Jane's psyche for clinging so tenaciously to such a set of beliefs, for whatever reasons, and angry at myself for not understanding any better than she did their extent and depth, and just how damaging they could be in ordinary terms. I'd also been reminded of material Seth himself had given a few weeks earlier, in a very important private session on April 16: "Many of Ruburt's beliefs have changed, but the core belief in the sinful self has been very stubborn. *(To me:)* While you do not possess it in the same fashion, you are also tainted by it, picking up such beliefs from early background, and primarily from your father in that regard. . . ."

It's impossible to present here all of Jane's own material on her sinful self—much as I'd like to—but shortly I do want to give portions of the first few pages to show readers how experiences from one's very early years can sometimes have the most profound effects in later life. As will be seen, that material obviously raises as many questions as it answers, but right now we can do little more than touch upon the whole affair. We have years of work ahead of us as we search for understanding. Certainly Jane *chose* all of her challenges in this life, just as I did, and as we believe each person does, but a major concomitant of focusing upon certain activities involves how one copes with them (often in close cooperation with others) as the years pass:

What new and original depths of feeling and idea are uncovered, layer by layer, what insights, what rebellions, and, yes, what acceptances. . . .

I could write many windy pages about the mysteries of life, I suppose, and how each of us does the best we can, although often we may not understand what we're doing; but what I really want to do is simply note that in her case, fortunately, and even if she may think she's failed in certain major areas of life, Jane has achieved some remarkable insights into her own situation (as I have into mine, being her marriage partner). She's managed to do this with the help of various portions of her own personality, the Seth material, and me. Our hope is that *her* case can help illuminate others. There are reasons—*creative reasons*— why she can't walk now, or write in longhand. We insist upon knowing what those reasons are. Some of them were obviously engendered by and within Jane's so-called sinful self. What challenges she and I have to meet! Once again, let me quote Seth from that private session Jane held just a year ago, on April 16, 1981: "Your kind of consciousness, relatively speaking, involves some intrinsic difficulties along with spectacular potentials. You are learning how to form reality from your own beliefs, while having at the same time the freedom to choose those beliefs—to chose your mental state in a way that the animals, for example, do not. In that larger picture (underlined) there are no errors, for each action, pleasant or not, will in its fashion be redeemed, both in relationship to itself and . . . to a larger picture that the conscious mind may not be able presently to perceive."

Fine. We agree with Seth's overall view, and that a sublime mystery is implied—but we also want to achieve as much as we can of that redemption now, and on conscious physical and psychological levels.

One small way in which I wanted to begin that quest was for me to teach Jane to write—print, actually—with her left hand, which functions much better now than her right one does. I thought this might be relatively easy for her to do, since she's often voiced her suspicion that she's one of those born "lefties" who at a very early age were forced to begin writing with their right hand. She has yet to do anything about my suggestion. (I spoke from my own related experience, since as a native right-hander I taught myself to print with my left hand just to see if I could do it. Now I always do crossword puzzles that way.)

At the end of May and early in June 1981 we published two books involving years of effort: Seth-Jane's *The Individual and the Nature of Mass Events*, and Jane's *The God of Jane: A Psychic Manifesto*. I was positive that those volumes contained much excellent work. I was also positive that with their publication Jane's symptoms—especially her walking difficulties—became considerably worse. On the surface at least, it was as though some powerful portion of her psyche were exacting a grim compensation for the books' appearance in the marketplace. Perhaps, I thought, that portion was creating a physical disability that allowed Jane to publish forbidden material while protectively isolating herself —and me—from rejection by the physical world. Both of us became terribly upset. Our joint lifework teetered upon the edge of a physical disaster.

It could hardly have been accidental, then, that beginning on June 17, 1981, our deep need led to Jane's spontaneous production of her own sinful-self material. The way had been illuminated by Seth himself in his private sessions, with his discussions of her sinful self and related challenges: Those sessions, the publication of the two books, Jane's personal sinful-self material and her worsening physical situation, all combined to serve as a complex trigger. Here are those promised, very revealing passages. I presented their beginning in the notes for Session 931, in Chapter 9 of *Dreams*. I repeat that material here but add considerably more to it. Again, my few insertions are bracketed.

Statement of the Sinful Self

I resent the designation unjustly given to me, for if I have believed in the phenomenon of sin and sought—apparently too rigidly—to avoid it, my intentions and interests always were not the avoidance of sin so much as the pursuit of eternal truths; the alliance with universal goals, the unity in spirit at least of self, whole self, and universal mind. Those goals ignite your creative powers and have (and still do) propelled you to explore all categories of existence possible, seeking to express those divine mysteries that lie within and behind each existence—yours, and mine as well.

Our explorations involved no secondhand evidence handed down by others, but the direct personal encounter of our consciousness and being with the vast elements of the unknown—a meeting of the self (human and vulnerable)

with the psychological realms of gods and eternities; giant
realms of mind that *our* nature felt attracted to . . . and [was]
uniquely equipped to perceive.

I believed in the soul's survival first of all, and inspired the
"creative self" to step out as freely as possible even while in
my heart I [also] believed in the existence of sin and devil. I
felt upon my heart the heavy unkind mark of Cain, sensing
that humanity carries (unfairly) the almost indelible strain—
the tragic flaw—[of] being tinged by sin and ancient
iniquities. Thusly I reasoned: If I am flawed I must
automatically distort even those experiences of the soul that
seem clearest. I must unwittingly fall into error when I trust
myself the most, since I share that sinful propensity. Yet
despite these feelings did I (did we) unswervingly set
forward.

The belief in sin and in the sinful self has been for
uncounted centuries embedded in man's concepts about
himself and God. Around those beliefs civilizations evolved
and religions orbited. So I maintain that I am being unfairly
attacked (perhaps that is too strong a word) for personally
accepting in my own understanding a philosophy to which
ten millions and more have also succumbed, and to
which the "wisest" of the species have given their loyalty
and trust.

Yet even in our [Jane's] childhood years I yearned to free
us from such doctrines, to search for alternate explanations,
to go where no man or woman had gone before, and to
venture outside the boundaries of *all* official beliefs.

And to me this was no play but the main challenge—to
discover while within one life all life's meaning; to acquire in
one life's vulnerable swiftness evidence of eternity's breadth
and depth, to sniff out its extended unknown dimensions. So
if in the pursuit of such goals I overdid my cautions and
overreacted, it certainly was not out of malice, but in a well-
meaning attempt to protect the creative self—to keep a hand
of caution on its course lest the centuries of man's belief in
sin carried a true weight that I shared but could not
comprehend.

Easy enough to discard this or that symbol of evil, but
suppose all such symbols hid some deep truth, and cast some
restraining base of force that in my ignorance I still did not
perceive? For by this time in our experience, yours and
mine, the creative self was rambunctiously rushing forward,

despite all the cautionary statements of many ancient and modern documents, and our books were being read by millions.

So the belief in man's sinful nature persisted in my mind, a constant reminder of man's ignorance of his own nature. How could I be sure that *our* sight wasn't also distorted; that our "sin" was in *not* accepting sin as a value? Perhaps sin *itself* contained some value that escaped beyond our calculations, still undiscovered.

So in a fashion [Jane's] physical symptoms became a psychological disclaimer, so that in some court of larger values we could not be "sued" for leading others astray from entrenched beliefs that we were still discarding, while not having any completed structure that would allow easy access or safe passage from one "life raft" to the new one that *we* were trying to provide. . . .

But—it now becomes evident—I was myself tinged not by sin in a metaphysical sense (as I thought I might be), but with a belief in sin (itself) that I had not dismissed. Therefore the disclaimer was necessary to protect myself and others from any fatal flaw in our work—a flaw that sin's blindness made invisible. . . .

And so on. It all was—and is—great material, and more accurate and penetrating than my own ideas as to why some portion of Jane's psyche might feel a need for protection from the world, or from another part of herself. While profoundly upsetting both of us, the revelations of her sinful self also seemed to provide a magical psychological key: the yearned-for understanding that would finally unlock Jane's bent physical body. But it didn't. Nothing did—not Seth, with all of his great material on the magical approach, not the publication of the new books, not even Jane's own work. The challenge of our learning enough to initiate her recovery was still with us during that summer of 1981.

And as for books, early in August I returned to our publisher, Prentice-Hall, the page proofs Jane had corrected for her book of poetry: *If We Live Again: Or, Public Magic and Private Love.* Ordinarily that event would have delighted us, since it meant that before the year was out she'd have another work published. Instead, we despaired over her physical condition as the weeks passed. Just how stubborn could those core beliefs held by her sinful self be? Finally, we were left hoping that the sinful self's very exposure through its own material would eventually bring about some physical improvement. That didn't happen either. I painted in the mornings, searching for a peace of mind that I couldn't obtain in any other way. Jane held a few widely scattered sessions for *Dreams*, and a number of private ones as fall came, then winter. Those sessions represented largely futile activity, I thought, yet I gladly admitted that each one of them was as unique and creative as ever, no matter what its subject. Perversely, beyond taking it down and typing it, I hardly looked at the Seth material for days at a time. Finally, early in December 1981 I told Jane I was on the verge of refusing to sit with her for any sessions at all, regular or private, for I'd become deeply afraid that the more sessions she held the worse she'd get. Again she refused to go into the hospital. At this time, Prentice-Hall sent us the first published copies of *If We Live Again*, but as proud as Jane and I are of that book, its appearance didn't help her. At our small, annual Christmas Eve party we gave autographed copies of the book to close friends—the best presents we could offer. After the holidays, though, we saw few friends and no strangers.

The winter turned into one that seemed to be the longest and coldest in years, although while heavy storms raged all around us, our immediate area of New York State received surprisingly little snow (a fact we were very grateful for!). As Jane had dictated to me in her own session for April 1—the first one presented in these essays—during those early weeks of 1982 her walking, writing, and hearing began to deteriorate markedly. In late February she was hospitalized. . . .

ESSAY 4
SATURDAY, APRIL 17, 1982

(7:30 P.M. After supper I told Jane I was going to work on the essays for Dreams. *Already this morning I'd typed from my notes last night's very encouraging private Seth session: "—and know that you have taken, both of you, important new strides." Jane said she'd*

like to do some more dictation of her own, so I agreed to take down that instead. Once again, however, she shied away from translating any more of that dirgelike Sumari song she'd sung to herself, and recorded, shortly before going into the hospital. I still had only that one great line she's interpreted for me in English: "Let my soul find shelter elsewhere."

I now read to her the last two pages of material Seth had given us last night. Jane was nodding in her chair as I finished, and I thought she wouldn't be doing any work this evening after all. Yet she roused herself: "I've got the first sentence, I guess." I lit her cigarette for her. Her voice was free of tremor and her rate of delivery was a little slow.)

There is no doubt that I was caught between life's contrasts, and only too aware of the endless questions that came to mind. On the one hand there was the Seth material itself, and Seth's performance in his books.

(Long pause at 7:34.) His ideas had somehow led me to the point where the very dimensions of experience should change. As he presented them, his concepts dealt with the spontaneous, rambunctious powers with which nature was endowed. Seth insisted that those powers, followed at least in principle, would raise man's estate and fill it with a brilliance and joy in which the old problems of the species would largely disappear.

Certainly our lives and the lives of others have been strongly influenced by the Seth material, changed for the better. Certainly our comprehensions have deepened as a result—yet in the face of that great promise, what was I doing barely able to leave my chair? And if spontaneous order was such a vital ingredient in the workings of the universe, then what was I doing trying to shut it down in my own daily life?

(Long pause at 7:40.) In the meantime, Rob and I often thought that this very book would never be completed. I might decide that I'd given enough years and energy to the Seth pursuit. Without making any conscious decision, I might simply cease having sessions. *(Long pause.)* I *did* continue with the sessions, of course. The book *is* finished. I realize more and more that life's experience is played out in a framework that stretches *between* life's contrasts. We live in a world slung between our dearest hopes and greatest fears, while seldom encountering either in their pure form.

(7:48. Jane spoke with much emphasis here. As if on cue, through an open front window a quickening breeze stirred the long glass wind chimes hanging just inside; their pealing harmony filled the living room. The chimes had been sent to us as a gift by fans we've never met.)

Value fulfillment is the largest issue here, both with Seth's book and my own experience, and if I really understood what Seth was saying in this book, I would not have needed to undergo such an uncomfortable drama in my daily life.

(Long pause at 7:51.) Our vitality wants to express itself. The whole world of nature is an irrepressible, expressible area of expansion. Old ideas of the survival of the fittest, conventional evolutionary processes, gods and goddesses, cannot hope to explain the "mystery of the universe"—but when we use our own abilities gladly and freely, we come so close to being what we are that sometimes we come close to being what the universe is. Then even our most unfortunate escapades, our most sorrowful ventures, are not dead-ended, but serve as doorways into a deeper comprehension and a more meaningful relationship with the universe of which we are such a vital part.

(7:58. "End of introduction," Jane abruptly said. "That doesn't mean that when you get it all typed up I won't want to add to it. I just want to make sure that my own experience keeps coming back to the book, 'cause that's what it's for. You could end up with a brief epilogue, according to what happens."

"I don't know," I said. "That's too far away to tell."

"Wait a minute, while I see if there's anything else. You can do a prologue or whatever else you want, too. . . ."

End at 8:01 P.M.)

ESSAY 5
SUNDAY, APRIL, 18, 1982

(9:03 A.M. Last night Jane had pronounced her work finished on the introductory material for Dreams. I hadn't said so, but I'd suspected that she had more to say. Then as we went to bed she brought up two additional subjects to discuss, for those who would wonder: why we hadn't more actively sought medical help in the past

for her physical condition; and the many private, or deleted, sessions
Seth himself has given for her over the years.

A third point came up this morning, one we've talked about often
lately. It concerned the other "Seths" who are revealing themselves
around the country these days. Later tonight I want to offer a little
more about this overall development—but people speak for their
Seths entirely without Jane's permission. Jane is most concerned that
she and I protect the integrity of the Seth material in its unique and
original form.

In fact, all of those topics were so much on Jane's mind that for
the second time in three days she went to "work" right after
breakfast. In a firmer voice, then, and following a quick look at the
Sunday-morning paper:)

Seth gave so many sessions that were devoted to my own
physical condition that I finally became embarrassed and
confused: The sessions were obviously terrific—why couldn't
I put them to more practical use?

I have no idea, of course, what physical state I'd be in if
the Seth phenomenon hadn't appeared in my life *(in late
1963)*, or if I hadn't had those sessions to rely upon. And
even in the most private-type sessions Seth always wound his
material into more public areas, so that we have reams of
unpublished (and very controversial) material dealing with
the connections between one's illness and other members of
the family, community relationships, and with the very belief
systems that underlie all of human activity. The kinds of
beliefs we have about people bring about the kinds of
illnesses we encounter. That is certainly one of Seth's clearest
messages. The individual is always in a state of change. To
name and dignify a group of symptoms only brings them
further into prominence, and offers them another
framework for permanency.

(9:10.) Seth couldn't lead my life for me, of course. He
couldn't lead other people's lives for *them* (underlined),
either—yet through the years I began to feel a greater and
greater sense of responsibility for people with physical
problems who wrote requiring Seth's aid, or mine. Their
needs—and my own—seemed to blot out the great hope
that Seth could and did offer: the infusion of understanding
and comprehension that could clear away the old belief
patterns that held the individual in bounds.

Since the later 1960s, when my own troubles began, I
stubbornly resisted medical assistance. If I had broken a leg

I would have gone to a doctor to get it set. I felt that I could handle my particular kind of difficulty alone. *(Long pause.)* The symptoms were obvious enough: stiffness, slowing down of motion, and general lack of mobility. I could keep track easily enough, I thought, of my own progress as I worked directly with my body, without drugs to confuse the issue, and with no one else between me and the reality I had so cunningly created. How else could I really learn anything? The more middlemen that I entertained between my physical condition and my personal beliefs, the more confused I thought I'd be.

(Long pause at 9:21.) I'm not sure where I drew the line. If I'd felt I was suffering a heart attack, for example, I knew I would rush to the hospital, but this was a chronic condition. The diagnosis—which I mentioned in my first session *(on April 1)*—gave a pinpointed, specific cause: a severely *under*active thyroid gland, a situation that in no way contradicts Seth's own larger interpretation of my physical state.

(9:25.) I still must have needed the doctors to tell me so. Seth was right: I *was* going too slow—*not* too fast, as I had feared. I had calmed myself down too far, disciplined myself overmuch, until my only hope was to change my course at once.

Doctors had terrified me as a child, when my mother was already bedridden with arthritis, and when I was diagnosed as having an *over*active thyroid gland—an affliction that could lead, so my mother told me, to insanity and death. If the medical profession had had anything to do with casting that medical spell, then apparently it could be quite effective in removing it.

(Long pause at 9:35.) By last year, as my symptoms worsened, I began to feel that life's frustrations outweighed its pleasures. Other annoying events were occurring in our private lives. The company that published my books, Prentice-Hall, was changing its structure and policy. My longtime friend and editor there, Tam Mossman, was considering leaving to work for another publishing firm. And—very troublesome to me—came the repeated news that various people were "speaking for Seth" publicly, and charging hefty-enough fees.

(9:43.) I felt that my work was being contaminated, and more, I was annoyed and disappointed by those readers who could apparently be so taken in by those other Seths. As he has said so many times, Seth speaks only through me, to protect the integrity of the material. And it is indeed that contract between him and me that always assures you of the authenticity of Seth's work.

In any case, all of those issues weighed upon my mind.

Now let's see. . . . Okay: I hope sometime to tell the entire story of my physical and creative challenges, which as of now of course is unfinished. Much of this present manuscript, *Dreams, "Evolution," and Value Fulfillment*, deals with the development of the individual as it is primarily concerned with the development of the universe: The two *are* one. *(Long pause.)* In man's desire to make creative adjustments, it often seems that instead he adds unfortunate blemishes to life's vitality. Yet in the long run even these *become*, finally, *constructive* manipulations whose purposes, perhaps, we did not understand at the time.

(9:49 A.M. "Well, I guess that's it," Jane said. "This stuff goes with last night's work."

"Actually," she continued much more emphatically now, as we discussed her rather mild comments about the other Seths, "I'm deeply outraged that some people who considered themselves 'followers' of mine or Seth can so easily fool themselves when they claim to be speaking for Seth—be so blind to their own motives, or not recognize the fact that they're taking advantage of people. They're also using my *work to validate their own. . . .")*

Concerning Jane's understandable desire to protect her work, long ago she published some very clear statements about that. In Chapter Nine of *The Seth Material* (1970) she wrote: "Several people have told me that Seth communicated with them through automatic writing, but Seth denies any such contacts, saying that his communications will be limited to his work with me, in order that the integrity of the Seth Material be preserved." And in her introduction to *Seth Speaks* (1972), she quoted Seth from the 510th session for January 19, 1970: "While my communications will come exclusively through Ruburt *(Jane)* at all times, to protect the integrity of the material, I will invite the reader to become aware of me as a personality. . . ."

After all, if he *does* come through others—or can if he wants to—why hasn't Seth himself simply said so, and repeatedly, in the books as we've published them over the years? We'd have respected his statements on that aspect of his abilities and intents as much as we did—and do—on any other. To have attempted to censor Seth since 1963, say, to "keep him to ourselves" on that particular subject, would have long ago turned into an impossibly complicated and dishonest task: Jane and I would have become involved in a constant distortion of his material as we rewrote the sessions. Such a procedure could have turned into a creative tragedy for us and for our readers.

Even in *God of Jane*, which was published in 1981, Jane presented some relatively late material from Seth to show that he doesn't independently communicate with others. The idea that he'd done so can be inspiring, however. In Chapter 20 of her book, see Session 876 for August 27, 1979. After explaining how a couple of women (among others) had recently claimed that he had been in contact with them, Seth stated: "Now, I did not communicate with those women—but their belief in me helped each of them use certain abilities."

This whole miniature tempest is almost enough to make one wonder: How come those other people made their "Seths" known *after* Jane began to speak for *her* Seth, and to publish the Jane-Seth material? Being inspired to use one's own abilities is a perfectly understandable development that we can be very happy about. But to claim to speak for Jane's Seth *per se*, as a means of expression, is quite another thing. . . .

ESSAY 6
TUESDAY, APRIL 20, 1982

(8:47 A.M. Our original idea was to insert the session Jane gave this morning in one of the earlier essays. This would have been a very mechanical approach. More, it would have involved altering dates, and changing or eliminating some of the copy to make the rest of it fit—all things I dislike doing. After Jane came through with her dictation I told myself I'd know what to do with it, and awoke the next morning with the clear understanding that her session should be

presented just as is, and when we received it. Jane said okay. The subjects discussed are deeply charged for us, and the physical and psychological aspects of some of them could be devastating if we allowed them to be. Presenting the session in a more isolated manner here, then, may give the reader a clearer idea of how we felt during Jane's early days in the hospital [and later too, for that matter]. This course also lets the session serve as an automatic bridge to some of the material in the earlier essays.

So last night, less than two days after she'd held her last session, I asked Jane for some material about the central theme of her days in the hospital, both from her own viewpoint and that of the doctors who probed, examined, and discussed her and her problems. Some of them talked about her right in front of her as though she weren't there—and, Jane said, with her hearing still much impaired at that time, she almost felt as though she wasn't *there.*

For the third time in five days she began dictating her own material right after breakfast. Once again from the card table in the living room:)

It seemed to me that once medical science got hold of you it wanted to justify its existence, to exercise its wonders for those fortunate or *un*fortunate enough to be considered "proper candidates" for its full ministrations.

Several of the brightest young rheumatologists and orthopedic surgeons had my future all mapped out for me, or so it appeared, as they discussed my case. When they spoke to Rob and me I tried to listen, but my hearing was still so poor that it was nearly impossible to make out one full sentence at a time. All the doctors seemed to agree that I had a kind of burned-out case of rheumatoid arthritis, with little active inflammation. But one doctor soberly told me that I'd never walk again, or even put my weight upon my feet again, unless I underwent a series of joint-replacement operations—*if*, he cautioned, I proved to be a "proper candidate."

Being a proper candidate meant that I would turn my life over to medical science in the hospital for at least a year: a year spent in therapy, surgical procedures, and more therapy, until I ended up having at least four separate operations. My knee joints and hip joints could thus be replaced.

My condition had certain drawbacks, however: The two sides of my body were uneven, so I could end up with four bright new metal and plastic joints and still not be able to walk properly. I might need a cane, or a walker. Medical science would be willing to *try*, however. Out of the goodness of its heart, all of its scientific procedures would be put at my disposal. True, the amount of money required for such surgical possibilities was staggering, but insurance of one kind or another could be found to carry the cost. (We didn't have nearly enough money, but could qualify for adequate insurance by fulfilling the terms of an 11-month waiting period.) But regardless of cost, one orthopedist saw me staying right in the hospital—now that I was there—until the entire procedure was finished. Particularly if, again, I proved to be a proper candidate.

(Long pause at 9:02.) Being a proper candidate meant getting rid of those bedsores, for one thing, as well as taking extensive physical therapy. As I listened to the doctor talk, poor hearing or no, I could almost feel medical science starting up all of its gears, ready to go to work on my behalf —and I wasn't ready to make any such decision right then. I wanted to see how my body would react to the synthetic thyroid hormone and to therapy first. I wished to hell I could (underlined) run, I thought, for boy, I'd have run right out of there, fast!

(9:05.) The particular group of young doctors I saw, the specialists, were probably the fanciest-looking dandies that Elmira has known. They were superlative-looking young men, dressed in the latest of fashions, and even in the hospital it was apparent that they were properly clothed in the finest of *social mores* as well. They were in their collective way like magicians, producing wonders out of the clear air, stunning you with their charming smiles and manners, trying to win you over to some strange cause.

(9:12.) In this case it was the *operation* cause. It was the only way to go: What a crime to accept less than full, complete motion at my age *(53)*!

(A one-minute pause at 9:13, eyes blinking, then closing.) One doctor told me that my body's mobility would be bound to change for the better as my thyroid gland . . .

    (After a long pause in midsentence Jane began to doze. Her head dipped down. Her body began to slowly lean against the right arm of her chair in what has become a characteristic pose, for both her thyroid activity, and therefore her energy, are still below par even

though she's been out of the hospital for 24 days now. By 9:17 she was asleep. Watching her tilt more and more, I wondered whether she truly had the psychic and physical reserves to heal herself— whether anybody *would under the circumstances. Perhaps her challenges* were *too much for her. What were her limits, how much more could she take after some 17 years of ever-increasing struggle, whether or not those challenges had been chosen—some of them far in advance—for whatever reasons?*

Jane came awake at 9:20. "Now that was just on the operation thing—"

"Did you know you were asleep?"

"Not until I woke up," she said with a half-guilty grin. "Now there's some stuff I want written down, but you won't approve because it's not for the intro—"

"I don't give a damn," I said. "If you don't want it in the book, okay. We can still get it, can't we?")

(9:25 A.M. "That's all of the stuff on the Introduction, then . . . ." And now Jane dictated the equivalent of three typewritten pages of "other hospital material" that she knew she'd eventually want to use somewhere.)

Actually, I came to realize, Jane was so terrified by the thought of those operations that mentally she shunted aside all such prospects. Only when she was home did she begin to fathom the possible depths of the physical reality she'd created for herself, with my help. To coin a phrase, she was "truly, deeply shocked." The doctors wanted to literally cut the major joints out of her body! To replace them with metal and plastic joints inserted into the bone ends and cemented in place. Jane cried. Her voice shook. "But in spite of everything, over all those years I never *felt sick* until I went into the hospital," she wailed. The glowing reports we heard and read about successful joint-replacement operations meant little to her. "Sure, for one joint, or two, maybe," I said, then shut up, not wanting to add my own fears to her fears. But *four* of those operations? And why stop there? If they fixed her knees and hips, what about her shoulders? She couldn't raise her arms level with them. "Oh, they'd operate on the shoulders, too," a doctor told me in front of Jane, without inflection, as though we were discussing an inanimate mechanism that needed rebuilding. *Six* operations, then. But what about my wife's elbows, and her fingers? Somebody at the hos-

pital—I forget who—told us that joint replacements for the fingers and/or knuckles usually weren't all that successful: The
bones in the hands were pretty small and delicate. But it could
well be argued that Jane needed to be able to *write* with a pen or
pencil, to express her basic creativity in that particular elemen-
tary fashion, even *more* than she needed to walk. (It would be
great if she could at least use a typewriter!) So there could be
eight operations, or ten, or . . . ?

What might happen to the body, I wondered, even if its
psychic tenant were willing to endure any or all of those "surgical
procedures"? I answered my own question by remembering accounts I had on file, explaining how people of various ages had
withstood numerous, incredible operations, sometimes over a
period of years. But I was horrified to think that my dear wife
might become involved in a similar reality, with or without my
unwitting compliance. I knew that she was far from making any
decisions about surgery, but I recoiled from pushing any such
suggestions upon her, no matter how fine it would be to see her
on her feet. Joint-replacement operations were irreversible procedures, and I also had on file material about how they sometimes failed.

Short of outright failure, however, some of the articles I've
collected contain the information that a conventional artificial
joint replacement—for a knee, say—usually lasts only from four
to seven years before loosening. A most discouraging prospect!
What does one do when the insert begins to wobble? None of
the doctors we'd talked to had mentioned such a possibility.
(One can always claim that being able to walk for even four years
is a lot better than not walking at all!) Jane and I also read that
through experiments with animals medical designers are working to perfect an artificial knee joint with porous surfaces, to
promote better bonding of bone to metal; it could last 15 years
or more. Someday, I told Jane, and regardless of whether or not
we ever choose to take advantage of any of them, we'll be questioning orthopedic surgeons very closely about what "surgical
procedures" are available.

As I wrote in the first essay, "the trouble with having something diagnosed as rheumatoid arthritis is that not only do you
have it when you go *into* the hospital, but when you *leave* it."
Even if Jane had all of those operations—even if she ended up

able to walk after a fashion—she'd still have arthritis. She was suffused with it. Our beliefs said so. So did her body, as everyone could see. "Your joints are destroyed," Dr. Mandali told Jane, after getting the opinion of the young out-of-town rheumatologist she'd asked to examine my wife. "Do you want to spend the rest of your life inside, in a wheelchair? That's a pretty limited existence you're talking about there. . . ." And Jane, trying to protect herself from the negative suggestions that had been administered to her like psychic hammerblows, ever since she'd entered the hospital, could only weakly demur on the subject of operations.

Let me quickly add that all of the doctors who examined her advanced their suggestions while trying to be helpful, and in the name of "truth" as they saw it—with individual variations, of course. To us, however, in all but one case their general unconscious biases were negative. The exception was the youngish doctor Jane had referred to at the very end of her last session. As it happened, he was the one who'd had her admitted to the hospital to begin with. He'd offered Jane encouragement *as she is*, and she had felt an immediate psychic rapport with him. But he was a neurologist, and we saw less and less of him as it was determined that his special skills wouldn't be of continuing help in Jane's situation. In the overwhelming medical view, then, as Jane said, the operations *were* the only way for her to go. . . .

ESSAY 7
FRIDAY, MAY 7, 1982

In this essay I'll touch upon a number of subjects. Some of them have already been mentioned. During our work on these pieces Jane and I have automatically been led back to earlier material again and again, but each time we've tried to plunge deeper into the topic under discussion, to uncover new layers of meaning and insight. (Doing this always reminds us of additional points to cover, of course!) Putting it all together is an extremely challenging endeavor as I try to summarize our years of committment to the Seth material—for inevitably we end up dealing with ideas lying outside society's generally accepted frameworks of belief. Forty-one days have now passed since Jane left the hospital, and this passage of "time" alone has given us more perspective on the whole affair of her illness, and on our beliefs, intents, and desires.

Among the subjects not discussed so far are Seth's (and our own) ideas on reincarnation, counterparts, probable realities, and Frameworks 1 and 2. Jane briefly referred to Seth's "magical approach" material in her dictation last month (see her own session of April 16, 1982, in Essay No. 3 on that date)—thus prefacing the long quotations from her "sinful self." So as counterpoint to her writings on the sinful self, I'll be presenting two excerpts to hint at what Seth does mean by his magical approach.

Aside from any books that he may produce himself (and on whatever subjects), I've already made plans to put together a short volume featuring Seth's discussions on the magical approach to reality. A year earlier Jane had begun a much more ambitious project involving this material, as she mentioned on April 16, but she laid it aside for reasons already covered. My version will mainly feature the dozen or so sessions Seth gave in August–September 1980, and the poetry Jane was inspired to write because of them. She may also contribute an introduction to the book, showing how Seth's and her own sinful-self information are related to the magical approach.

If, as Jane dictated in her session for April 17, "We live in a world slung between our dearest hopes and greatest fears," then surely it can be said that she's chosen to delve into at least some of her "greatest fears." Her present impaired condition is certainly generating powerful physical and psychic conflicts and challenges, and it's my personal assessment that she's dealing with these in her own unique way. That way is different from anybody else's way. I think that if parts of her psyche "fear those fears," other parts do not—or that at least they chose to confront them, and actually began doing so many years ago. Otherwise Jane's "symptoms" couldn't exist on any level. Nor am I implying ideas of predestination. The chances here for exploration are very extensive, of course. And I still implicitly believe the quotation Seth gave on April 16, 1981, over a year ago now: "In that larger picture there are no errors, for each action, pleasant or not, will in its fashion be redeemed, both in relation to itself and . . . to a larger picture that the conscious mind may not be able presently to perceive."

I'm certainly not writing here about the idea of redemption in the ordinary religious sense, although I think it's perfectly possible that in some other frameworks, larger than our taken-for-granted physical and psychological one, the idea of redemption —of *understanding* and *embracing*—may be involved in a "religious" sense, as part of an intuitive grasp of All That Is.

Since I'm so closely related to Jane in this life, through marriage, as well as through at least several reincarnational and counterpart roles (according to Seth and our own feelings), I'm as deeply involved in this search for redemption as she is. Given our present ideas about the limitless nature of consciousness, we think our joint quest has been underway since before our births —*by choice*—and we expect it to continue for the rest of our physical lives. I don't mean that physical or psychic healings, for example, can't or won't take place "this time around," but that if they *do* happen they too will be deeply connected with those overall, much broader patterns of our lives. To me, redemption means a continuous search or journey, then, involving whatever events and interchanges we choose to create, for whatever purposes, along the way—and truly, I think, some of those purposes will involve things "the conscious mind may not be able presently to perceive." That we believe such things speaks for our own brands of faith, then, and also signifies that Jane and I think we have much to learn. And we try to keep in our minds Seth's statement that "your intellect does not have to know the answers to all of your questions."

Jane and I live our physical lives on mundane levels, though, as everyone else does, so it's inevitable that we often find ourselves meeting our daily challenges within those frameworks. We practice one big difference, however—for we hold within ourselves Seth's ideas on a host of subjects. It seems that we can feel his concepts—intermingled with our own questions, ideas, and accomplishments—constantly turning within a kind of special excitement and revelatory insight. This is true for us even when things aren't going well, when we feel "dumb" or blocked about whatever we may be trying to do.

At such times I'm apt to think about ideas of reincarnation

and counterparts. Right here I'm dealing with just two of Seth's larger concepts. But without dwelling upon them too heavily, I may consider the notion of my larger, nonphysical "whole self" or "entity" being made up of a number of other psychically related *physical* selves projected into time. For Seth, basically there is no time, only a great "spacious present" that's a manifestation of a sublime, indescribable All That Is. Our gross physical senses, and indeed our very bodies, insist upon interpreting the spacious present in linear terms, however—through the inevitable processes of birth, aging, and death—so to help us get his point here Seth advances his ideas of reincarnational selves and counterpart selves in ways we can understand sensually.

He tells us that our reincarnational selves explore the past, present, and future—*but basically all at once*, since time as he defines it is simultaneous. I've written before that as physical creatures we're always going to find the contradictory notion of "simultaneous time" hard to comprehend, intellectually at least.

Before proceeding I want to make clear just what I mean by "reincarnational selves" (while confining this discussion to "past" lives for the moment). For it's also contradictory to say, for example, that "I was a serf in the 12th-century Germanic state of Bavaria." As Seth and I both noted in Volume 2 of *"Unknown" Reality*, each of us has our focus of identity *now*—not in some other portion of the spacious present, just as each reincarnational self has his or her own historical focus of identity. How could it be otherwise?

Could one return to that 12th-century life, even as an observer, what would the traveler find? An individual—and one not about to surrender his or her identity to anyone, or have it thought of simply as a manifestation of some "future" self! I think that when they blithely talk about having lived other lives people forget that those living before were—*are*—fully independent creatures, even if they are psychically related to others. The traveler could hardly move in on one of his or her own personalities! Interesting question: How would our 20th-century individual react when told by a visitor from the year 2355 (for example) that he or she represented one of our futurian's "past" lives?

The serf will invariably be looking at his time through a different focus than his future self could ever do. And think of the added challenges of feeling and perception where sexual changes between present and past incarnations are involved! Eroticism—and yes, outright sexual curiosity and arousal over reversed genitalia, for instance—must enter in sometimes, although in print at least these specifics of sex in connection with reincarnation seem to be a taboo subject. By contrast, there's plenty of material in the reincarnational literature on the generalized patterns of sexual behavior, from promiscuity to repression. (I wonder whether a long-term past-life sexual *fantasy* could be connected to a *real* sexual problem or challenge in a present—or future—life.)

But would our time traveler ever want to give up his or her present mental and physical focus to enter completely into an earlier personality? I think not, in the overwhelming majority of cases—and perhaps never—for in those terms it would mean surrendering a portion of the whole self or entity that had, through a projection into our scheme of "present" time, attained a certain consciousness and physical form of a unique degree. Yet, on second thought I wouldn't dare rule out completely such bizarre developments. Perhaps transfers like that can and *do* take place within the vast arena of probable realities (which I'll also be discussing in this essay). If so, then, they would be strange only from our limited viewpoints.

Further, Jane and I believe that what really happens during a "past-life regression" under hypnosis is that the subject (aside from any responses given to the hypnotist's own witting or unwitting suggestions) very cosily views his or her previous lives from the comfort and safety of a present existence. This would be the case even when the subject is very unhappy with present challenges, and is trying to assign their origin to events in one or more former existences. All well and good to announce that one was a serf some 900 years ago—but one is much more likely to be either tuning into minute signals surrounding the actual physical and mental reality of the serf (poor fellow), or to be picking up on elements of that individual's personality as they're associated with the serf's whole self or entity. Either possibility makes it much safer—and much more entertaining—to proclaim one's serfdom.

There's so much I could discuss here that the lack of time and space is very frustrating. I can only hint at what I consider to be important points. The books and magazines dealing with reincarnation—and the tapes, too, these days—swarm with tales of journeys to past lives, and some of those accounts are most spectacular. Yet, even given ancient concepts like that of Seth's spacious present, the participants in such adventures usually quite happily ignore the conclusion that reincarnation should also operate from the opposite direction—the future—just as well! As a very perceptive young lady wrote Jane and me recently, why can't people be *progressed* to their future lives just as successfully as they're *regressed* to their past lives? Indeed. Our rather copious mail brings us questions like that very rarely. (The key word there, I think, is "successfully.")

Back in 1974 Seth responded to my own musings on the subject by commenting: "You are afraid to consider future lives because then you have to face the death that must be met first, in your terms." (See Appendix 12 for Volume 2 of *"Unknown" Reality*.) Seth referred to the conventional, culturally instilled fear of death that most of us carry, of course. Surely one's death to come is a much more personal and penetrating prospect—a much more frightening one—than "facing" any past-life deaths one may encounter: *Those* deaths have already happened! But it certainly seems that in those terms present challenges could be illuminated through exploring "future" lives as well as those of the past.

I referred to a "successful" progression because reaching into the future is evidently much more difficult. By its very nature a future life cannot be proven—records checked, and so forth. Anything goes. Jane and I have read of many systems designed to regress the individual to past lives. Often such "trips" are mediated by hypnosis. It can even happen spontaneously, and I had a most exhilarating glimpse of a past life of my own that way. (See Session 721 in Volume 2 of *"Unknown" Reality*.) However, neither of us have had such an outright encounter with a future self—*that we know of.* I'd say that under hypnosis the urge to fantasize the future lives must be a tempting one; but what's the explanation for achieving little more than a formless future state while "under," no matter how hard one tries? The failure to get there, to turn time around, could be taken as a sign of resistance on the part of the present self. (Or even a past self or selves, but that's too complicated a subject to go into here.)

And how about reaching a future life through the dream state, perhaps abetted by hypnosis or self-suggestion before sleep? Our own results have been ambiguous at best, in contrast with the "ordinary" precognitive *dreams* Jane and I have had, which we can document through our written records. Future-life dream recall may be thoroughly disguised so as to not alarm the guardian, conscious present self. I've often speculated that clues to oncoming lives must exist within the hundreds of dreams I've recorded.

Accounts of projecting into distant future lives seem rare: Perhaps the conscious self deeply hesitates at swimming in such uncharted pools of consciousness, even though present and future relationships are assumed.

My main point is that I also feel, without having asked Seth, that the farther one travels ahead in time the greater the play of probable realities and probable lives he or she encounters. To venture into such a skein requires that one constantly picks and chooses among them—for each move, each thought, even, can launch the traveler into a different probability. In some cases there will be a great fear of becoming lost among all of those realities. (What if one *doesn't want* a probable reality they choose? But that must happen all of the time!) The uncertainty perceived here by the conscious self, however, can act as a great restraint toward knowing a future life or lives—just as much as might the fear of tuning into one's physical death ahead of time in this life. Hook up those two factors with the quite natural concern that at least some events in any life to come will inevitably be unpleasant, or worse, and we have at least three powerful restraints, or psychic blocks, inhibiting awareness of future lives. There would be others. Everything considered, we may just not want to know about future lives most of the time.

I'll digress a moment to note that it's quite obvious that when conducted by skilled therapists past-life regression has proven to be of great benefit to certain individuals. Whether or not reincarnation has been proven objectively, the belief structures surrounding that concept, or even the idea of it, have served very well as a forum within which certain present-life challenges have been worked out, through the therapists' use of hypnosis, allegory, association, symbolism, and other very respectable methods.

How richly creative we are: Each of our presents is part of the future from the standpoint of the past; each of our presents is also part of the past from the standpoint of the future.

I think it quite humorous (and ironic) that whether or not they realize it, those who engage in past-life regressions play with the notion of future selves all of the time—for from the standpoint of any "past" lives they reach their present lives obviously represent future existences. In a way, and in those terms, this also applies in Jane's case when she contacts Seth, even on the "psychological bridge" those two have constructed between them: When Seth tells us that his last physical life was in Denmark in the 1600s, then Jane and I represent future physical selves of his. I put it this way because Seth himself has commented that the three of us are "offshoots of the same entity." (This time, see Appendix 18 for Volume 2 of *"Unknown" Reality*.) Yet we are all of us *different* now: "Ruburt *(Jane)* is <u>not</u> myself <u>now</u>, in his present life. He is nevertheless an <u>extension and materialization of the Seth that I was at one time.</u>"

All of this is most simplified. One ought to be very careful about assigning past and future status to various portions of a self, for ultimately, as one moves further into the spacious present, such constructions as the past, present, and future begin to melt away. And, as in Seth's case and Jane's case, probabilities and choices come much more prominently into play.

However, Jane and I don't particularly think that in our present lives we've been that greatly influenced by any successes, failures, or illnesses chosen from other lives except in the broadest of terms: general bodily and personality characteristics and abilities, say. I freely note, and with some humor, that this can be somewhat of a jointly contradictory attitude for us. Perhaps we're too stubborn about agreeing wholeheartedly that such possibilities exist, or perhaps we're just too enamored of our "present" physical lives, even with all of our challenges, to want to fully concur with Seth.

Our attitudes, then, may point up our unconscious strengths and weaknesses when it comes to our acceptance and use, or nonuse, of at least portions of the Seth material. We may be more "prisoners," or more deeply rooted in our times and concepts, than we like to admit. Consciously, however, Jane has never been overly enthusiastic about the idea of reincarnation to begin with. I've noted in other books that she seldom talks about it. She was brought up as a Roman Catholic, and more than passionately embraced that faith. Yet she was early subjected to the church's rigid opposition to the whole idea of reincarnation because, strangely enough, even in her very youthful poetry she dealt with the forbidden subject (although not by name). Jane does believe that long ago she left behind the church's dogmas on reincarnation. She doesn't want to use the concept as a crutch; her caution stems from other beliefs, on which I'll quote her shortly. (As for myself, while growing up I knew nothing of reincarnation beyond its name.) But we'll be the first ones to agree that in certain Seth sessions, and in her very evocative poetry, Jane has encouraged her intuitive and creative selves to seriously discuss reincarnation. This is very evident in her second and latest book of poetry, *If We Live Again: Or, Public Magic and Private Love*, which was published in December of last year (1981). From the beginning of Section 3 of "I Am Alive Again":

> *I am alive again,*
> *remembering a thousand seasons,*
> *arranging and rearranging*
> *Aprils and Septembers*
> *in my mind's transparent vase*
> *and placing it on the shelf*
> *of my attention—*
> *a miniature still life.*

It can be seen from even this tiny quotation that Jane's poetry reflects that same mystical, intuitive innocence before nature (and thus, ultimately, All That Is) that I tried to describe in the first essay. It could well be that her psyche has derived from her whole self, or entity, the "facts" of reality a lot better than either of us consciously knows them. Both of us have had our psychic expressions (really isolated episodes) involving what can be called simultaneously existing reincarnational selves, and we've published accounts of a few of these. Some of our experiences have come in dream states. Our independence relative to reincarnation may represent just conscious cussedness on our parts, but we believe that each of us (meaning anyone, that is) always has the freedom to accept or reject any such choice or causality

—*whatever we choose to do*. No, instead we think of our current challenges as *contributing to* the knowledge of our whole selves in most specific ways, rather than our being swayed that much by our reincarnational and/or counterpart associations. However, I'm not at all sure how many others feel that way. I do know that regardless of local variations an acceptance of reincarnation has encircled the earth for millennia, and that in our country recent polls show a quarter of the population believing in it.

I also know that in a couple of chapters for *Dreams* itself Seth referred to the genetic factors involving reincarnation. He said that basically both our genetic structure and our reincarnational history are systems of consciousness, that they're "intermixed." The former is physical, the latter is psychic, a part of our inner bank of knowledge. I don't doubt that he's right—that is, in our temporal lifetimes we call upon whatever systems of consciousness we desire to, at whatever "time": a matter of choice and free will operating within the broad parameters of our sexual orientation and other personality factors.

I keep wondering about the results of an individual's choosing not to call upon *any* of his or her bank of reincarnational lives, though, whether from the past or the future. This approach would very nicely eliminate having to deal with one's "karma" this time around—should there really be a system of consciousness embodying that ancient concept. Think of the fun a person could have who decided at an early age—or even before physical birth—to experience a life unencumbered by other psychic relationships; wherein it had little or nothing to "work out." What freedoms might lie ahead—and yes, what challenges, too! Buddhism and Hinduism would banish the very thought: How dare one even *think* of escaping, or just simply ignoring, his or her "fate or destiny" (to put it loosely)! Yet our mass reality obviously is large enough to allow me room to generate such fanatical thoughts. . . .

All of this reminds me that lately the media have carried a number of stories detailing how medical science is not only trying hard to approach cures for scourges like cancer (in cancer's case, possibly through the exploration and understanding of the role played in the cell nucleus by altered normal cells called oncogenes), but is already claiming to have narrowed down its search to specific genes that affect imponderables like *behavior*—depression, for example. Not only that, sociobiologists are advancing their very controversial ideas that much of human behavior has an ultimate genetic basis, which in turn influences cultural change, and so on.

Well, one may ask, if a so-called negative quality like depression has a genetic foundation, what about the genetics for a positive attribute like joy—or, even, something like reincarnation? (I haven't come across anything in the media yet about either one of those.) If reincarnational and genetic systems *are* intermixed, then it could be said that even a person's decision to ignore his or her reincarnational heritage was in itself genetically based—and it could be fun to explore the contradictory ramifications of such a state. What other wonders might our cells contain? While amusing myself I'm simplifying to a great degree: If traces of one's "successive" lives are genetically embedded, sorting them out would be an enormous task.

It would be impossible at this time, I'm certain, for a researcher to find any evidence that reincarnational heritages are coded for among the approximately 100,000 genes lined up on the 46 chromosomes we carry in the nucleus of each of our cells. We say that a certain gene contains the instructions for the manufacture of a certain protein the body uses in the construction or function of an eye, for instance, and that in expressing that code the gene passes on characteristics inherited from physical ancestors—but is that endowment influenced or directed in any fashion by reincarnational attributes as well? Might those factors be just as potent as those inherited from a grandfather, say? The genes in each cell have their individual jobs to do in furnishing the quivering templates for the manufacture (via the nucleic acids DNA and messenger RNA) of all of our bodily proteins. But if we think of our genetic endowment as first being a system of consciousness as our reincarnational history is, we can see how the two nonphysical systems could be intermixed, as Seth put it, with one influencing the other. Conceivably, each of us could be a mixed bag of ancestral and reincarnational heritages, then— more "mongrelized" than we may care to admit. Interesting. . . . What we choose to do with those possibilities that we present ourselves with at each temporal birth may be another matter entirely.

And nowhere in this part of my discussion, in order to keep it within manageable bounds in this essay, have I mentioned the inherent ramifications involving genetics and reincarnation and *probable* realities.

"I think that a too-specific 'reading' of reincarnational material leads us to forget time's simultaneous nature and promotes a 'nitty-gritty' attitude," Jane wrote for me as I was working on these passages. "We may want to know the place and the time of a past self, for example—and the very concentration upon the 'past' simply deepens our commitment to time. The search for detail leads us further away from the larger sensed dimensions in which those facts must lie.

"I feel that Rob and I have lived our lives together many times, for example, and in many relationships. But I don't want to spend a lot of 'time' learning about those lives. I 'know' we change and replenish those other existences.

"When I write poetry I can often feel that translife focus, and catch the 'real facts.' "

We're not against reincarnation, then, only careful about our beliefs concerning it. Within the context of my discussion, reincarnation is Seth's historical version of his counterpart concept, which is that each of us is physically connected with certain other males and females who are living at the same time we are, and who are exploring physical life from a variety of viewpoints in ways that no one physical self could possibly match. This means that each reincarnational self has its own cluster of counterpart selves within its own time period, and that all are interconnected on nonphysical levels, joining together like magical gears meshing in constantly changing patterns across time and reality. And once one understands ideas of reincarnation and counterparts in these terms, it becomes difficult to think of one without the other, so inevitable do they appear to be.

(Obviously, some counterpart selves can meet physically, as reincarnational selves cannot. Under circumstances and in ways explained in Volume 2 of *"Unknown" Reality*, again, Jane and I think we've encountered a few of our counterpart selves. Just for fun, try to imagine the complicated relationships that can obtain within only a family of five, say, when each member exists within his or her much larger family of reincarnational and counterpart selves. Let the mathematicians among our readers calculate the number of possible psychic interchanges alone that can arise in the "past, present, and future" involving the reincarnational and counterpart selves of these five people!)

Now what kinds of "redemption" can be found amid the interchanges among any combination of reincarnational and/or counterpart lives, for instance? Some, certainly, and no doubt the reader can think of at least a few creative interpretations of redemptive qualities, but I'd rather let the question search for its own approximate answers as I continue work upon this essay. Jane and I do feel sure, however, that the experiences of our current lifetimes have so many psychic and physical ramifications that their numbers are literally beyond our grasp—and that many of those developments are certain to be quite "alien" to us here in our own everday realities. (All of this applies to everyone, of course.)

I don't really think we can conceive of anything to be truly "alien," though, so I use the word here only to lead into the next of Seth's larger concepts that I want to mention: that of probable realities, or probabilities, as Jane and I usually say. Not only does Seth stress the constant psychic motion of reincarnational and counterpart selves upon this earth we know—but he also tells us that each of those selves can move into *other* or parallel realities. I quote him from Session 681 in Volume 1 of *"Unknown" Reality*:

"All probable worlds exist now. All probable variations on the most minute aspect in any reality exist now. You weave in and out of probabilities constantly, picking and choosing as you go along. The cells within your body do the same thing."

So if Jane undergoes illness in *this* reality, in another she does not—but in between those extremes she also explores all stages of her illness in a series of probable universes, flashing among them in "no time at all," basically. . . . In some of those realitites I accompany her in various relationships. In others *I* am the one who becomes ill! In some I don't even physically coexist with her. But as Seth has said, since I live with her in this probable reality from which I write, then my existence is always at least probable within any of her realities. The same applies to me from Jane's standpoint. And although Seth hasn't said so yet (that I remember), I also think that within the spontaneous plan of probable realities each of us—anyone, that is—explores all aspects of sexuality and parenthood at the same time.

Within the idea of probable realities, then, there are innumerable opportunities for redemption to take place, between or among creatures—or even between or among *ideas*—and in all manner of ways. In how many ways? Seth remarked a long time ago that we humans can at least *approach* the notion of infinity by considering the ramifications inherent within probabilities. For my own amusement, in recent years I've often tried to objectify that statement by equating the possible number of probable realities with the current scientific estimate of the number of atoms in the universe: 10^{79}, or a 1 followed by 79 zeroes. But even if that rather simple number is inconceivable to us it still won't do, of course, for it represents only a limit of measurement inside the "physical" universe we think we know. Within the limitless realms of consciousness, 10^{79} is still but a doorway to vastly greater imaginative quantities and qualities of either numbers or probable realities. Fascinating! There are multitudinous possibilities for a redemption—or equalization or love or *forgiveness*, say—to take place amid such a dazzling array of probable realities. As far as our understanding can go, such a redemptive quality can be psychic, physical, both, or simply based on explorations of feeling and accomplishment we have yet to know.

Then beyond those human-oriented parameters must lie a host of probable realities involving changes in psychic and physical form: *non*human aspects of ourselves that in ordinary terms we'd have great difficulty relating to. This discussion could be carried further into such realms, but instead I'll note that even here I don't conceive of anything that would prohibit at least some exchanges between certain of those far probable realities and our own mundane universe. It all depends upon where you want to stop in your thinking, upon what you can conceive of. . . .

We've presented lengthy quotations from Seth on his Framework 1 and Framework 2 material both in his *Mass Events* and in Jane's *God of Jane*. His discussions on the subject are an excellent example of how a very creative idea, capable of helping many people, can arise from an attempt to deal with a personal situation—for on September 17, 1977, Seth introduced his Frameworks 1 and 2 concept in a private session designed to help Jane contend with her physical symptoms.

For Seth, Framework 1 is simply a term representing the

everyday, linear, conscious "working reality" we take for granted, the one in which "time" and events automatically unfold in moment after undeniable moment. It's the milieu in which most of us unthinkingly live out our physical lives. Beyond Framework 1, however, exists Framework 2, and it represents the great timeless or simultaneous spacious present that's so dearly a manifestation of All That Is. All of our dreams, plans, thoughts, actions, and choices live in Framework 2; all flow from Framework 2 into Framework 1 according to our beliefs.

As Seth told us in that introductory session, over four and a half years ago, Jane's "body itself has nothing wrong with it except the application of beliefs. . . . Even if you think the body does have something wrong with it, then the necessary adjustments would be made in another kind of time [in Framework 2] that in Framework 1 would take no time at all—or, the amount of time you thought required." For emphasis I myself underlined that last phrase, because it's easy to miss how very important it really is: Our individual concept of the amount of time necessary to accomplish an action like a healing will govern its progress. Then, a bit later, Seth made a statement that I've thought most ironic ever since: "In terms of creativity, however, Ruburt has long been operating in Framework 2, and this session should help him make certain correlations so that he can automatically begin to use such methods in regard to his physical conditon."

There followed many sessions, both regular and private (or deleted, as we sometimes call them), in which Seth discussed Frameworks 1 and 2. As can happen when we're consciously too close to a deep-seated situation, some little time passed before Jane and I realized the obvious: It wasn't that we were *unable* to tune into Framework 2, say, for help in effecting a healing for her in the joint reality we'd created in Framework 1—but that in physical reality we were drawing from Framework 2 *exactly what we wanted to*, even if often on unconscious or unwitting levels. Again, a matter of choices, and hard truths to face. As I've tried to show in these essays, we didn't suspend our efforts to reach into that larger framework. In a variety of ways we kept trying to do just that through the screens of our emotions and intellects. In those terms, communication between frameworks is unstoppable, really: I think that if one could halt the interchanges, physical death would result. For us, the learning processes were there for the changing anytime we decided that a physical illness was "wrong." But it would be wrong only when we decided that we didn't need it anymore.

I should note that Seth has briefly—very briefly—referred to the existence of Frameworks 3 and 4. He says, I believe, that initially his encounters with Jane take place in a Framework 3 environment. It's my own guess that Framework 4 might involve our communication—*through* the first three frameworks—with some of those nonhuman probable realities I mentioned not long ago.

But if the interactions between or among frameworks exist for everybody, in our terms, then as far as I'm concerned they exist for each *thing* as well—and I do mean the so-called "inanimate." (This isn't the place to go into it, but Seth maintains that for many reasons we arbitrarily decide what's living and nonliving.) Each reincarnational self, each counterpart self and probable self has its complement of frameworks. So does the most minute living or nonliving entity and the most gigantic. So, "probably," do most of the far-out probable realities one can imagine—for I won't go so far as to deny that some probable realities may exist without such framework structures. Strange one-dimensional "flatlands" indeed! But in each case where those framework interactions operate, they help each creation, each presence, each essence or vital principle fulfill "a larger picture that the conscious mind may not be able presently to perceive." In ways I can't even begin to describe here, all frameworks must ultimately be joined within the ineffable context of All That Is.

Early in this essay (which I began on May 7, 1982), I mentioned the series of sessions Seth gave in 1980 on his magical approach to reality, and the different approaches Jane and I took toward doing books on the subject. We were becoming so harried by her worsening physical symptoms when that material started to come through that she gave up working on *Dreams* and concentrated on those private sessions instead. For many months she considered doing a book on the magical approach (with my encouragement), and collected much information of her own for it. In other words, she viewed the book as helping herself as much as anyone else. Then when Seth and Jane both came through with material on her sinful self (see Essay No. 3

for April 16, 1982), those data took precedence over everything else. That was to be expected, of course, for by then our concentration was directed almost wholly into the area of symptoms. Jane didn't return to work on *Dreams* until July 1981, when the two blocks of sinful-self material had run their courses. By then, she'd held only one session for *Dreams* in the last 13 months.

Her focus on her book about the magical approach never jelled enough for her to carry it through, even though she continued experimenting with it. Our own general psychological unease certainly contributed to that failure, but Jane's writing became bogged down in details about dates, quotations from old sessions, and elaborate studies built upon our dream accounts and other psychic and daily records, for example. Not her way of working, really, even though all of those ingredients were—and are—excellent.

Before presenting the promised excerpts on the magical approach, I want to note that Seth is simply saying that from Framework 2 (and possibly from other frameworks) we draw whatever information we want in whatever *way* we choose to focus upon it: positively, negatively, magically, literally, skeptically, and so forth. As he told us in a private session way back on February 26, 1972: "You get what you concentrate upon. There is no other main rule." Every reincarnational and counterpart and probable self, located in whatever neatly packaged compartment of time—past, present, or future—can utilize the magical approach as a matter of choice, then. That simple declaration of use involves a world of understanding and experience, however, and one that Jane and I have found extremely difficult to initiate in the way we consciously think we want to—although according to their letters, at least, many of our readers are able to work with various portions of the Seth material with little or no trouble at all.

Seth, from the private session for August 17, 1980—the third one in his series on the magical approach:

"The magical approach takes it for granted, in the simplest terms, that the life of any individual will fulfill itself, will develop and mature, that the environment and the individual are uniquely suited and work together. This sounds very simple. In verbal terms, however, those are the beliefs (if you will) of each c-e-l-l *(spelled)*. They are imprinted in each chromosome, in each atom. They provide a built-in faith that pervades each living creature, each snail, each hair on your head. Those ingrained beliefs are of course biologically pertinent, providing the impetus of all growth and development.

"Each cell believes in a better tomorrow *(quietly, with amusement)*. I am, I admit, personifying our cell here, but the statement has a firm truth. Furthermore, each cell contains within itself a belief and an understanding of its own inevitability. It knows it lives beyond its death, in other words. . . ."

And: "The magical approach takes it for granted that the human being is a united creature, fulfilling purposes in nature even as the animals do, whether or not those purposes are understood. The magical approach takes it for granted that each individual has a future, a fulfilling one, even though death may be tomorrow. The magical approach takes it for granted that the means for development are within each individual, and that fulfillment will happen naturally. Overall, that approach operates in your world. If it did not, there would be no world. If the worst was bound to happen, as the scientists certainly think, even evolution in their terms would have been impossible, of course —a nice point to put in somewhere *(all intently, but also with considerable humor)*.

"You needed this background, for I want to build up the atmosphere in which this magical approach can be comprehended."

In the first essay I described how Dr. Mandali had told Jane that her thyroid gland had "simply ceased functioning," and how the doctor had started to cautiously rejuvenate my wife's endocrine system with 50 micrograms daily of a synthetic thyroid hormone. Jane is supposed to take these pills in some still-to-be-determined strength for the rest of her life (although in his session for April 16 Seth had explained that her thyroid gland "has repaired itself" on several occasions; see the essay for the same date.)

After nine weeks, however, Jane and I are more than ready for an increase in the strength of the pills, for she obviously needs the boost. I've mentioned several times her dozing or falling asleep outright in her chair. Dr. Mandali agrees that the low thyroid activity is directly related to these episodes. Yet there's more involved with the dozing—effects I haven't gone into yet, and can only briefly refer to here. We haven't discussed these with her doctor, either—clear signs of the secretive aspects of our own natures—but Jane believes she's had a number of part-hallucinatory, part-psychic experiences as a result of the thyroid-medication situation.

"I've had several new experiences with altered states of consciousness," she wrote in labored script, "and these are quite different than anything I've done before. For this reason they are difficult to classify. . . ." Also, she's indulged in long conversations with me—and on occasion with certain friends—when we apparently were present in out-of-body states. Related here are actions she thought she was participating in with me, say, yet when she "woke up," she discovered we hadn't done any of those things. She's referred often to "gaps in my consciousness" while dozing. "I don't know what I was doing in my chair," she said at 11:05 A.M. yesterday; she'd fallen asleep after telling me she had to use the commode. "I don't like the way the thyroid business is making me feel. . . . I feel like I'm in your way, or in life's way. . . ." She had certainly been depressed on that occasion, and I'd tried to cheer her up.

In addition, Jane has described some unique versions of out-of-body episodes that have grown out of the thyroid-medication connection. These haven't been like the typical experience, wherein she'd feel her psyche rising out of a physical organism that was securely anchored by gravity to her chair to the floor, for example. Instead, she had felt her body *in the chair* lift most convincingly toward the ceiling. . . . Sometimes those events became curious indeed—for in her chair Jane flipped over and approached the ceiling of our bedroom feet first. Below her, then, was an upside-down television screen, and a pair of windows with the café curtains at the top instead of the bottom. Not only that, but with her double vision Jane sometimes saw *two* television screens and *four* windows! She hasn't seen her own body sitting below her yet, though, as can happen in the out-of-body state, and she hasn't seen or talked with any deceased individuals.

At this time Jane doesn't know just how, or to what extent, hallucination was involved in any of these episodes, if at all; sometimes the dream state definitely was. But the experiences

I've mentioned here, plus others, have uncovered some surprising new dimensions of her abilities, and later she wants to thoroughly investigate and write about them.

ESSAY 8
SUNDAY, MAY 23, 1982

It should be obvious by now that in a large measure all of the selves and approaches I've delineated in these essays simply represent Seth playing around semantically, as he tries to get various portions of his ideas through our heads at certain times. All is one, basically, as he knows—and can *feel*—far better from his vantage point than we can from ours. (Yet, "Our lives and deaths are now," Jane wrote in Chapter 10 of *God of Jane*, quoting herself from her own "psychic library.")

That all seeming divisions reflect portions of a unified whole is surely one of our oldest concepts, growing, in those terms, with us out of our prehistory as we struggled to grasp the "true" nature of reality. Traditionally we've cast that feeling or knowledge in religious terms, for want of a better framework, but I think that more and more now the search is also on within science for a theory—even a hypothesis—that will lock up our often subjective variables into what might be called a more human equivalent of the still-sought-for unified theory in physics. What are human beings, anyhow? From what Jane and I can gather (through our reading especially), at least some of the world's leading scientists are becoming willing to contend with consciousness itself. (Including *their own* consciousnesses? I can't help wondering!) Portions of the latest scientific literature I have on hand, particularly that produced by physicists, contain references that not long ago would have been branded as metaphysical, or even worse.

But I note with some amusement that science absorbs such heresies by weaving them into and developing them out of current establishment thinking—concepts, say, like the many-worlds interpretation of quantum mechanics. Put very simplistically, this "quantum approach" allows for the theme that each of us inhabits but one of innumerable probable or parallel worlds.

Even the theory of evolution is invoked, for those other worlds are said to *evolve* in parallel with the one we inhabit. Yet there is no answer within quantum mechanics as to how or why one's personal identity *chooses* to follow a certain probable pathway, and consciousness *per se* is not considered. (Some physicists, however, have implied that subatomic particles—photons—*communicate with each other* as they take their separate but "sympathetic" paths.) Pardon my irony here, but Seth has always dealt with the ramifications of consciousness and maintained also that we do not inhabit just one probable world, but constantly move among them by choice—and by the microsecond, if one chooses.

(I'll add that both Seth and quantum theory predict the spontaneous creation of particles of matter out of or in "empty" space —events that, it seems to me, go against some of the laws of conservation. One of these states that matter cannot be created from nothing. Seth says this spontaneous creation happens all of the time through the actions of consciousness. In the theoretical quantum world, however, certain conditions are needed: superheavy nuclei amid strong electrical fields, and so forth.)

Some of our readers, sending us recent books and copies of articles written by scientists working on these subjects, have noted that it must be nice for Jane and me to have concepts that Seth has been discussing for years "corroborated" by the establishment (often we already had the material on file, by the way). But once again irony enters in on my part, for I'm afraid our answer is that in general science isn't even aware of the existence of the Seth material, notwithstanding the letters of approval and/or encouragement we receive from individual scientists, representing a variety of disciplines. We feel no sense of corroboration. As I wrote to a fan just last week: "No matter what he or she may think of it personally, no reputable scientist is going to publicly espouse a belief in the Seth material. Certainly not career-wise. Not for a long time yet, in our opinion, and for many reasons."

Some day, for our own amusement—but hardly with the idea of convincing others, let alone influential scientists—I'll ask Seth to comment upon whatever connections may exist between his ideas and those embedded in quantum mechanics. I'm sure he's quite entertained by the whole situation—yet also compassionate toward the human strivings involved. He's never mentioned the concept, nor have we asked him to. I think that Jane has little (if any) interest in whether any connections might exist between the Seth material and the mathematical theory of quantum mechanics. Any discussion of this in our books is strictly my own doing, my own speculation: I think it fun to play creatively with a theory that is, after all, there for anyone to consider, from whatever standpoint. And I maintain that the theory of quantum mechanics does contain strong paranormal aspects, whether or not science admits this.

I also think that if asked Seth would point out that since the concept of quantum mechanics is based upon the idea that everything we "know"—matter, energy, our sensual information —is made up of quanta, or the interactions of insubstantial fields that in turn, and quite paradoxically, produce very active subatomic packets or particles, then quantum mechanics is at least analogous with his statements that basically the universe is composed of consciousness itself. But I think that the continuum of consciousness, or All That Is, contains not only the phenomena of quantum mechanics, but also Seth's nonphysical EE (electromagnetic energy) units, and his CU's (or units of consciousness). In those terms, then, quantum mechanics is a theory that doesn't penetrate deeply enough into basic reality, even if physicists these days are basing their unified field theories upon quantum thinking. (These theories are themselves quite incomplete, since at this time they incorporate only three of the four basic interactions in nature: electromagnetism, and the strong and weak nuclear forces. So far, gravitation remains outside all attempts at integration.)

To me, consciousness or All That Is is an omnipresent, really indescribable *awareness* that to us human beings has no limits, "one" containing not only the attributes of time and space and of all feeling, thought, and objectivity, but numberless other properties, manifestations, and probabilities that lie outside our very limited interior and exterior perceptions. In terms of physics, then, reality is still unknowable.

Even if she's to remain in something like her present impaired state, Jane said as I wrote the above paragraph, still it seems we're better off for having the Seth material than not: "I'd sure as hell rather take my chances *with* it than *without*!" she exclaimed, if somewhat ruefully.

Six days ago, on May 18, and to our great relief, Dr. Mandali finally stepped up the strength of the thyroid hormone pills she is prescribing for my wife—from 50 to 70 micrograms daily. "But the benefits are still weeks away," she told Jane. The increase followed the positive results of a blood test the doctor had ordered a few days previously: A hospital technician had come to our hill house to draw blood from Jane—performing a "phlebotomy service." Now Jane must have such a test before each increase in her thyroid medication.

In our ceaseless search for answers to an unending list of personal questions, we discussed the notion that in her own way Jane has described a circle from her childhood: Her parents, Marie and Delmer, were married in Saratoga Springs, a well-known resort town in upper New York State, in 1928. They were divorced in 1931, when Jane was two years old. (Jane didn't see her father again—he came from a broken home himself—until she was 21.) By the time Jane was three years old, her mother was having serious problems with rheumatoid arthritis. Indeed, the daughter has only one conscious memory of seeing her mother on her feet. All we have are a few photographs Del took of Marie not long after their marriage. They show a beautiful woman wearing a bathing suit, standing on a beach in Florida.

Some of our other books contain more information on how Jane grew up fatherless, and with a Marie who soon became bedridden and embittered. Mother and child were supported by welfare, and assisted over the years by a series of itinerant housekeepers—a number of these were prostitutes who, according to Jane, were periodically thrown out of "work" when town officials would shut down the "houses," try to clean up gambling, and so forth. Marie was a brilliant, angry woman who lived in near-constant pain, and who regularly abused her daughter through behavior that, if not psychotic, was certainly close to it. (She would terrify the young Jane by stuffing cotton in her mouth and pretending she'd committed suicide, for example.) Jane also spent time in a strictly run Catholic orphanage. Her father died in 1971, when he was 68. Her mother died in 1972, at the same age; Jane, who hadn't seen Marie for a number of years, did not attend the funeral. I didn't urge her to do so, either. For my part, I'd always felt distinctly uneasy in Marie's presence on the few occasions we met.

None of the doctors we talked to would say outright that rheumatoid arthritis is inherited—only that "it seems to run in families," and that more women than men develop it. Even today we saw a well-known specialist say the same thing on a national television program. Yet except for her mother's case there's no history of arthritis in Jane's family, outside of a "routine" trace of rheumatism in a couple of grandparents. The curious question arises: Why, then, did first Marie and then Jane begin showing their symptoms? (As closely as we can determine, Marie was about 26 years old at their onset. Jane was 35; she'll be 53 tomorrow.)

My own belief, which I've held for some 15 years, is that in Jane's case at least the young girl's *psychological conditioning* was far more important—far more damaging, in those terms—than any physical tendency to inherit. I think that Marie's domineering rage at the world (chosen by her, never forget) deeply penetrated Jane's developing psyche, and—again in those terms—caused her to set up repressive, protective inner barriers that could be activated and transformed into physical signs at any time, under certain circumstances. Out of many possibilities, the daughter's conditioning was psychically chosen and accepted, and through that focus she meant to interact with the mother's behavior. This, to me, is an example of the way a course of probable activity can be agreed upon by all involved.

I even think there's good medical evidence these days for my view of Jane's "symptoms," as we've called them for many years. In recent years rheumatoid arthritis has been found to be an amazingly complicated disease involving a great number of the body's immune factors. In the progression of rheumatoid arthritis one's own immunologic system turns on the body and damages it. A very simplified explanation is that in a process repeated over and over, a variety of defender cells called phagocytic monocytes turn into macrophages, or scavenger cells that, in turn, release enzymes which consume healthy joint tissue. The resulting debris attracts more monocytes, and so on. An inflammatory accumulation of cellular detritus finally destroys the joint's cartilage and eats away bone.

This isn't all, however, for experiments have now shown that the brain/mind connection can influence immunity, through stressful conditioning either enhancing its effects or subduing them. Until a very few years ago it was medical dogma that the immune system was entirely independent of any "outside" influence. But recently certain brain chemicals were discovered paired off with cellular chemical "receptors" in the immune system, and researchers expect to find many more of these associations. In physical terms, then, I think it quite possible that in Jane's case long-term stress, beginning in her early childhood, consistently overstimulated her immune system. Over and over Marie told Jane that she was no good, that the daughter's birth had caused the mother's illness. Well before she was 10 years old Jane had developed persistent symptoms of colitis, an inflammation of the large intestine/bowel that is often associated with emotional stress. By her early teens she had an overactive thyroid gland. Marie—and others—told her that she would burn herself out and die before she was 20 years old. Her vision was poor; she required very strong glasses (which she seldom wore). Finally in her mid-30s there came the beginning of rheumatoid arthritis: Jane's immune system greatly increased its attack upon her body.

(I believe that current medical thinking about the immune system and arthritis will be much enlarged upon by the time this book is published, though I haven't given that much thought to just what new information may be acquired. However, I do think I'm accurate concerning the connections between Jane's early psychological conditioning and her present challenges.)

A moment ago, I referred to the way all involved with my wife could agree upon a course of probable activity. There are as many possibilities—and probabilities—as one can think of. I can hardly begin to list them all here. In Framework 2, for example, Marie, pregnant with Jane, could have decided with her daughter-to-be upon certain sequences of action to be pursued during their lives. Or in Framework 2 the two of them could have co-operated upon such a decision before *Marie's* birth, even. If reincarnation is to be considered, their disturbed relationship this time might reflect past connections of a different yet analogous nature, and may also have important effects upon any future ones. Additionally, Jane could have chosen the present relationship to eventually help her temper her reception of and reaction to the Seth material, making her extra-cautious; this, even though she'd seen to it ahead of time that she would be born with that certain combination of fortitude and innocence necessary for her to press on with her chosen abilities. She could have made a pact ahead of time to "borrow" certain strong mystical qualities from her maternal grandfather, who was part French Canadian and part Canadian Indian (specific tribe unknown by us), and with whom she strongly identified as a child. And Jane's resolve, her will that, according to Seth, "is amazingly strong" (in Volume 2 of *"Unknown" Reality*, see the 713th session for October 21, 1974), may buttress the understanding and determination of one or more of her counterparts in this life; she may meet (or have met) such an individual; another may live across an ocean, say, with no meeting ever to take place in physical terms.

In all of this I've barely hinted at the complicated relationships involving *other* family members from the past, present, and future. The mathematical combinations possible are vast. And what's *my* role in all of this, for heaven's sake (to make a pun)? Or that of members of my own family? What part do I play, and have yet to play, in Jane's redemption—as well as my own—and on what level or levels? When did the two of us make our own pacts in Framework 2 (or other frameworks), and how will they work out in Framework 1? But it's even possible that all together Marie, Jane, her grandfather, and I set up the original situation before the physical births of *any* of us—and in some probable reality (if not in this one) we did do just that! Words become terribly inadequate tools to express what I feel and am trying to write here, for I want to record at once every combination of relationships I can conceive of. . . .

Whatever the initial course of action agreed to in just this probable reality by everyone involved, from whatever point in the "past," in Framework 1 the participants have subjected it to an almost infinite variety of choices and modifications through the years: but always—always—within nature's great structure, and accompanied by the utter freedom of each person concerned to accept, reject, abort, or change the whole affair from their individual perspective at any moment. . . .

To return to just Jane and Marie, then, I think that their long-range cyclical behavior and interaction, no matter how painful it may seem on the surface, represented deep challenges set up by mother and daughter for certain overall purposes that they wanted to experience, separately and jointly. Not only would the two women be emotionally tested and enriched across physical and psychological time, but so would their entities or whole selves.

One of their common creations within the same time scheme was rheumatoid arthritis, of course, for Jane began to show *her* version of it some eight years before Marie died. That mutual illness obviously became a deeply charged subject for both of them. However, with that fine stubbornness I mentioned in the first essay, Jane never told Marie of her own affliction; since the two no longer saw each other, consciously Marie never knew. Both of us think she *did* know psychically, though. I even think that mother and daughter shared the *same* case of arthritis—there weren't two separate instances of it.

"Oh, why did you have to put *that* in!" Jane cried in anguish as she read that last sentence. It happened to mark the end of my day's work, which I'd showed to her after supper. "It's a fantastic idea, but—"

"Well, I know it's a good idea," I said. "I think people do it all the time. Something like it must happen in epidemics, too. But I didn't mean to hurt you—don't pay any attention to it."

In these last few pages (since I began discussing my beliefs about Jane's early psychological conditioning), I've indicated the only kind of thinking by which I can personally make sense out of our world these days. Particularly when I consider the "news" on the typical front page of the typical daily newspaper: All too accurately the "stories" of war, pollution, corruption, and poverty and crime show just how little we human beings know or understand ourselves at this time—and how far we have to go, individually and *en masse*. As the years have passed, I've come to trust more and more my own insights into our behavior as a species within the framework of a nature that I believe our kind has co-created with every other species on the planet (to confine my theme to just our immediate environment for the moment). It all seems very complicated, certainly, but as I manipulate in everyday life I don't consciously dwell upon all of the ramifications I've mentioned in these essays. Instead I try to hold them in the back of my mind as parts of a greater whole. So, I believe, does Jane.

Granted that our species' best human understanding of "the mystery of life" and of the universe is exceedingly inadequate, still Jane and I do not think that nature is totally objective, indifferently cruel, or simply uncaring, as science would have us believe. (We also have deep reservations about the theory of evolution and its "survival of the fittest" dogmas, but this isn't the place to go into those subjects.) Far more basic and satisfactory to us are the intuitive comprehensions that this "nature" we've helped create is a living manifestation of All That Is, and that someplace, somewhere within its grand panorama, each action has meaning and *is* truly redeemed. We are not dwarfed. How could we be? For if, as I wrote earlier, Jane and I agree with the ancient idea that "all seeming divisions reflect portions of a unified whole," we also think that in some fashion the whole is enclosed within *each* of its parts. Science calls the idea holonomy, but Seth has been saying the same thing for years without ever mentioning the word. Jane didn't even know it.

I've written these passages knowing, of course, that many of Seth's points and our own are at best theories, if very intriguing ones. Some may contend that they're not even theories, but only hypotheses—tentatively inferred explanations requiring much further experimentation and examination. Worse still (I write with some humor), they may "only" be ideas. Whatever their status, Jane and I take heart from the letters sent us by many thousands of readers, who have time and again explained how they put the Seth material to use in very positive physical and mental ways. (Except for a few early instances when we inadvertently lost some of our correspondence, we've saved all of it. The cartons are piling up in a cellar storeroom. We hope that eventually our "fan mail" will serve as the foundation for a study concerning the ways in which society reacts to new ideas, through the viewpoints, say, of science, philosophy and psychology, religion, the "occult," skepticism, generalized deep curiosity, and mental illness. Very abusive responses are also involved, as well as surprising near-illiterate ones.)

Because of its very nature, however, and even though it comprises enough "evidence" in favor of a generalized principle that explains the workings of certain phenomena, a theory inevitably contains errors, since it's based upon incomplete data to begin with. It's therefore vulnerable to later theories through which investigators attempt to reduce or eliminate those errors. A continuous refining of detail takes place in the search for a final truth that can become "fact." (I also note that that truth being sought may end up as so abstract a quality that it loses its emotional and intellectual meanings for us, and moves out of our generalized perception. I'm noting, then, that we can analyze something right out of our own reality by ultimately declaring it to be impossible—when actually it, and other versions of it, continue to exist in related probable realities.)

Considering the views of Seth, Jane, and me, reincarnational and counterpart existences and their ramifications may enter in as portions of such a refining process as we attempt to search out the dimensions of consciousness. This may be true whether or not we believe in past and future lives, and/or counterparts, yet I can see no way such postulated manifestations can be "proven" at this time.

I think the beliefs the three of us hold are very creative ones; we accept them on that basis; they are as good "proofs" as we can currently get, and offer their own answers by sparking us into new ways of trying to make sense out of our reality. Science and philosophy will not agree with any of this, I know—at least for the most part, for I've read that there's never an idea so wild that it can't find a home in the mind of some scientist or philosopher. Jane and I aren't so naive as to think that we can offer any hard proofs for what we believe, and certainly Seth doesn't worry about it. Not even when I play around with his ideas relative to quantum theory can such proof be found—yet I let Jane's "amazingly strong" will be the measuring and observing device that automatically causes "waves" of knowing or consciousness—in Framework 2, for example—to coalesce into the "particles" that make up the physical forms she perceives as her reality in Framework 1, either psychically from a distance or right here.

ESSAY 9
MONDAY, MAY 31, 1982

Just over nine weeks have passed now since I brought my wife home from the hospital. And just last week (after another routine blood test) Jane's doctor again raised the dosage of the synthetic thyroid hormone she's taking, this time from 75 to 100 micrograms per day.

In the first essay I referred to Jane's unique combination of stubbornness, innocence, and mysticism, and in that respect nothing has changed. In spite of her horror at the medical practices and suggestions she's encountered, and in spite of her dismay at the physical damage the arthritis has caused in her temporal body, Jane will give up nothing until she—and/or her whole self—get out of the entire illness syndrome exactly what she wants to get. She has an incredible stubborn patience with physical life. This quality has sustained her throughout all of her challenges as well as her successes, and I think it must have been particularly important during her early frightening years with her mother, Marie. Her determination even shows somehow in photographs taken when she was of preschool age. Jane learned to refuse to strike back at the invalid Marie's rage and sarcasm, to inhibit her spontaneity and impulses, and so habits of repression entered in. Yet she was—and is—free of guile and sophistication.

She learned of the concept of sin through her intense early involvement with the Roman Catholic church. It's easy to see how, in Jane's case at least, the church's teachings about sin began to grow as the innocent child started protecting her spontaneous natural mysticism—that prime attribute she'd chosen for exploration in this life. I don't think of her "sinful self" could have risen to such prominence without feeding upon those repressions, clamping down more and more within the psyche as the years passed, continuing its misguided but "well-meaning attempt to protect the creative self . . . to keep a hand of caution on its course lest the centuries of men's belief in sin carried a true weight that I shared but could not comprehend." And so, of couse, the sinful self's own overreactions, although carried out without "malice," became themselves a portion of Jane's long-range learning challenges this time.

Until she became so ill that she was practically forced to go into the hospital, I'd always felt that my wife's single-minded yet literal focus of intent was capable of lasting however long it took to reach a particular goal—whether for five minutes or fifty years. Her illness led me to question that premise, but now it's back in place. Jane may not be always conscious of what she wants as she confronts her own projections in physical reality, but strong portions of her psyche are (and I think this applies to everyone).

When in the earlier days of our marriage I used to tell her that she had her "symptoms" regardless of what I thought or wanted, she would deny it. Yet I thought she *did*, and so I was driven to grope for larger understandings. I had to learn that if I shared a marriage in which my wife had developed a chronic illness, then certain portions of me had also participated in that joint creation. Eventually nothing made sense to me otherwise. I believe implicitly now that each one of us *does* create our own reality. "Interactions with others do occur, of course," Seth told us long ago, "yet there are none that you do not accept or draw to you by your thoughts, attitudes, or emotions." (In Chapter 1 of *The Nature of Personal Reality*, see the 613th session, for September 11, 1972.) And Jane and I are still exploring, still searching—together—for the factors within those larger frameworks of existence which make qualities like illness possible and understandable.

Throughout these essays I've been unable to go very far into most of the subjects Jane and I wanted to discuss, to do much more than approximate in words a welter of feelings and actions. There's much that I haven't even mentioned, so to that extent this record is quite incomplete. And regardless of whether our space and time are limited here, still it seems impossible to really penetrate to the deeper core of any subject or belief. Perhaps if Jane and I could do that, a great metamorphosis would take place: The closer we moved through probabilities toward All That Is, the more the tensions associated with the subject in question would transform themselves into profoundly joyous answers and challenges.

I've hardly mentioned our dreams. As related to Jane's physical symptoms, they have remained largely unconscious phenomena: We knew all along that we were often having "symptom dreams," but didn't recall them consistently enough to be able to do much conscious work with them. That's still the case. Obviously, we made our choices in that respect long ago: As far as the deeply charged subject of Jane's illness was concerned, we decided to keep most of our dream work on intuitive and unconscious levels. We took from Framework 2, then, exactly what we wanted to.

But that simple statement also means that our dream work

relative to Jane's challenges has often been powerfully abetted by Seth in many of the 347 completely private and 159 partially private sessions he's given us since November 1965. Much of the fascinating and informative material in which Seth discussed various aspects of Jane's symptoms is generalized enough for publication, and could help others, but because of its very intense personal connotations it's a project we haven't started yet. (Not that I haven't presented excerpts from a few of those sessions in other Seth books.)

There must be a vast amount of pertinent dream information ready for the tapping, however, and maybe with Seth's help Jane and I can eventually learn more about the undoubtedly therapeutic roles our joint and individual dreams have played as we contended with the challenges posed by her physical difficulties. Many questions arise: Even granting our personal reservations about influences being exerted within our current lives through past, future, as well as *other* present existences, what about exchanges on dream levels concerning Jane's symptoms between or among any of our reincarnational selves, our counterpart selves, or various combinations of the two? How am I involved in any of these, and how are Jane's and my families—and reaching how many generations back in ordinary time? To what extent does Jane's physical infirmity mushroom into other probable realities through the dream state? I think that Jane herself can deal with many such questions; possibly tuning into them on her own, should she decide to, or through the mediation of her "psychic library." A book could automatically develop out of the investigation—even, I joked with Jane, a "world-view" book.

As Jane wrote in Chapter 1 of *The World View of Paul Cézanne: A Psychic Interpretation* (1977): "Seth maintains that each of us forms a psychic world view, composed of our own ideas, feelings, and beliefs, as we encounter our private corner of reality." The world view of every creature that has ever lived continues to exist, and can be turned into under certain conditions. So can the psychic patterns of those now living, and even of those not yet born. Yet none of this means that contact will be made directly with the creator of the world view in question—only the bank of experiences originated through that individual's unique version of reality. And since world views are far from being static, interactions and combinations involving all time periods take place among them constantly.

Jane's book would be called *The World View of Jane Roberts*, of course. And, I thought, why not? If she could tune into the world views of the philosopher and psychologist William James, and the artist Paul Cézanne, why couldn't she do it for the writer and mystic Jane Roberts? The results would be even more intimate than those in *James* and *Cézanne*. A work like that would furnish invaluable clues concerning her redemption, on many levels, and mine as well.

The morning after showing her this material, I asked Jane what she thought about such a book. "I don't like to talk about it," she said, "but I've been potting around with the idea—getting some thoughts about something like that. But I'd rather not discuss it."

"Okay," I said. I was pleasantly surprised by her reaction, for her reluctance to talk about a certain subject often was a sign that she'd end up doing something creative with it.

Actually, of course, each *second* of any creature's life represents a creative act of the keenest sort, for it signals that physical entity's decision to continue living in physical terms. I think Jane has made some remarkable gains since leaving the hospital. Our friends all tell her she looks better each time they see her. She has beautiful clear skin. (*Irish* skin, I joke with her, although she's really but a quarter Irish.) She has additional freedom of movement in various joints, such as her knees and hips, although she's far from being able to walk. She can now type—if rather awkwardly—perhaps half a page of copy per day. "During those frightening-enough hospital episodes I learned under combat conditions, so to speak, how to trust my body," she wrote one day—an apt-enough analogy, I think.

She's also done her first two colored-ink sketches, using one of the 4″ x 6″ watercolor pads I'd bought for her last year. In these sketches, with their simple but very effective patterns of line and primary colors, Jane somehow bypasses her everyday challenges and very clearly reflects her basically mystical view of the world. She does the same with the little poems she's worked upon, most of which she regards as being not only incomplete but quite inconsequential: "I wouldn't even type them up, like you did," she commented. Yet I like lines like: "Let the dirge be heard, sweeping all things before it," and: "I've developed a sense of death, when someone takes a few steps off the known path almost unknowing," and: "I breathed in the public air and it became private." Jane also sings in Sumari occasionally, and has written down a few short songs in that "language" without translating them. I've been careful to collect for our own records the prose, sketches, poetry, and Sumari she's produced during this time of healing and testing.

For Jane's situation continues to be a time of testing. Writing with her right hand is still quite difficult for her. She's made no effort to learn to write with her better-functioning left hand, as I suggested she do a couple of months ago, so I've dropped that idea. "But I could start another book tomorrow," she said, "only I don't know what good it would do. . . ."

She has a lesser degree of double vision these days, but still may require surgery to correct imbalances in her optic muscles. An experimental treatment that's just been announced, involving injections into certain eye muscles of a drug derived from the toxin of botulism, may ultimately benefit her; the procedure, which apparently has no side effects, can eliminate the need for surgery by encouraging the realignment of the eyes. Jane is still very much against drugs and surgery, though—even while she's well aware of the contradictions in her beliefs as she continues to take daily the synthetic thyroid hormone and the liquid salicylate medication prescribed by Dr. Mandali. In his session for April 16 (see the essay for the same date), Seth told us that on several occasions Jane's thyroid gland has "repaired itself," but we don't think that has fully happened yet this time. In a recent private session (for May 10) Seth told us: "The gland is activating itself by itself—off and on, so to speak, giving a sputtering effect. Overall, the body is exploring the best rhythm of metabolism, and fitting itself in with the medication."

(Which makes us wonder: Just how will Jane's body let us know when it finally wants to divest itself entirely of the thyroid supplement? We're telling ourselves that that little challenge will automatically work itself out at the right time. We haven't posed the question to Seth.)

The quotation from Seth just presented will certainly lead the reader to wonder about additional sessions we may have acquired from him since April 16, and from Jane since April 20 (see the essays for those dates). The answer is that we've held 13 more sessions—4 of them given by Jane "herself," and 9 by Seth speaking through her. The last session in that baker's dozen was delivered by Seth on June 7. Most of the sessions are rather short, and not all of them are strictly personal. For those that do concern us I've written lengthy notes, often recording the minutiae of our daily lives for our own reference.

Even if those sessions can't be quoted in these essays because of the obvious space limitations, I can note that Jane and Seth each continued to develop the themes already laid down in the sessions that *have* been presented. What they really signify for the long term is (as I wrote in the essay for April 16) a continuing program of intense study for Jane and me—and yes, for Seth, too—as we seek to better understand our chosen commitments in our present physical lives. Our questions reflect those that everyone has, whether consciously or unconsciously—and among them is that eternally human "Why?" behind each event that we know. The material in the sessions is exhilarating, painful, enlightening, perceptive, frustrating, and maddening by turn—and sometimes, it seems, all of those things at once. We'd like to publish much of it, even though it's hardly all flattering, and even though some of it, because of our ordinary human limitations, may not be very useful in everyday life. For if the information arouses such mixed emotions in Jane and me, surely it will do so in others too, serving as an impetus or goad to learn more even while it highlights one's strengths and weaknesses. You create your own reality. The anger I'd felt at Jane and myself when she began recording her sinful-self material (see the essay for April 16) has long since dissipated. I won't claim that residues of it may not be buried within my psyche (and within Jane's), but it's very difficult to stay mad when one agrees with the simple but most basic and profound idea that you *do* create your own reality.

At times Jane still becomes depressed, just as she still dozes in her chair. While at work in my own writing room I occasionally hear her talking to herself as she sits at her card table in the living room, just down the hall: I've learned that on such occasions, she's asleep and often dreaming aloud, solving the psychological equations continually arising among the levels of her psyche as she pursues her chosen learning processes. I help her as much as I can. While I spend all of this time working on these essays for *Dreams*, I'm always afraid I'm leaving her alone too much. Jane does get lonely, she says.

Of course these essays reflect our particular chosen stances in life, both with and without the Seth material. I know that to some we're sure to have appeared slow in putting to use much of the material, but in a most basic respect we're way ahead in the situation: If we hadn't almost instantaneously begun to encourage the flow of information from Seth when Jane started to express it some 18 years ago, *and to write it down*, then it wouldn't even exist—at least in its present form. So we do take credit for doing some things right. Learning experiences can show themselves in a vast number of ways, then, and independently of sequential time, too; and if Jane and I don't like certain aspects of the realities we've created, we can try to change them, together and separately.

Already we've given up many old living patterns since Jane came home from the hospital, and in a strange way we now have the freedom to focus daily upon just a few main things. We've been reminded anew—more accurately, *we've taught ourselves*—that physical life itself is a wondrous medium of expression, and terrifically varied in that respect.

Our joint concentration has become like a brilliant light directed upon first one event and then another. Because Jane still requires regular care, our sleeping patterns remain much more evenly divided between the daylight and nighttime hours (see the essay for April 16). Since I can no longer work for hours at a time on the Seth books, or with the Seth material, I'm training myself to "put out" copy in concentrated bursts of energy that are usually of an hour's duration, say. I work around these creative outpourings by ministering to my wife, running our house and the many errands connected with our daily living, handling our publishing affairs, seeing visitors—expected and unexpected—and trying to answer at least some of the mail, which is threatening to accumulate beyond control. Once again I'm becoming aware of my dreams, and so is Jane. I haven't been able to get back to painting since Jane left the hospital, and I've had to hire help to mow the grass. Nor have I resumed the midnight walks I used to take over the hilly streets of our neighborhood;

I used to look forward to seeing the shadowy deer as they moved down into the streets from the woods north of the hill house. Jane's nurse now visits but twice a week, which is all that's necessary (my wife's decubiti are under control, for example).

At the request of Dr. Mandali, a few days ago Jane underwent her routine phlebotomy, or bloodletting, here at the house. Today (on June 18), the doctor informed us by telephone that as one result of the test we can increase Jane's thyroid hormone dosage from 100 to 125 micrograms—a most welcome development, for we hope it will add to her daily energy. Yet there was *unwelcome* news, too—for the test also showed that the level of liquid salicylate medication (the aspirin substitute) in Jane's blood is too low. She's been taking that product four times a day for almost *16 weeks* (see the first essay). Dr. Mandali instructed us to put Jane back on aspirin, to keep any arthritic pain and inflammation under control: "You can take up to sixteen tablets a day."

Jane rejected that total at once, feeling it's far too high, and announced that she'll probably go back to her old routine of eight to ten aspirin a day. We're angry and dismayed. It's very unsettling for us to learn that the prescribed medication isn't doing its job after all. It is, I remarked somewhat bitterly, another sign of the frustrating, mixed results one must learn to expect, at least in some instances, from the imperfect practice of medicine. To treat rheumatoid arthritis with *aspirin*? We'd always found that incredible. Yet it's still the best way to go, Dr. Mandali said, even with the new anti-inflammatory, nonsteroidal drugs that the FDA (the U.S. Food and Drug Administration) has released to the marketplace recently, for often they produce more side effects than aspirin. And her advice is reinforced by published material I've collected lately for our files.

It seems that once again we must learn the hard way that in Jane's case any improvements we achieve are going to come from within *ourselves* (for I'm certainly as involved in and "responsible" for her illnesses as she is). That such feelings are rearoused in us at this time is hardly coincidental in view of our lifelong habits and belief systems; our tendencies toward secretiveness and our desires to be as self-sufficient as possible—even with Jane's very dependent situation. Different modes of behavior don't fit our chosen courses of action in physical life "this time." Once again I note that in my opinion Jane's dependency represents, at least in part, a search for a "redemption" that encompasses other motivations and realities than those concerned with "just" our temporal lives; that indeed, her impaired state grew out of her mystical nature itself (but was hardly *caused by* it!).

So, although I think that Jane *has* made some "remarkable gains" during recent weeks, I also think that basically she has yet to resolve the entire issue of her illnesses—or even whether to continue physical life. Seth put it beautifully a couple of months ago in the session for April 12—the first time Jane spoke for him since leaving the hospital—and I return to it again and again. See the essay for April 16: "The entire issue *(of Jane's living)* had been going on for some time, and the argument— the argument being somewhat in the nature of a soul facing its own legislature, or perhaps standing as a jury before itself, setting its own case in a kind of private yet public psychic trial. Life decisions are often made in just such a fashion. With Ruburt they carried a psychic and physical logic and economy. . . ."

Obviously, Jane's deliberations over whether to continue physical life are much easier to appreciate when she's depressed and/ or physically uncomfortable, and during those times I can sense the fluctuations in her examination of her psyche. Portions of her are still quite deliberately thinking it all over, I'm sure, although she doesn't mention this outside the session frameworks she provides for Seth and herself.

"I probably didn't want to write any more," she dictated in her own session for May 27. " I feared I'd lost all inspiration—that 20 years of answers weren't enough, and that perhaps my life had no place to go if that were the case. I plan to work with the rest of that sinful-self material. . . ."

But she hasn't begun to do so yet.

I should add that I don't think Jane has started to "set . . . aside" the medical interpretation regarding her "arthritis situation," as Seth suggested she might do when he came through on April 12. (That session is presented in the essay for April 16.) Any decision Jane makes about altering the deeply set beliefs involved in her condition will require the cooperation of a number of portions of her psyche, including her sinful self, and it appears that at this time neither of us is ready to try achieving that kind of overall effect. Our fear of failure undoubtedly plays a strong part here. Ironically, Jane's sinful self is one of the main creators of and participants in her illness syndrome, so any beneficial changes she can bring about will first call for a major shift in the attitude of that very stubborn portion of her psyche. It will be a triumph indeed if and when we can create an alteration like that. And all of this presupposes that each of us will be ready to draw "new facts" into our daily lives from Framework 2.

At my age (63), then, I'm learning once again that I can't live Jane's life for her, or protect her from the motivations of her own physical and psychic explorations and *choices*, no matter how much I may want to. Nor could she do that for me. On many levels that kind of psychic interference is quite simply ignored by the individual in question, and rightly so. Jane's determination would see to her own protection in any case. And her innate mystical nature must fully know and accept that the time, manner, and method of her physical death, *whenever* it occurs, is as much a part of her body's life as its life is. I deeply believe that her psyche would insist that she doesn't need any sort of basic protection by me (or anyone else) to begin with— only understanding. I live daily with the proposition that my wife is in the process of making profound decisions, and that once she's made them she'll respond accordingly both physically and mentally.

In that sense Jane's whole self or entity accepts her actions completely, as part of the learning processes available to "it" through her individuality—nor do I mean it does so in any passive or remote sense at all, but in the most intimate, sensitive terms possible, and also, probably, in ways we cannot appreciate now. At that moment of joining with her whole self, whenever her "death" does take place, all will be resolved with the finest creativity and understanding, for I believe that Jane herself will certainly continue "living" as an individual.

I also believe that these kinds of challenges—involving decisions about whether to continue physical life—have always existed for every creature on earth (just as they have for the earth itself as a living entity). Jane and I have no idea of how our personal story is going to work out, but we do want to tell it.

Apropos of the material I've been covering in these pages, I want to close this essay with quotations from two sessions that I've always thought are among the best Seth has given. These sessions still live, and in them he reinforces the idea that each of us does create our own reality. Both can be found in Chapter 1 of *Personal Reality*.

From Session 610 for June 7, 1972: "You always know what you are doing, even when you do not realize it. Your eye knows it sees, though it cannot see itself except through the use of reflection. In the same way the world as you see it is a reflection of what you are, a reflection not in glass but in three-dimensional reality. You project your thoughts, feelings, and expectations outward, then you perceive them as the outside reality. When it seems to you that others are observing you, you are observing yourself from the standpoint of your own projections."

And from Session 613 for September 11, 1972: "Interactions with others do occur, of course, yet there are none that you do not accept or draw to you by your thoughts, attitudes, or emotions. This applies in each area of life. In your terms, it applies both before life and after it. In the most miraculous fashion you are given the gift of creating your experience."

ESSAY 10
WEDNESDAY, JUNE 23, 1982

Finally, since I opened the first essay with a line from one of Jane's songs in Sumari, I think it appropriate to close the last essay with Sumari, too.

This time, though, I have the translation of a whole composition to present. Jane spontaneously gave voice to her song yesterday afternoon while sitting in the glass-enclosed front porch of our hill house. The day was mild and sunny and breezy, and I'd opened all of the windows for her. The rich green lawn sloped down to the great maple and the sumac trees lining the road. I hadn't asked her to do a song for this last essay; she told me afterward that she hadn't realized I was that close to finishing it. (The whole series has taken much longer than I expected it to, though.) I only know that Jane began to sing in very melodious tones that flowed through the house. I easily heard her from my writing room. "Oh, your singing is so clear and sweet!" her visiting nurse had exclaimed the other day, when my wife had begun to sing while the nurse was changing the dressings on her decubiti. And that present clarity of voice, almost free of tremor, showed how much Jane has improved since returning home. How different her singing is now from that very mournful Sumari song she'd recorded last February, a few days before going into the hospital. "Let my soul find shelter elsewhere," she'd lamented then.

Jane didn't tape this new Sumari, though—which we regretted—for she wasn't able to get out of her chair to hunt for her recorder; I was too charmed just listening to her sing to think of a tape. She wrote down the translation as soon as she finished the song. When she read it to me I knew at once that it would go here, for a few words she certainly sang of the basic theme of these essays—of the sublime, immortal consciounesses of the earth and All That Is, of that loving redemption that consciousness always make possible somehow, somewhere, in the eternal private world of each of us, and that each of us always seeks:

Sumari Healing Song

While you were
sleeping,
all the cupboards
of the earth
were filled.
Mother Earth
sought out each
need.

While you were
weeping,
your tears fell
as sweet rain
drops on small
parched hills
that rise in worlds
you cannot see,
though you are known
there.

While you were
sleeping,
Mother Earth
filled all the
cupboards of your
flesh
to overflowing.
Not one atom went
uncomforted
in worlds that
are yours,
but beyond your
knowing.

PREFACE
BY SETH

PRIVATE SESSION, SEPTEMBER 13, 1979
8:40 P.M. THURSDAY

PRELIMINARY NOTES

(Seth actually began his Preface for this book, Dreams, "Evolution," and Value Fulfillment, *with the next, 881st session, which Jane delivered for him 12 days later [on September 25]. I chose to present this private session first because in it Seth offers certain information about Jane and me that I think applies to all of our work with him, through the session and books, and to our own separate creative lives as well. Especially do I like to interpret his material tonight as meaning that Jane is "a psychic or a mystic," for to me, at least, this means that in this physical life she's chosen to penetrate as deeply as she can the depths of reality, or consciousness.*

Later in these notes I also plan to include, as a partial answer to many who have written us on the subject, material Seth gave on animal consciousness; this information came through just three days ago, in the 878th session for September 10. In the meantime I want to tie together Dreams *and the last Seth-Jane book,* The Individual and the Nature of Mass Events. *Seth completed his work on* Mass Events *about a month ago [on August 15], and a week later I began finishing my notes for it. This will require at least several months. At the same time I'll be taking Jane's dictation for* Dreams. *Along with my painting and dream recording, both of which I do in the mornings, all of these activities come together in just the kind of busy, creative life I greatly enjoy. As for Jane, she couldn't be more pleased to be so involved with all she's doing.*

95

I wrote quite a bit in Mass Events *about our publishing activities, just to show for the record how complicated certain aspects of the creative life can be as we juggled sessions, manuscripts, proofreading, and deadlines [to list a few of our endeavors]; we "worked" at any time of the day or night—which didn't bother us at all. Since a lot of that kind of information was presented in* Mass Events, *Jane and I don't intend for much of it in* Dreams. *Rather, after indicating in this Preface the continuity between the two books, I'll discuss briefly a few other subjects we feel deeply about. All of them are related to our work with the Seth material and* Mass Events, *however, and will, I'm sure, be reflected in* Dreams. *Beyond that, I have little idea of how many notes of Jane's and mine, or quotations from nonbook sessions, for example, we'll be adding to this book.*

Our lives do indeed seem to revolve around book projects and events! First, let me update the creative activities Jane was involved in while Seth and she were finishing Mass Events.

As of last May, when she laid it aside to begin work on her own The God of Jane: A Psychic Manifesto, *Jane had some 17 chapters in fairly good shape for her third Seven novel,* Oversoul Seven and the Museum of Time. *By now she's written 15 chapters, rough first draft, for* God of Jane, *and done notes for a number of others, out of a total of perhaps 25; she knows she'll return to* Seven *when she's through with the much more personal* God of Jane. *Since she's finished her Seth part of the work for* Mass Events, *three days ago she began writing the Introduction to that book. She's been painting, answering mail, and writing poetry. Jane would especially like to do another book of poetry, since she published* Dialogues of the Soul and Mortal Self in Time *way back in 1975. She talks about doing this rather often, then reads through the collections of poems she's built up over the years. She's even made a few notes about such a venture. [Personally, I just wish I had more time to sit quietly and reread some of her poetry.]*

Right now our friend Sue Watkins, who lives better than an hour's drive upstate, is well past the 15th chapter of Conversations With Seth, *the book she's writing about the ESP classes Jane held from September 1967 to February 1975. Prentice-Hall will publish it. Jane hasn't seen* Conversations *yet. Next month she'll get together with Sue to go over it, then start writing the Introduction for the book soon afterward.*

Within a few days we expect to receive from Delacorte Press the first copies of Emir's Education in the Proper Use of Magical Powers.

Emir *is Jane's children's book—or the one for "readers of all ages," as she puts it. At the same time, Tam Mossman, Jane's editor at Prentice-Hall, is trying to find out whether the Dutch edition of* Seth Speaks *has been published. He thinks it has. As soon as Prentice-Hall receives its shipment of books from the Netherlands, Tam will forward the copies due us. The German-language edition of* Seth Speaks *was published in Switzerland four months ago [in May], and just three weeks ago we received our first fan letter from that country. The author wrote in English, and her appreciation of the work Jane and I are trying to do is amazingly similar to certain letters we receive from readers here at home. Even if that initial response was slow in coming [partly because of the language barrier, we think], we were glad to get it, for it indicated a commonality of interest in human potential, regardless of nationality. We expect the same kind of response from those who will seek out the Dutch* Seth Speaks. *We know the mail from European readers will very gradually increase, just as it did after Jane published* The Seth Material *in the United States in 1970.)*

(Late last night I stepped out onto the screened-in back porch of the hill house. Our black-and-white cat, Mitzi, followed me. We're having the house painted, and I could smell the acrylic odor. The woods on the hill in back of the house echoed with the stridulations of the cicadas and katydids. When I went outside I made sure the porch door was latched so that Mitzi couldn't get out; she sat silhouetted against the light coming from the kitchen window as she watched me walk down the driveway. It was the natural time for her to be free, I thought. We'd had Mitzi spayed three weeks ago, when she was seven months old. [Our veterinarian has told us we have to wait until early next year before Mitzi's littermate, Billy, can be neutered; he has some more growing to do first.] Seth's recent material on animal consciousness has assuaged to some degree the guilt Jane and I feel at depriving the innocent cats of their reproductive roles. We've also felt bad over our long-standing decision to keep them in the house; they can roam no farther than the front and back porches. Both porches are screened in down to the floor and furnish the only contacts Billy and Mitzi have with the outside environment.

As I moved down the driveway I was thinking of what I wanted to cover next in these notes. The night was warm, heavily overcast, and mysterious: The streetlight down at the corner of our lot cast long shadows up the road running past the house and into the woods. The rhythmic, almost harsh sounds of the insects were strongly reminiscent of the long camping seasons my father had treated his family to many years ago. [I remembered holding an amazingly delicate, green-colored katydid in my hand as a child. My father had taken my brother and me into the woods one night, at first tracking one of the insects by its sound, until finally he'd been able to illuminate with his flashlight the katydid as it perched on a branch at just the right height for us.]

I'd looked for the shape of a rabbit last night, hopping across the silent road like an upright shadow casting a shadow, as I'd seen one do the other evening. I didn't see a rabbit, but I did hear a flight of geese approaching from the north above the cloud cover. And that growing cacophony, perhaps my favorite sound in all of nature, reminded me that I'd closed out Mass Events *by writing about geese. I'd also mentioned the status of Three Mile Island, however, the nuclear energy generating plant located some 130 airline miles south of us, in Pennsylvania. Because of a combination of mechanical failure and human error, one of the two reactors at TMI had come very close to a meltdown of the uranium fuel in its core. A potentially disastrous situation had developed, one that could have involved many thousands of people and several thousand square miles of land. It seemed incredible now that that accident had taken place only six months ago.*

Enjoying the sounds of life in the mysterious nighttime, I intuitively understood that not only did I want to mention in this Preface the feelings Jane and I have about Three Mile Island as a technological and scientific entity, embodying man's attempts to extract new forms of energy [and yes, consciousness, in our joint opinion] from the far more basic and profound quality Seth calls All That Is; I also knew that I wanted to indicate how the very idea of nuclear energy, as an attribute of a national focus, compared with the situation in the Middle Eastern country of Iran. Iran is undergoing a revolution of a strongly religious, fundamentalist-Islamic character. [Islam means "peace," by the way.] The force of Iran's upheaval makes the growing Christian fundamentalist movement in the United States seem tame indeed by comparison; therefore I want to concentrate upon the Iranian dilemma rather than the religious conflicts in our own country.

In Mass Events, *along with TMI Seth had discussed the tragedy of Jonestown—where in November 1978 over 900 Americans had died [by murder or suicide] for a religious cause in faraway Guyana, South America. Last night I realized that in these notes for* Dreams *I also wanted to refer to the religious revolution in Iran while reminding the reader of the events in Jonestown. For to me, and to Jane also, I'm sure,*

Three Mile Island and Jonestown-Iran represent powerful extremes or directions in large-scale human behavior: certain aspects of religion and science seemingly at opposite poles of the human psyche, as it were.

Just as though it had been waiting for the right moment last night, a screech owl began to sound its sorrowful descending cry in the black woods on the hill behind our house. The barking of the geese started to fade. At least from my viewpoint, each of nature's rhythmic signs implied a continuity, an inevitability and security, that I've often felt is lacking in our all-too-human affairs—this, even though I wrote in Mass Events *that Jane and I are aware, of course, of all the "good things" we humans have constructed in our mass reality. Actually, I thought, our concepts of religion and science aren't as contradictory as at first they may seem to be. In* Mass Events *Seth spent considerable time discussing the deeper and very similar meanings behind both of those belief systems—or cults, as he called them—and Jane and I hope he continues to do so in* Dreams. *Now it even seems to us that in* Mass Events *Seth began preparing us for* Dreams *long before Jane and he ever mentioned that work by name.*

Iran's fundamentalist Islamic orientation is directly opposed to the secular or worldly view of government espoused in Western lands. Horrendous as the situation at Jonestown turned out to be, with religious fanaticism furnishing a framework for all of those deaths, I think it obvious that developments in Iran are already far more serious. Iran is an entire country, whereas Jonestown was one fragile settlement confined within the jungles of an alien land. Iran can "infect" other nations or peoples with an ancient religious force, or consciousness, if allowed to do so. Nuclear power can do the same thing with a new scientific force that can be even more devastating if not carefully "controlled" [in our terms]. To Jane and me these particular aspects of science and religion represent the way large-scale events can escape their well-meaning creators and literally take on lives of their own. And really, I thought, it could have hardly been an accident on consciousness's part that as the events at tiny Jonestown receded from world attention, the revolution in Iran began to dramatically increase. To me the religious correlations are obvious.

After six months, then, Three Mile Island is still "a closed enigma," as I wrote in finishing Mass Events—*only now the costs for the repair and cleanup of its damaged reactor have been projected as being well over $1 billion instead of the $40 million to $400 million of just a month ago, and into many years of "time" instead of just four. TMI has become the unfortunate symbol of our unprepared experimentation with* *a nature that contains all sorts of surprises for us; especially when, as Seth maintains, each of those "surprises," once created, becomes conscious in its own way. [I do believe that this kind of thinking is totally unacceptable to most businessmen, as well as generally to the public they serve, the irony here being that neither businessman or scientist can explain what that fantastic nuclear energy—or* any *energy, for that matter—really is. In the frontmatter, see the first of the four quotations from Seth; the one taken from a private session given just two months ago: "All energy contains consciousness (underlined). . . . A recognition of that simple statement would indeed change your world."]*

I'd rather write about the nature that Jane and I live amid here at the hill house, I suppose, but it seems that in the beginning each great secret we uncover in our world is a "natural" one. Nuclear energy was supposed to transform life on our planet—until we began to encounter unexpected challenges with safety, the disposal of radioactive wastes, corrosion, cost, poor workmanship, aging equipment, and many other obstacles. Nuclear energy's science and technology had always been isolated from most of us. Very gradually its ambience actually became threatening and psychologically "unnatural." In the case of Three Mile Island, that energy, that consciousness, balanced on the edge of running out of our mundane control.

If the hassles surrounding TMI have engendered forces of a scientifically oriented *consciousness, then, certainly those in Iran have released a very strong* religiously oriented *consciousness. Religious drives of whatever nature are much more comprehensible to us than scientific ones: I think it quite safe to note that in ordinary terms our species began struggling with religious expression long before it began recording history. This year [1979], Iran has turned into a land in which all Western nations—but particularly the United States—have become anathema. Iran's religious leaders actually run the country now, operating behind a weak secular and probably temporary government appointed by its Western-leaning and departed leader before he fled his country last January. [Now, looking tired and ill, he travels the world with his expensive entourage, looking for a safe place to live after leading 25 years of savage oppression in his homeland.]*

Within the context of Islamic culture, law is intrinsically religious law; there is no real separation of state and church unless by force. Iran seethes. Many hundreds have died in bitter internal factional disputes. Under the clergy this year several hundred others have already been executed as Islamic law is enforced, and thousands more are to die. Last

February some 70 Americans were taken hostage when a mob of Marxist-led Iranian fedayeen [or sacrificers] overran the United States embassy in Iran's capital, Tehran. The captives were quickly freed by secular negotiators loyal to the Iranian clergy, but certainly that kind of virulent anti-Americanism can happen again. Our citizens began a large-scale evacuation of Iran by air, as did those of several other Western countries. The official and unofficial call has gone out from millions of Iranian throats to purge the country of all Western thought. . . .

The religious and scientific mass consciousnesses released in Iran and the United States respectively reach far beyond their countries of origin, obviously. Indeed, I think those attributes of All That Is must have long ago formed strong portions of the psychic atmosphere that, one might say, encircles the earth and affects all below. Those forces or consciousnesses must also constantly replenish themselves: Iran's religious leaders devoutly nourish their country's hatred for the United States, while here at home no less than six separate teams or commissions have begun investigations—on private, state, and federal levels—of what went wrong at Three Mile Island. Many younger people [and not only in the United States] have become very fatalistic over the possibility of nuclear accident, or worse, war. Some even refuse to bring children into a world they believe their elders have created for them [in those terms]. And most older people avoid seriously considering what nuclear war would really mean for them, out of fear closing their minds to certain aspects of that psychic atmosphere.

Jane and I try to keep in mind Seth's ideas, as well as our own, concerning the great challenges our species has chosen to deal with these days, but I must admit that we often have trouble doing so. It seems to us that even if they privately agreed with us, our world leaders would have even more trouble implementing such thinking, for in their positions of "power" they're quite locked into their national statuses by centuries of custom and history. To initiate truly original and/or revolutionary forms of beneficial governmental and mass behavior would be extraordinarily difficult.

In my opinion these are hardly predictions, but instead very conservative projections of already well-established phenomena: I don't for a minute think that any country, let alone our species as a whole, will give up on nuclear power. Nor will Iran, or the United States, or a number of other nations, dispense with fundamentalist religion of whatever kind. I believe that those particular aspects of scientific consciousness and religious consciousness will be with us for a very long time, for in our chosen earthly reality a larger consciousness—and, ultimately, All That Is—has opted for much long-range exploration of those two closely related portions of itself. In our probability we can create both very transcendent and very painful portions of that dual exploration. I think those particular aspects of mankind's search for answers will grow ever more powerful for a number of years, until their very excesses finally lead to their "evolution" into forces that are much more controlled and compassionate and understanding.

In our terms, then, it's certainly foolish for scientists to expect that the peoples of the world are simply going to dispense with religion just because scientists want them to, calling them "deluded" or worse. It's just as foolish for those who are religious, even though they outnumber the scientists by far, to expect most scientists to embrace religion, to surrender their agnosticism or atheism, to give up their mechanistic, reductionist views of life—their attempts to use a series of "logical" steps to reduce the human being, say, to his or her ever-lower components, right down to the atomic level. [God is, therefore, unnecessary.] And this, of course, even though the scientists cannot explain where the universe we know came from, or where "it" may be going. They can only speculate about such massive concepts via theories like the currently popular "big bang" origin of the universe, with all of its implied consequences, or through the much lesser-known "inflationary model." Nor can scientists tell us, any better than the religious-minded can, what life itself is, or where "it" came from, or where "it" may be going.

I vividly remember that in the last chapter [7] of Mass Events *Seth remarked: "The universe is—and you can pick your own terms—a spiritual or mental or psychological manifestation, and not, in your usual vocabulary, an objective manifestation." [See the 855th session for May 21, 1979. I find it amazing that Jane came through with that session only four months ago.]*

The feelings Jane and I have for animals almost automatically lead us to associate at least some of the implications of Seth's statement with another one he'd given earlier in Mass Events. *I remember it equally well, and find it fascinating. In Chapter 5, see the 832nd session for January 29, 1979: "Nature in all of its varieties is so richly <u>encountered</u> by the animals that it becomes their equivalent of your structures of culture and civilization. They respond to its rich nuances in ways impossible to describe, so that their 'civilizations' are built up through the interweavings of sense data that you cannot possibly perceive."*

I often consider those insights when observing both the wild and do-

mesticated animal life, as well as the bird life, around the hill house.
Much earlier in these preliminary notes I wrote that we'd had our cat
Mitzi spayed almost three weeks ago [on August 27, to be exact], and
that her littermate, Billy, is to be neutered early next year. I mentioned
the guilt Jane and I feel because we're depriving the cats of their repro-
ductive roles in life, and because we don't let them run free in the
environment. I also noted that in a session on animal consciousness Jane
held just three days ago, Seth had to some extend assuaged our feelings
on such questions, and that his information will be of value to others.
The session, the 878th, was held on September 10, 1979, and it began
at 9:07 P.M. Monday—just five regular sessions after Seth had com-
pleted his work on Mass Events, *and three before he began* Dreams.
Earlier that day I'd made a wadded-up paper ball for Mitzi to play with.
Using her lightning-quick reflexes, she kept knocking it around the living
room and beneath Jane's rocker as my wife went into trance, then began
to speak. Here are session excerpts:)

Good evening.

("Good evening, Seth.")

Observing the antics of your Mitzi gives me an excuse to begin
the topic of the evening: animal consciousness.

I want to begin simply by having you question some concepts
taken quite for granted—to question much *(emphatically)*.

(Pause.) It is somewhat fashionable to see man as always nature's despoiler, as the destructive member of nature's family, or
even to consider him apart from nature, who was given nature
as his living grounds.

It is somewhat fashionable to see man as . . . the creature who
dirties his own nest, and I am not condoning much of man's
behavior in that regard. However, there are other issues, and
questions seldom asked. You ignore the fact that [overall] the
consciousness of animals has its own purposes and intents. It is
true that animals are slaughtered under the most cruel of circumstances for human consumption—for then (underlined)
they are treated simply as foodstuff.

(Pause.) Buffaloes do not roam as they did before. There are
thousands of farm-bred animals, however [and have been], all
throughout civilization, alive for a time, well-cared-for for a time
—animals who in usual terms would not exist except for man's
"gluttonous" appetite for meat. That is the way the issue is often

considered. It seldom occurs to anyone that certain forms of animal consciousness came in physical form [by choice], that certain species are prized by man and protected, or that the consciousnesses of such animals had anything at all to do with such an [overall] arrangement.

You cannot say that such animals came out ahead of the bargain, but you _can_ say that the species of man and certain species of animals together formed an arrangement . . . that did have benefits for both. Man is more a part of nature than he realizes, and in the greater realm of activity he cannot take any . . . actions with which the rest of nature does not agree for its own reasons.

Remember here other material given about cellular communication, for example, and the vast web of intercommunication that unites all species. Of course animals _can_ communicate with man, and of course man can communicate with other species— with _all_ species. Such communication has always gone on. Man cannot afford to become aware of such communication at this point, simply because your entire culture is based upon the idea of the animals' "natural" subordinate position. The men who slaughter animals cannot afford to treat those animals as possessors of living consciousnesses.

(Long pause at 9:26.) There _is_, beneath it all, an important unity, a sense of communion, _as_ one portion of earth's living consciousness dies to insure the continued life of _all_ nature. That natural sacrament, however, turns into something else entirely when the gift is so misunderstood, and when the donor is treated so poorly. . . .

Basically [many farmers love] animals for themselves, and delight in their ways—but by itself "delighting in animals" is not considered particularly virile enough. In your society, if you like animals you must not like them for themselves, but for other reasons. If you want to be with animals then you must become a farmer, or a veterinarian, or a cattleman, or whatever. . . .

Many animals enjoy work and purpose. They enjoy working with man. Horses enjoyed the contributions they made to man's world. They understood their riders far more than their riders understood them. Many dogs enjoy being family protectors. There are deep emotional bonds between men and many species of animals. There is emotional response. Dolphins, for example, respond emotionally to man's world. The animals on a farm are emotionally aware of the overall psychological content of the farmer's life and [that of each member of] his family. . . .

Consciousness is filled with content—any kind of consciousness. [The farmer's] animals understand that in a certain fashion he is a midwife, responsible for some of their births. Food comes from his hands. The animals understand, on their own, that life on any terms that are physical ends with death—that the physical properties must be returned to the earth from which they came. . . .

(Pause at 9:45.) [Animals] do not blame [human beings] for anything. If as a species you really found yourselves communicating with the animals, you would have an entirely different culture, a culture that would indeed bring about an alteration of consciousness of the most profound nature.

You have forgotten, conveniently, how much you learned from all of the animals, as I have mentioned in past sessions. You learned a good deal of medicine from watching animal behavior: You learned what plants to avoid, and which to cultivate. You learned how to rid yourself of lice by going into the water. You learned social behavior by watching the animals. At one time you could identify with animals, and they with you to a remarkable degree. They have been your teachers, though they did not choose your path. Obviously, you could not have gone your way [as a species] had it not been for the animals.

Domesticated animals have their own reasons for choosing such a state. It is, for example, usual enough to think that your cats (Billy and Mitzi) should ideally run outside in the open, because in the wild that is what cats would do.

Cats in the wild were, in those terms of time, exploring one kind of nature. In that kind of nature, with a natural population taken care of in the environment, there would be far fewer cats than there are now. Your cats would not exist. Why does it seem antinatural, even slightly perverse, for a household cat to, say, prefer fine cat food from a can, when it seems that he should be eating mice, perhaps, or dining upon grasshoppers? The household cat is exploring a different kind of nature, in which he has a certain relationship to human consciousness, a relationship that changes the reality of his particular kind of consciousness.

Your cats are as alive in all ways inside of the house as out.

They understand their relationship with your human reality. They enjoy contributing in your life as much as any wild animal enjoys being a part of its group. Their consciousnesses lean in a new direction, feel about the edges of concepts, sense openings of awareness of a different kind, and form alliances of consciousness quite as natural as any other.

(10:01. Now Seth discussed a couple of other questions Jane and I had, then ended the session at 10:27 P.M.

Inevitably, Seth's specific references to cats had reminded me of certain other intriguing passages of his in Mass Events. *I found I'd presented them therein as excerpts from nonbook sessions in Chapter 6: See Note 2 for the 840th session. Both of the following quotations from that material contain vast implications—and should these ideas ever become well known, Jane and I feel, they'll be sure to arouse the deep opposition of a number of vested interests.*

From Session 837 for February 28, 1979: "There is no such things as a cat consciousness, basically speaking, or a bird consciousness. In those terms, there are instead simply consciousnesses that choose to take certain focuses."

From Session 838 for March 5, 1979: "If there is no consciousness 'tailored' to be a cat's or a dog's, then there is no prepackaged, predestined, particular consciousness that is meant to be human, either. . . .")

(Actually, it's taken me a long time—a little over three years—to round out these preliminary notes for the session that follows. When I finished them, then, it was nighttime again, September 23, 1982, late, and once again I stepped off the back porch of the hill house for some fresh air. [Mitzi didn't watch me this time.] Much has taken place in Jane's and my lives since 1979, as it has for everyone else, but here in the light of the corner streetlight the scene outside our place was just as magical and mysterious as ever. That's what we love about it. In the warm evening the silent road still ran uphill past the house and into the woods. The cicadas and the katydids still sounded their hypnotic rhythms, I've heard geese often lately, moving south in noisy waves, and we've had deer in our driveway several times. I looked for rabbits or 'coon or deer now, but didn't see any of those creatures.

Once more, as I've done often in recent years, I expressed the hope to myself that in another probable reality very similar to this one I opted for the outdoor life in a much stronger way—even to living outside night and day for most of the year. I must be doing so right now! In that

*probable life I use a tent sometimes, but I cook and sleep outside as much
as possible, except in the worst weather. What a different life! I'm still a
painter, I often think, but perhaps not a writer. I might be a Milton
Avery or a Paul Cézanne type of artist. More and more I've come to
admire—revere, even—the single-minded, childlike devotion artists like
Avery and Cézanne had for their art. Not that I want to copy Cézanne,
for instance [I couldn't even if I wanted to], but in that other reality I
too chose to live the natural life in a more naive or clear-eyed manner—
to sublimate myself before nature while at the same time trying to become
master of whatever means of expression I can achieve.*

*How strange a desire to have in these days of scientific and religious
turmoil, of computers and nuclear debate and space technology. It's
almost like trying to wish oneself back into an earlier, seemingly less
complicated time. That, surely,* would *be an illusory goal! But no matter
what we may accomplish as a species, or how far we may travel, in those
terms we started out utterly dependent upon our earth, with its fantastic
variety of resources and life forms. That sublime framework still exists
for us in all of its great beauty, and I want to always return to it: We
create our human version of it each day, and I think that even now we've
hardly begun to understand what we are and have. I've come to believe
that the predominantly outdoor life would give me a certain understanding of our temporal and spiritual worlds impossible to grasp otherwise,
and that my painting would inevitably mirror that greater comprehension. Sometimes I simply yearn for that way of living. Of course, what
I'm really stressing here is living the independent life as much as possible
within our ever-more-complicated national and world cultures. But we
all have our dreams.*

*Even though she values the idea of independence as much as I do, the
idea of such a life doesn't appeal to Jane at all. Not that she didn't take
to camping, for instance, when I introduced her to it after we married in
1954. She grew up in a quite different physical and psychological environment, however, and the outdoor, athletic life was not a part of that
ambience. But she more than proved her own intuitive grasp of nature,
and of my own desires, by producing for me as a Christmas present [©
1977] her excellent book,* The World View of Paul Cézanne: A
Psychic Interpretation. *. . . .*

*Now here is the private session listed at the beginning of these advance
notes—the one I chose to present just before Seth's actual Preface for*
Dreams. *The opening notes that follow are pretty much as I wrote them
before Jane began delivering the session on Thursday evening at 8:40,*

September 13, 1979. [That night, however, I could do no more than barely indicate the "extra" material I've just finished giving, although even then I knew much of what I wanted to cover.])

(Jane had been so relaxed, so physically at ease yesterday—as she has been often lately—that we'd passed up our regularly scheduled Wednesday night session. At the same time she's been extremely inspired and creative recently, working on her own God of Jane *and the Introduction for Seth's* Mass Events, *turning out many pages of excellent material for those works. Even though she was again very relaxed today, she was also active writing. In fact, after supper she produced two more pages of notes that she "picked up" from Seth on his new book* Dreams, "Evolution," and Value Fulfillment.

We held the session in the living room, as usual. Jane yawned, then laughed as we waited for Seth to come through. "I keep trying to change that title, though. . . ." After a prolonged juggling of titles and themes on her own, she'd finally acquired the book's title directly from Seth some seven weeks ago, or shortly before July 30, 1979; see the closing note for Session 869 in Chapter 10 of Mass Events. *"I just think that 'value fulfillment' is a strange phrase to use in a book title," Jane said. "It's too unfamiliar—I'm afraid it'll confuse the reader. I keep thinking of something simpler, like* Dreams and Evolution: A Seth Book. *And without 'Evolution' being in quotes, too. Or how about* Dreams, Evolution, and Creativity . . . ?"*

I've been expecting Seth to begin Dreams *at any time. From him we've derived the idea that "value fulfillment" represents the creative development of hard-to-define values which increase the quality of life for any being, whether human or not—and not only in moral terms.*

Jane had suggested an earlier session, although I hadn't really thought she'd hold one at all. My only recent concern has been that she not let the sessions go on a regular basis just because I'm working on the notes for Mass Events.

"I think I'm about ready. . . ." After she went so easily into trance, Jane's delivery was very active and energetic—in most definite contrast to the near-bleary-eyed state she'd been in before Seth began speaking. This is a transformation that I've seen happen often: that familiar but always exciting and mysterious influx of energy and/or consciousness.)

(With amusement:) Comments.

("Okay. Good evening, Seth.")

(Pause.) The two of you thought of yourselves specifically as a

writer—or rather a poet—and an artist before our sessions began. I would like to clear up some important points.

You identified, primarily now, as a poet and an artist because those designations, up to that time, seemed most closely to fit your abilities and temperaments. Ruburt's[1] writing set him apart. Your painting set you apart. These were recognizable, tangible proofs of creativity. You therefore identified with elements, characteristics, and traditions that seemed to suit you best.

To some extent you had your own niches, recognizable by society even if they were relatively (underlined) unusual. You did not know that there was a deeper, older, or richer tradition —a more ancient heritage—to which you belonged, because you found no hint of it in your society. It seemed at different times since our sessions began that there were disruptive conflicts. For example: Was Ruburt a writer or was he a psychic? Were you an artist, or weren't you? What about the writing you did—both for our books, and the writing that you sometimes plan to do on your own?

Those kinds of conflicts can only exist in a society in which the entire concept of creativity is segmented, in which the creative processes are often seen as inner assembly lines leading to specific products: a society in which the very nature of creativity itself is largely ignored unless its "products" serve specific ends.

Ruburt was correct in his introductory notes (*for* Mass Events) today—about the poet's long-forgotten abilities, and his role. Ruburt has been a poet all of the time in the most profound meaning of that term. For the poet did not simply string words together, but sent out a syntax of consciousness, using rhythm and the voice, rhyme and refrain as methods to form steps up which his own consciousness could rush.

(*8:53.*) Early artists hoped to understand the very nature of creativity itself as they tried to mimic earth's forms. Poetry and painting were both functional in ways that I will describe in our next book (*humorously, elaborately casual*), and "esthetic," but poetry and painting have always involved primarily man's attempt to understand himself and his world. The original functions of art—meaning poetry and painting here specifically— have been largely forgotten. The true artist in those terms was always primarily—in your terms again—a psychic or a mystic.

His specific art *(pause)* was both his method of understanding his own creativity and a way of exploring the vast creativity of the universe—and also served as a container or showcase that displayed his knowledge as best he could.

That is the heritage that both of you follow, and have followed faithfully. It has an honored tradition. Also involved is, as Ruburt correctly picked up from me, a group of accomplishments that we will call the psychological arts. You are involved in those also.

(To me:) I want you to specifically understand that there is and can be no conflict, for example, between your writing and painting, for in the most basic of ways they represent different methods of exploring the meaning and the source of creativity itself.

The sessions I give you, in usual (underlined) terms, are a new extension of that creativity—but again, that extension has an ancient heritage. *(To me again:)* Your own writing, of course, is art. It is also a method of perceiving and understanding creativity. It is a method of learning that redoubles upon itself, and you are uniquely equipped *(pause)* to discover comprehensions from a standpoint that is most unusual.

Explore, for example, your own feelings toward me: whether or not they have changed through the years, how much I seem to be myself, or part Jane, or part Ruburt, or part you, or part Joseph, or whatever. Realizing that you are in the position you wanted to be [in], and realizing that your abilities are not in conflict with each other, nor you with them, will automatically fulfill and develop all of those abilities, in a new kind of overall creativity that is itself beyond specifics.

Now: When Ruburt begins to trust himself, as he has, the physical *(arthritic)* armor loosens. The creative abilities become even more available, hence his new creativity, and the new physical steps he has taken. They all go together.

He believed in the specific nature of the creative self, so that it could only be trusted in certain areas. He believed he needed strong mental barriers as well as physical ones, set up against his own spontaneity. He is beginning to understand that the spontaneous and creative aspects of personality are the life-giving ones. They can and must be trusted. He knows now he does not have to slow down, and that relaxation leads to motion.

(9:09.) He did indeed pick up from me a partial list of the

subject matters to be covered in our new book—which will be called *Dreams, "Evolution," and Value Fulfillment.*

(Pause.) The book will necessarily of course include much material on the true nature of creativity and its uses and misuses by civilizations. You do not have to fight to trust the thrust of your own life. That thrust is always meant to lead you toward your own best fulfillment, in a way that will benefit the species as well.

When you trust the thrust of your own life, you are always supported. Tell Ruburt that.

I want you both, then, to understand that in the greater light of creativity, understanding its true meaning, you have taken the right course, and therefore drop from your minds any lingering ideas of conflict and doubt. Such a stand will automatically clear up all problems involving things like taxes, sex roles, or whatever—on both of your parts.

You (both) are studying the nature of creativity as few others have done or can do—and that is bound to make possible new creative frameworks, and to offer new solutions to situations that cause difficulty only within smaller frameworks.

Do you have questions?

("No. Jane's been doing great lately, and I'm very pleased to see that.")

He should—meaning predictive, he will. End of session.

("Thank you.")

A fond good evening.

("Good night, Seth.")

(9:16 P.M. And right at the end of the session, Jane's head flopped down loosely as she quickly returned to the very relaxed state she'd been in before speaking for Seth.)

NOTE: PRIVATE SESSION, SEPTEMBER 13, 1979

1. Those who are familiar with the Seth material know this, so I ask their forbearance while I reproduce for "new" readers Note 3 for Session 679, in Volume 1 of *"Unknown" Reality:*

Almost always Seth refers to Jane by her male entity name, "Ruburt"—and so "he," "his," and "him."

To sum up Seth's somewhat amused comments in the 12th session for January 2, 1964: "Sex, regardless of all of your fleshy takes, is a psychic phenomenon, merely certain qualities which you call male and female. The qualities are real, however, and permeate other planes as well as your own. They are opposites which are nevertheless complementary, and which merge into one. When I say as I have that the overall entity [or whole self] is neither male or female, and yet refer to [some] entities by definitely male names such as 'Ruburt' and 'Joseph' [as Seth calls me], I merely mean that in the overall essence, the [given] entity identifies itself more with the so-called male characteristics than with the female."

SESSION 881, SEPTEMBER 25, 1979
8:50 P.M. TUESDAY

(Saturday afternoon Jane finished typing the final version of her Introduction for Mass Events, *and yesterday morning I mailed it to Tam Mossman at Prentice-Hall.*

Today my wife was once again very much at ease for most of a day— so much so, in fact, that she slept several times. Many beneficial muscular changes appear to be taking place in her body. After supper I suggested that if she had a session tonight Seth could comment upon her current series of relaxations. At 8:30 she called me out of my writing room. Now she was nervous, for she felt that Seth was ready to dictate his Preface for Dreams.

I especially liked the first sentence Seth offered for his latest book. He promised something Jane and I could really focus upon . . . an exciting yet thoughtful time of "work" and new information. Quietly, with many pauses, a few of which are indicated:)

(Whispering:) Good evening.

(I laughed. "Good evening, Seth.")

Preface: This book will be my most ambitious project thus far. Period.

It may be said by some that any book at all is an ambitious endeavor, when it originates from a psychological source (underlined) so far divorced from your ordinary ideas of creativity. It is one thing, for example, for a physical writer to produce a manuscript—and even that kind of creativity involves vast and hidden psychological maneuvers that never appear in the manuscript itself.

As most of my readers know, I make no claims of now having a physical personhood. *(Pause.)* I do claim an independent reality at another level of existence. My status and origins seem strange only because you have understood so little about your own origins. I am beginning this book this evening. I have already given the title, and at another level of consciousness Jane Roberts was able *(12 days ago, for example)* to perceive some glimpses of some of the subject matter that will be included here. So far, however, physically there is only the page of paper upon which Robert Butts is writing down these words I speak.

Someday, in terms of time, there will be a thick book. Although the manuscript does not yet exist in a physical book, the book itself, the ideas and words, are in the most important fashions quite real now. Certain qualities are implied in all kinds of creativity that are generally overlooked, and so they are not apparent. The kind of creative procedures we are involved in can serve to bring some of those qualities to light, and to shed illumination upon many aspects of the human psyche that usually remain hidden.

I speak through Ruburt—or through Jane Roberts, if you prefer. Ruburt has his own creative abilities, and uses them well, and it is to a large extent because of those abilities that our contact first took place *(in December 1963)*. Scientists like to say that if you look outward at the universe, you look backward in time. That statement is only partially true. When you move inward through the psyche, however, you do begin to thrust, in your terms, "backward" toward the origins of existence. Your creative abilities do not simply allow you to paint pictures, to tell or write stories, to create sculpture or architecture. They do not simply provide you with a basis for your religions, sciences, and civilizations. They are your contact with the source of existence itself.

(Jane took a long pause in trance at 9:10.) Give us a moment. . . . *(Long pause.)* They provide the power that allows you to form a belief system to begin with.

(Pause.) Now: While you believe that consciousness somehow emerges from dead matter, you will never understand yourselves, and you will always be looking for the point at which life took on form. You will always have to wonder about a kind of mechanical birth of the universe—and it will indeed seem as if

your own world was made up of the spare parts that somehow fell together in just such a fashion so that life later emerged.

You are filled with questions about when and where the various species appeared, and how the rocks were formed, when some reptiles grew wings, when some fish emerged from the oceans and learned to breathe air, and you are bound to wonder what happened in the times in between.

How many reptiles tried for wings, for example, and failed, or could not fly—or how many millions of reptiles did it take, and how many trials, before the first triumphant bird flew above the landscape? How many fish died with only half-formed lungs, who were too far from the water's edge to dip again beneath the waves? *(More intently now:)* Or how many fish flopped backward to the water, finding themselves in such an in-between stage that they could no longer live in the water nor breathe the air?

So in those terms, how many water dwellers died before the first mammal stood securely with fully completed lungs, breathing earth's early air?

Scientists say now that energy and matter are one. They must take the next full step to realize that <u>consciousness</u> and energy and matter are one.

(Pause at 9:22.) Give us a moment. . . . In this book, then, we will look at the origin of the universe, the origin of the species, the origin of life from another viewpoint. This viewpoint will, I hope, provide another framework through which you can understand and study physical reality, your part in it, and sense the immense creative complexity that unites each individual with the source of consciousness itself.

To do this, I hope to explore a more meaningful concept of evolution[1]—and that concept must involve a discussion of subjective reality and its effect upon the "evolution" of man's consciousness.

The universe did not originate from what you like to think of as an external, objectified source. Your own physical body provides you with sturdy corporal images, exterior presentations. Your dreams do not suddenly appear exteriorized upon your images <u>in place of your features</u>, for example. They remain hidden. Your dreams appear on the interior screen of your mind.

I never want any of my remarks to be construed in such a

fashion that it seems I am in any way negating the fullness, validity, and magnificence of physical existence. I do want to point out, however, that a state you usually call dreaming is but a dim indication of an <u>inner</u> reality of events *(intently)*, an inner order of events from which the physical world emerges. I hope to show how the nature of dreams has helped shape man's consciousness. I hope to show that <u>consciousness forms the environment,</u> and not the other way around *(with many gestures).*

I hope to show that all species are motivated by what I call <u>value fulfillment,</u> in which each seeks to enhance the quality of <u>life for itself and</u> for all other species at the same time.

This further unites all species in a cooperative venture that has remained largely invisible because of beliefs projected outward upon the world by both your sciences and religions, generally speaking. All of your grandest civilizations have existed first in the world of dreams. You might say that the universe dreamed itself into being.

(A one-minute pause at 9:40.) Give us a moment. . . . Generally speaking, the states of waking and sleeping are the only levels of consciousness with which you have been primarily concerned. It seems to you that this is the result of your evolutionary progress —but there have been civilizations upon the earth that specialized in the use of many focuses of consciousness, as for example you are focused upon the use of tools.

Dreams can be highly specific. They can be used to provide sources of information. I hope to show their practical importance, both as a part of man's "evolutionary development" and their possibilities in what you think of as modern life. The answers are where you have least looked for them. The universe is still being created, even as each person is in each moment.

(9:47.) End of Preface. That should make Ruburt feel better *(with amusement),* and give us a moment. Rest your fingers. . . . Will you open that *(wine)*?

(After giving a little information for Jane,[2] Seth wound up the session:)

We begin again with a new book, and I am sure your own lively mind will bring questions to the forefront that will be of interest.

A fond good evening.

("Thank you, Seth. Good night.")

(9:56 P.M. *"I could feel him around when I was doing the supper dishes," Jane said as soon as she was out of trance. "And I could feel him around more and more after that, but I still get cold feet when I know he's going to start a new book. . . . Was it good?"*

I nodded a very pleased yes. "He said this one will be his most ambitious project to date."

"Well, I don't want to think about that. If I do, then I'll start worrying about my responsibility again and forget what Seth says about having the sessions because they're fun. Wow—I'm really out of it. I'll be curious as hell to read it," Jane said as she headed for the couch.

"So," I joked, "the day wasn't a total waste after all. We did get something done." Even Jane laughed.

It's impossible, of course, for us not to have a sense of responsibility about the sessions. I'm sure Seth knows this, but it's obvious that he wants us to maintain a light rather than a heavy psychological touch. Sometimes that's rather difficult to achieve, though. Recently we received an excellent, rather lengthy paper about our work in which the writer, a psychologist, discussed among other things the import of Seth's material, as well as various explanations of his origin. We think about those subjects too, but in order to have the sessions on a week-to-week basis we concentrate upon the simple creative achievement embodied in each session itself, and let go of the larger implications. Those implications are usually in the background of our joint awareness, however.)

NOTES: SESSION 881

1. Recently, I bought two books written by "scientific creationists." The authors strongly disagree with ideas of evolution. I've read halfway through one of the books, and have discussed it with Jane to some extent. After the session I suggested that she start reading it also, in order to acquaint herself with theories radically different from the "ordinary" scientific ones espoused by evolutionists. Very briefly: The creationists believe that God created the universe (including the earth, obviously) around 10,000 years ago. They maintain that all of the earth's living forms have remained essentially unchanged since that prime creative event; they can account for the disappearance of the dinosaurs, for example, and the vast number of other life forms we no longer see around us. On the other hand, evolutionary

science believes that the universe came into being between 10 billion and 20 billion years ago; that the earth itself is about 4.6 billion years old, and that according to the fossil record and other evidence, its living organisms first arose and began evolving at least 3.5 billion years ago. Science also believes, however, that the study of a "first cause" involves not scientific but philosophical and theological questions. For instance, why did the universe we think we know so well come into existence at all, and what was the *cause* of that beginning?

I know that Jane is interested in the book in question, but also a bit afraid of it: "I don't want to be so influenced by it—or by any other book—that it starts coming out in the material," she's said more than once recently. I agree, since I think that in their own ways the views expressed by the scientific creationists are just as limited as those held by the conventional scientific establishment. But Jane has an excellent critical mind. I'm not concerned that anything she reads will unduly influence her—or Seth.

2. I'm presenting the private portion of tonight's session for two reasons: Seth comments a bit upon the creative production of the sessions, and he shows how we can habitually impose upon our physical selves our conscious ideas of what we "should be doing"—not paying enough attention to our impulsive, natural, bodily messages.

"Today, Ruburt's body wanted to relax. He has been doing very well, and he tried to approve, but since he lost work time yesterday, his approval barely went skin deep *(louder)*.

"When you mentioned his ink sketches he instantly wanted to play at painting again, but felt, guiltily, that he should not. He forgot, once again, that the creative self is aware of his entire life, and that his impulses have a creative purpose.

"These sessions themselves involve the highest levels of creative productivity, at many levels, so he should refresh himself painting or doing whatever he likes, for that refreshment adds to his creativity, of course. He will finish his book *(God of Jane)*, and do beautifully with it. He should follow the rhythms of his own creativity without being overly concerned with the time. For a while, again, have him write three hours of free writing, and paint or whatever. His book will be provided for. You can see how your own creativity is emerging in the notes for *Mass Events*. Granted, you need time to write physically, but the basic creativity has its own 'time.'

"End of session, and a fond good evening."

("Can I ask a question?")

"You may."

("What was that feeling he had today in his chest, back, and body, like an electric pulsation?")

"Because he did not approve of his own relaxation. He put brakes upon it."

("Okay.")

CHAPTER 1

BEFORE THE BEGINNING

SESSION 882, SEPTEMBER 26, 1979
9:14 P.M. WEDNESDAY

(Jane was rather relaxed tonight—again—but decided to try for the session. She's been reading the book on scientific creationism I suggested to her. Her feelings about it are both ambiguous and funny: "You've got to watch those guys," she said more than once, meaning the creationists, "or they'll lead you right where they want you to go. You've got to keep thinking. I can only read so many pages at a time. . . ." Adding to the humor of the situation is the fact that we've had people write or say the same thing about the Seth material. But Jane didn't mention any of those events.

However, aside from being in outright conflict with the theory of evolution [and the idea of an ancient universe], the beliefs of the creationists do pose a number of questions that are quite intriguing from our joint viewpoint. My statement doesn't mean that Jane and I endorse creationism just because we question the doctrines of evolution. We think that either one of those belief systems is much too inadequate to explain reality in any sort of comprehensive way.

Jane expected Seth to work on his new book this evening. "Yeah, I've got sentences about it in my head. I'm just waiting for him to put them in order," she said as we sat for the session. Then, without calling his material Chapter 1, dictation, or whatever:)

119

(Whispering:) Good evening.

("Good evening, Seth.")

Now. *(Long pause, one of many.)* The universe will begin yesterday. The universe began tomorrow. Both of these statements are quite meaningless. The tenses are wrong, and perhaps your time sense is completely outraged. Yet the statement: "The universe began in some distant past," is, in basic terms, just as meaningless.

In fact, the first two statements, while making no logical sense, do indeed hint of *(pause)* phenomena that show time itself to be no more than a creative construct. Time and space are in a fashion part of the furniture of your universe.

The very experience of passing moments belongs to your psychological rooms in the same way that clocks are attached to your walls. Whenever science or religion seeks the origin of the universe, they search for it in the past. The universe is being created now (underlined). Creation occurs in each moment, in your terms. The illusion of time itself is being created now. It is therefore somewhat futile to look for the origins of the universe by using a time scheme that is in itself, at the very least, highly relative.

Your now (underlined), or present moment, is a psychological platform. It seems that the universe began with an initial burst of energy of some kind *(the "big bang")*. Evolutionists cannot account for its cause. Many religious people believe that a god exists in a larger dimension of reality, and that he created the universe while being himself outside of it. He set it into motion. Many individuals, following either persuasion, believe that regardless of its source, the [universe][1] must run out of energy. Established science is quite certain that no energy can now be created or destroyed, but only transformed *(as stated in the first law of thermodynamics)*. Science sees energy and matter as being basically the same thing, appearing differently under varying circumstances.

(9:31.) In certain terms, science and religion are both dealing with the idea of an objectively created universe. Either God "made it," or physical matter, in some unexplained manner, was formed after an initial explosion of energy, and consciousness emerged from that initially dead matter in a way yet to be explained.

Instead, consciousness formed matter. As I have said before, each atom and molecule has its own consciousness. Consciousness and matter and energy are one, but consciousness initiates the transformation of energy into matter. In those terms, the "beginning" of your universe was a triumph in the expansion of consciousness, as it learned to translate itself into physical form. The universe emerged into actuality in the same way (underlined), but to a different degree, that any idea emerges from what you think of as subjectivity into physical expression.

The consciousness of each reader of this book existed before the universe was formed—in parentheses: (in your terms)—but that consciousness was unmanifest. Your closest approximation —and it is an approximation only—of the state of being that existed before the universe was formed is the dream state. *(Long pause.)* In that state before the beginning, your consciousness existed free of space and time, aware of immense probabilities. This is extremely difficult to verbalize, yet it is very important that such an attempt be made. *(Long pause.)* Your consciousness is a part of an infinitely original creative process.

I will purposely avoid using the word "God" because of the connotations placed upon it by conventional religion. I will make an attempt to explain the characteristics of this divine process throughout this book. I call the process "All That Is." All That Is is so much a part of its creations that it is almost impossible to separate the "creator from the creations," for each creation also carries indelibly within it the characteristics of its source.

If you have thought that the universe followed a mechanistic model, then you would have to say that each portion of this "cosmic machine" created itself, knowing its position in the entire "future construction." You would have to say further that each portion came gladly out of its own source individually, neatly tailored to its position, while at the same time that individual source was also as intimately the source of each other individual portion.

I am not saying that the universe is the result of some "psychological machine," either, but that each portion of consciousness is a part of All That Is, and that the universe falls together in a spontaneous, divine order *(intently)*—and that each portion of consciousness carries within it indelibly the knowledge of the whole.

The birth of the world represented a divine psychological awakening. Each consciousness that takes a part in the physical universe dreamed of such a physical existence, in your terms, before the earth was formed. In greater terms than yours, it is quite true to say that the universe is not formed yet, or that the universe has vanished. In still vaster terms, however, the fact is that in one state or another the universe has always existed.

Your closest approximation of the purpose of the universe can be found in those loving emotions that you have toward the development of your children, in your intent to have them develop their fullest capacities.

(9:58.) Your finest aspirations can give you some dim clue as to the great creative thrust that is behind your own smallest act, for your own smallest act is possible only because your body has already been provided for in the physical world. Your life is given. In each moment it is renewed. So smoothly and effortlessly do you ride that thrust of life's energy that you are sometimes scarcely aware of it. *(Pause.)* You are not equipped with a certain amount of energy that then wears out and dies. Instead you are, again, newly created in each moment.

That is enough for now. End of session, and a fond good evening.

("Thank you, Seth. Good night.")

(10:02 P.M. "That was short, but I don't care," Jane said right after coming out of her trance state. "I thought that was what there was tonight. I never stop when there's more, like you'd turn off a faucet."

"I assume that's Chapter 1?"

"Oh yeah, he never said. Well, tomorrow I'll paint and forget the whole business about evolution. . . ."

But as I type this material two evenings later [on Friday], I can note that Jane didn't paint at all. Instead she continued to work on her own God of Jane. *She also finished reading the book on creationism, and at my request today wrote a page or so about her reactions to it. Her little essay is given as Note 2. Then see Note 3 for my own comments about evolution as I discussed that subject in Volume 2 of* "Unknown" Reality.*)*

Notes: Session 882

1. Originally Jane said "world" here, where I'm sure Seth wanted her to say "universe." Anytime I make such a change in Seth's copy, or insert a clarifying word or phrase as though it came from him, or might have, the alteration is in brackets [like this]. Occasionally Jane or I may recast a sentence of Seth's, but this isn't necessary even once per session. Our rule is that otherwise we do not change or delete any of his material without noting it.

Insertions I make in parentheses and italics, like "*(as stated in the first law of thermodynamics)*," are meant to be informative and obviously aren't from Seth.

2. "Rob wanted me to do a paragraph or so about my reactions to the book on scientific creationism that I've just finished reading," Jane wrote, "so here goes. The book follows the idea that an objectified God made the universe (and the earth) in a perfect condition, and that instead of evolving toward more complicated forms, it's running down; that decay and catastrophe are breakdowns of previous better conditions, but that even these will finally be removed by the Creator after they have served their own special purposes. The book states that the universe is around 10,000 years old. (Seth has said more than once that in those terms it's even older than the evolutionists believe.) The reasons given for this young age seem reasonable enough, though I hardly have the background knowledge to know how good they'd sound to an evolutionary geologist, say. . . .

"Maybe between one and two thousand years after the Creation a worldwide flood destroyed practically everything, though some species, including man, survived. (No even approximate date for the flood is given in the book. Noah, the 10th male in descent from Adam—Noah and his family, and the divine command he received to build the Ark—aren't even mentioned. But how could they be, in a book on scientific creationism?) There was no evolution. All species were created as they now appear. Oddly, if you postulate a god in that fashion, a personified one, then you wonder why he couldn't—or didn't choose to—maintain the perfection of his original creation. Why man's sin, resulting in the catastrophic flood, to which all species fell victim? The regular theory of evolution doesn't have to contend with such questions, of course, but in the book I just read no explanations for questions like that are given—I don't even remember that they were raised.

"The creationists put down other species, as do the evolutionists, taking it as fact that no other species is capable of conceptual thought, where I think that statement is extremely dubious generally, and even specifically in light of the work being done with dolphins, for example. The explanation for man's use of language sounded a bit pat, too: God just made him that way.

"I'd say that both the creation and evolution models suffer from logical and emotional sloppiness, and that neither one presents a reasonable view of man's origins. Both concepts seem equally implausible when you think of them with any objectivity, and neither can be proven, of course. They ultimately rest upon the *faith* of the believer! I get a spooky feeling that I've had before, thinking that here we are, alive and conscious, technologically accomplished, and we really haven't the slightest idea of where the universe came from or why we're alive, though as a species we're gifted with both intellect and intuition. At best our established concepts seem grossly insufficient. So Seth's version of All That Is being both within and without the universe makes more sense to me, and I'm very curious about where he'll go with this in his book. This morning, looking over the few pages we have so far, I got the idea that the title for the first chapter is going to be: 'Before the Beginning'—so we'll see. . . .

"In a magazine on parapsychology I recently read an article containing ideas that I think are at least a little more reasonable than those of creationism or evolutionism: Though the writer *did* take evolution for granted, he also put *consciousness* within matter."

I was surprised after the session tonight when Jane said that she still wants to read the second of the two books on creationism I'd bought, not long before she began delivering *Dreams* for Seth.

3. I've known Seth planned to discuss evolution—that sensitized subject—ever since Jane tuned into the title of his new book a couple of months ago. However, my interest in one of my favor-

ite fields of inquiry lay relatively dormant until Seth confirmed the title earlier this month (September); then I felt the impulse to jump right into producing notes on the subject. Better wait, I told myself and Jane, until we had an idea of how Seth is going to handle his own material on evolution.

I had finished Appendix 12 for Volume 2 of *"Unknown" Reality* by August 1977. I'd devoted the piece to a study of the establishment theory of evolution versus ideas Seth, Jane, and I have on that theme, and noted that I'd accumulated much information from a number of sources. I've amassed much more data by now, of course. Perhaps, I thought when putting together the Preface for *Dreams*, I just wanted to use some of our later material in the new book.

Yet most of what I wrote in Appendix 12 is still valid, to my mind, even though I've always wanted to expand (and expound?) upon all of it. There are a few things I'd put somewhat differently now, given the advantage of a couple of years' hindsight, but Jane and I don't really want to revise the material. We'd rather let it stand as is, representing our best knowledge and feeling of that time, including the way we put to use Seth's own information on the subject. If that "best knowledge" was groping and imperfect, then so be it. I think it most interesting that the theory of evolution is now challenged by those who, like Jane and I, simply want to know whether it has a basis in scientific fact; and that it's also come under virulent attack by those who generally believe in fundamentalist religions. The controversy over whether evolution ever really happened—and/or *is* happening—is far from resolved, whether in scientific, religious, or lay terms.

But why, I asked Jane, haven't our best minds—at least those who have operated throughout the centuries of our recorded history—been able to arrive at some sort of reasonable consensus about the "origin" of our universe (if it had one), its processes, and our human place in it? In their many forms religion and science haven't provided satisfactory answers, nor have agnosticism or atheism. Why have so many human beings (an estimated *50 billion* of them) had to exist along the way before we arrived at our present point—from which point we in our collective wisdom think we might begin to provide meaningful answers to such questions? If true, this proposition means that for all of that time, all of those people lived pretty useless lives as far as having any real understanding of their universe goes—hardly a natural situation, I told Jane. Life can't really be that way. The whole set of questions must be meaningless in deeper terms.

So why do Jane and I think we're on to something with the Seth material—that it can help if given the chance? Why haven't others—our scientific, religious, and political leaders, or those in the fine arts, say—come up with ideas similar to those espoused by a Seth, and why aren't those ideas common today? Seth's kind of information must have surfaced innumerable times, I think, and for many reasons fallen short as broad coherent systems of thought. How would theology, or the sociology of science, answer any or all of these questions?

SESSION 883, OCTOBER 1, 1979
9:06 P.M. MONDAY

(Last Saturday night, Jane and I presided over a "class" reminiscent of the weekly ESP classes we used to hold in our downtown apartments before we moved to the hill house, just outside Elmira, in 1975. A large group of former students attended from New York City, as well as some from the local area. The evening was a great success. Since each person knew everyone else so well, the verbal exchanges were many and often blindingly rapid. They were also hilarious: I laughed so often and so hard that my stomach ended up hurting. My voice was gone by the end of the meeting [and the next day it was still very hoarse]. Seth came through again and again, as he'd often done in class, and Jane thoroughly enjoyed herself. We're to get transcripts of the several tapes made.

Through it all each one of us felt a penetrating nostalgia for those vanished classes, for they'd been truly unique; I don't think it would be possible to recapture their particular, innocent, lasting sense of excitement and exploration. As might be expected, I appreciate Jane's accomplishments in them much more now than I did during the nearly seven years they were underway.

Almost three weeks ago I wrote in the Preface for Dreams that we were waiting to receive the first published copies of Jane's Emir's Education in the Proper Use of Magical Powers. Today the books arrived. Eleanor Friede, Jane's editor at Delacorte Press, has done a fine

job of supervising the illustration and production of a handsome little
volume. All of us hope Emir *does well in the marketplace.*

This evening it was obvious that Jane really wanted to have the ses-
sion, because she told me she was ready for it early. For a change we
decided to do our thing in her writing room, or den, at the back of the
house. She started out speaking for Seth very quietly, but her delivery
soon became much more intent—then often louder and impassioned:
Jane used many more gestures than usual, staring wide-eyed at me,
leaning forward again and again in her rocker, crossing and uncrossing
her legs. She was turned on in trance, wound up, her pace considerably
faster than it's been lately.)

(Whispering:) Good evening.

("Good evening, Seth.")

Dictation. The heading of the chapter—I forgot to give it to
you—is: "Before the Beginning."

Now: You cannot prove scientifically that [your] world was
created *(pause)* by a god who set it into motion, but remained
outside of its dominion. Nor can you <u>prove</u> scientifically that the
creation of the world was the result of a chance occurrence—so
you will not be able to prove what I am going to tell you either.
Not in usual terms.

I hope however to present, along with my explanations, certain hints and clues that will show you where to look for <u>subjec-</u>
tive evidence. Period.

You live your lives through your own subjective knowing, to
begin with, and I will try to arouse within your own consciousnesses memories of events with which your own inner psyches
were intimately involved as the world was formed—and though
these may <u>appear</u> to be past events, they are even now occurring.

Before the beginning of the universe, we will postulate the
existence of an omnipotent, creative source. *(Pause.)* We will
hope to show that this divine subjectivity is as present in the
world of your experience as it was before the beginning of the
universe. Again, I refer to this original subjectivity as All That
Is. I am making an attempt to verbalize concepts that almost
defy the edges of the intellect, unless that intellect is thoroughly
reinforced by the intuition's strength. So you will need to use
your mind and your own intuitions as you read this book.

All That Is, before the beginning contained within itself the
infinite thrust of all <u>possible</u> creations. All That Is possessed

(pause) a creativity of such magnificence that its slightest imaginings, dreams, thoughts, feelings or moods attained a kind of reality, a vividness, an intensity, that almost demanded freedom. Freedom from what? Freedom to do what? Freedom to be what?

The experience, the subjective universe, the "mind" of All That Is, was so brilliant, so distinct, that All That Is almost became lost, mentally wandering within this ever-flourishing, ever-growing interior landscape. Each thought, feeling, dream, or mood was itself indelibly marked with all of the attributes of this infinite subjectivity. Each glowed and quivered with its own creativity, its own desire to create as it had been created.

Before the beginning there existed an interior universe that had no beginning or ending, for I am using the term "before the beginning" to make matters easier for you to assimilate. In parentheses: (That same infinite interior universe exists now, for example.)

(Pause at 9:31.) All That Is contained within itself the knowledge of all existences, with their infinite probabilities, and "as soon as" All That Is imagined those numberless circumstances, they existed in what I will call divine fact.

All That Is knew of itself only. It was engrossed with its own subjective experiences, even divinely astonished as its own thoughts and imaginings attained their own vitality, and inherited the creativity of their subjective creator. [Those thoughts and imaginings] began to have a dialogue with their "Maker" *(all very emphatically)*.

Thoughts of such magnificent vigor began to think their own thoughts—and their thoughts thought thoughts. As if in divine astonishment and surprise, All That Is began to listen, and began to respond to these "generations" of thoughts and dreams, for the thoughts and dreams related to each other also. There was no time, so all of this "was happening" simultaneously. The order of events is being simplified. In the meantime, then, in your terms, All That Is spontaneously thought new thoughts and dreamed new dreams, and became involved in new imaginings—and all of these also related to those now-infinite generations of interweaving and interrelating thoughts and dreams that "already" existed *(with many gestures and much emphasis)*.

So beside this spontaneous creation, this simultaneous

"stream" of divine rousing, All That Is began to watch the inter-actions that occurred among his own subjective progeny. *(Pause.)* He listened, began to respond and to answer a thought or a dream. He began to purposefully bring about those mental con-ditions that were requested by these generations of mental prog-eny. If he had been lonely before, he was no longer.

Your language causes some difficulty here, so please accept the pronoun "he" as innocuously as possible. "It" sounds too neutral for my purpose, and I want to reserve the pronoun "she" for some later differentiations. In basic terms, of course, All That Is is quite beyond any designations having to do with any one species or sex. All That Is, then, began to feel a growing sense of pressure as it[1] realized that its own ever-multiplying thoughts and dreams themselves yearned to enjoy those greater gifts of creativity with which they were innately endowed.

It is very difficult to try to assign anything like human moti-vation to All That Is. I can only say that it is possessed by "the need" to lovingly create from its own being; to lovingly trans-form its own reality in such a way that each most slight probable consciousness can come to be *(long pause)*; and with the need to see that any and all possible orchestrations of consciousness have the chance to emerge, to perceive and to love.

We will later discuss the fuller connotations of the word "love" as it is meant here, but this chapter is a kind of outline of other material to come.

All That Is, then, became aware of a kind of creative tumult as each of its superlative thoughts and dreams, moods and feel-ings, strained at the very edges of their beings, looking for some then-unknown, undiscovered, as of then unthought-of release. I am saying that this mental progeny included all of the con-sciousnesses that [have] ever appeared or will appear upon your earth—all tenderly couched: the first human being, the first insect—each with an inner knowledge of the possibilities of its development. All That Is, loving its own progeny, sought within itself the answer to this divine dilemma *(all very intently, with eyes wide and dark, and with numerous gestures).*

(Pause at 9:57.) When that answer came, it involved previously unimaginable leaps of divine inspiration, and it occurred thusly: All That Is searched through the truly infinite assortment of its incredible progeny to see what conditions were needed for this

even more magnificent dream, this dream of a freedom of objectivity. What door could open to let physical reality emerge from such an inner realm? When All That Is, in your terms, put all of those conditions together it saw, of course, in a flash, the mental creation of those objective worlds that would be needed—and as it imagined those worlds, in your terms, they were physically created.

[All That Is] did not separate itself from those worlds, however, for they were created from its thoughts, and each one has divine content. The worlds are all created by that divine content, so that while they are on the one hand exterior, they are on the other also made of divine stuff, and each hypothetical point in your universe *(pause)* is in direct contact with All That Is in the most basic terms. The knowledge of the whole is within all of its parts—and yet All That Is is more than its parts.

Divine subjectivity is indeed infinite. It can never be entirely objectified. When the worlds, yours and others, were thus created, there was indeed an explosion of unimaginable proportions, as the divine spark of inspiration exploded into objectivity.

The first "object" was an almost unendurable mass, though it had no weight, and it exploded, instantaneously beginning processes that formed the universe—but no time was involved. The process that you might imagine took up eons occurred in the twinkling of an eye, and the initial objective materialization of the massive thought of All That Is burst into reality. In your terms this was a physical explosion—but in the terms of the consciousnesses involved in that breakthrough, this was experienced as a triumphant "first" inspirational frenzy, a breakthrough into another kind of being *(most intently)*.

The earth then appeared as consciousness transformed itself into the many facets of nature. The atoms and molecules were alive, aware—they were no longer simply a part of a divine syntax, but they spoke themselves through the very nature of their being *(gesturing)*. They became the living, aware vowels and syllables through which consciousness could form matter.

But in your terms this was still largely a dream world, though it was fully fashioned. It had, generally speaking, all of the species that you now know. These all correlated with the multitudinous kinds of consciousnesses that had clamored for release, and those consciousnesses were spontaneously endowed by All That Is with those forms that fit their requirements. You had the birth of individualized consciousness as you think of it into physical context. Those consciousnesses were individualized before the beginning, but not manifest. But individualized consciousness was not quite all that bold. It did not attach itself completely to its earthly forms at the start, but rested often within its "ancient" divine heritage. In your terms, it is as if the earth and all of its creatures were partially dreaming, and not as focused within physical reality as they are now.

(10:08.) For one thing, while individualized consciousness was within the massive subjectivity of All That Is, it enjoyed, beside its own uniqueness, a feeling of supporting unity, a comforting knowledge that it was one with its source. So in the beginning of [your] world, consciousness fluctuated greatly, focusing gently at the start, but not quite as willing to be as fully independent as its first intent might seem.

You had the sleepwalkers,[2] early members of your species, whose main concentration was still veiled in that earlier subjectivity, and they were your true ancestors, in those terms.

Are you tired?

("I'm okay.")

For one thing, early man needed to rely upon his great inner knowledge. Take your break.

(10:23. Seth's call for a break was abrupt. "Is one of the cats out?" Jane asked right away, looking around. Billy, our eight-month-old tiger cat, was sleeping on a chair near us. A couple of minutes ago he'd started making some odd high-pitched sounds I hadn't heard him produce before. I'd wondered if those noises might bother Jane in trance—and they had. I didn't know where Billy's littermate Mitzi was, though. I found her locked out on the screened-in front porch.

("I don't want to lose it," Jane said. She went quickly back into trance. Purring and rubbing, Mitzi began to climb all over me as I tried to take notes. Resume at 10:30.)

All of the species began by emphasizing a great subjective orientation that was most necessary as they learned to manipulate within the new physical environment.

(Jane paused, eyes closed. Mitzi was still loving me up. Then:)

End of session.

(10:31 P.M. "Oh," I said in some surprise.

"I'll tell you," Jane said, "I was getting more. It was fun to do, and I knew what was coming, but going back like that I couldn't get it."

I told Jane the session is brilliant, the best she's ever given. I told her *it raised many questions, but that I didn't think anyone, at any time, had dealt better with the "origin" of our universe, our world, our history.*

"I got some of it before the session—about the initial ones before the earth was formed—you could call them nonphysical entities. But it sounds dumb when you say it now: Physical *entities couldn't hold all that much consciousness. I didn't know it was that definite until the end of the session, though. . . . Boy, that was a really good state," she said with satisfaction. "I really enjoyed it. . . ."*

But I had to admit that I was also surprised. Seth had come through so rapidly and emphatically that while taking notes I'd hardly had time to think about questions. What's he trying to do, I asked Jane—combine something like science's theoretical "big-bang" origin of the universe, all of those billions of years ago, with creationism's theory of a recent spontaneous, divine creation of that same universe? Has our earth and all of its creatures "evolved," or not? Could you have simultaneous evolution? [Here we go again, I speculated, back to struggling with that contradictory notion of "simultaneous time."] How does Seth's instantaneous "beginning processes that formed the universe"—with no time involved—square with fossils in the earth? Isn't he saying that the universe grew/evolved through a series of dream states?

I told Jane that as far as I know the unimaginable explosion of the primordial superdense state, or entity, that resulted in the formation of our universe had been a straightforward event: Once begun, it kept going. There hadn't been any fluctuations or on-off states balancing between the physical and nonphysical, for example. Science currently postulates this theory as its "standard model" for the creation of the universe.[3]

So how do Seth's own ideas of probable universes and probable earths fit in with his material tonight—as I'm sure they do? I quickly saw that my questions could go on and on. Seth's book is young, I told myself. Wait. Wait. . . .

And Mitzi, her affectionate display long finished, had jumped down from my lap and disappeared as Jane and I talked.)

Notes: Session 883

1. Seth was evidently experimenting here, for right away he went back to using "it," instead of "he," when referring to All That Is. "It" may not be entirely satisfactory either, but Jane and

I didn't question Seth about it: We prefer that designation because it encompasses any kind of sexual orientation and/or function within All That Is. (When Seth used "he" while talking about All That Is a couple of times later in the session, I substituted "it" in my notes and let it go at that.)

2. Seth first discussed the "sleepwalkers" in Volume 2 of *"Unknown" Reality*—see Session 708 for September 30, 1974. Here's a much-condensed version of that he told us that night after break ended at 9:56:

"Imagine a body with a fully operating body consciousness, not diseased or defective, but without the overriding ego-directed consciousness that you have. The sleepwalkers' physical abilities surpassed yours. They were as agile as animals, their purpose simply to be. Their main points of consciousness were elsewhere, their primary focuses scarcely aware of the bodies they had created. Yet they learned 'through experience,' and began to 'awaken,' to become aware of themselves, to discover time, or to create it.

"They were not asleep to themselves, only from your viewpoint. There were several such races of human beings. To them the real was the dream life, which contained the highest stimuli. This is the other side of your own experience. Such races left the physical earth much as they found it. In what you would call the physical waking state, these individuals slept, yet they behaved with great natural physical grace. They did not saddle the body with negative beliefs of disease or limitation. They did not age to the extent that you do."

In *"Unknown" Reality*, then, Seth's material on the sleepwalkers heralded one of the main themes of *Dreams*, which he began five years later. *Dreams* was unsuspected by us then, of course; so what books to come will have their genesis in *this* one?

(I'll add that Jane and I have received several thousand letters since the publication of Volume 2 of *"Unknown" Reality*. As best I can remember, however, not a single writer has mentioned the sleepwalkers—one of Seth's most intriguing concepts.)

3. Theoretical physicists have charted (assuming that the big-bang origin of the universe was a hot event) how the first explosion may have "evolved" from one with a temperature well in excess of 100,000 million degrees Kelvin into a cooler one of

"only" a few thousand degrees Kelvin around 500,000 years later, so that atoms could begin to form. Jane has heard of this standard model, of course, but knows little about its supposed details.

In ordinary terms, she knows practically nothing concerning several other less prominent theories regarding the beginning of the universe. I haven't discussed these with her. One of them is the "inflationary model," which may become much better known. It incorporates many of the features of the big-bang theory, and actually may answer certain questions in a better scientific fashion. One of the big differences between the two is that in the big-bang theory all of the matter in the universe was already present, though existing in an extremely dense state which then began to expand; the inflationary model suggests that the universe was created out of nothing, or out of just about nothing—meaning that through unforeseeable rhythms sub-atomic particles spontaneously came into being, with sufficient energy behind them to enable them to persist as matter. A fantastic, inflationary expansion then began. Yet this creation of matter out of nothing, so to speak, violates at least some of the laws of conservation—laws that are indeed among the most basic and cherished tenets of physics.

From my reading of Seth's ideas of "in the beginning," however, I'm sure he couldn't agree with either the big-bang or inflationary models of the creation of the universe, even though his material may be evocative of portions of both theories. In physics, we're asked to believe that this "extremely dense state" which began to expand was in actuality many billions of times smaller than a proton. (Protons are subatomic components of the nuclei of atoms.) Matter is a form of energy. Even so, I have trouble conceptualizing the idea that *all matter* in our universe, out to the farthest-away galaxy of billions of stars, grew from this unimaginably small and dense, unimaginably hot "original" state or area of being. I can see how such a concept can be postulated mathematically—but could it ever have really happened in ordinary terms?

SESSION 884, OCTOBER 3, 1979
9:13 P.M. WEDNESDAY

(The weather has been exceptionally warm this fall—warm and often rainy or misty, but most welcome for this time of year. The trees seem way behind schedule; we've seen the first signs of their leaves turning color just recently. The grass has even started growing again, after lying dry and dormant for a long period this summer.

Yesterday morning I heard geese flying south for the first time this season, but they were invisible above a heavy overcast. This afternoon I both heard and saw them, and called them to Jane's attention—a wide, straggling, shifting, V-shaped flight vanishing over the valley holding the city just below us. The geese looked very vulnerable against the massive roll of the earth beneath them, but this was an illusion: Like every other entity on earth, each one of those birds knew very well what it was doing. Each was well equipped to seek out its individual value fulfillment.

I finished typing last Monday night's session a few minutes before we sat for this one, and Jane just had time to read it before she felt Seth around: "Okay, I'm ready. . . .")

Now. *(Smile. Then elaborately:)* Let us return to our tale or origins.

We are sitting here on a specific autumn evening. I am obviously dictating this book, speaking through Ruburt, while Joseph sits on the couch across from a very specific coffee table, taking down my words.

This is the year 1979, and the idea of time and of dates seems to be indelibly mixed into [everyone's] psychology. You can remember last year, and to some extent recall the past years of your lives. It appears to you that your present consciousness wanders backward into the past, until finally you can remember no longer—and on a conscious level, at least, you must take the very event of your birth under secondhanded evidence. Few people have conscious memory of it.

For the purposes of our discussion, I must necessarily couch this book to some degree in the framework of time. I must honor your specifics. Otherwise you would not understand what I am trying to say.

(Pause, one of many.) Even though this book is being dictated

within time's tradition, therefore, I must remind you that basically (underlined) that tradition is not mine—and more, basically (underlined), it is not yours either.

I used the term "before the beginning," then, and I will speak of earth's events in certain sequences. In the deepest of terms, however, and in ways that quite scandalize the intellect when it tries to operate alone, the beginning is now. That critical explosion of divine subjectivity into objectivity is always happening, and you are being given life "in each moment" because of the simultaneous nature of that divine subjectivity.

(Pause.) We will nevertheless call our next chapter "In the Beginning," laying certain events out for you in serial form. I hope that in other portions of this book certain mental exercises will allow you to leap over the tradition of time's framework and sense with the united intellect and intuitions your own individual part in a spacious present that is large enough to contain all of time's segments.

CHAPTER 2

IN THE BEGINNING

Chapter Two: "In the Beginning."

Once again, in terms of your equations, energy and consciousness and matter are one. And in those terms—in parentheses: (the qualifications are necessary)—consciousness is the agent that directs the transformation of energy into form and of form into energy. All possible visible or invisible particles that you discover or imagine—meaning hypothesized particles—possess consciousness. They are energized consciousness.

There are certain characteristics inherent in energy itself, quite aside from any that you ascribe to it, since of course to date you do not consider energy conscious.

(9:35.) Energy is above all things infinitely creative, innovative, original. Energy is imaginative. In parentheses: (Any scientists who might be reading this book may as well stop here.) I am not assigning human traits to energy. Instead, your human traits are the result of energy's characteristics—a rather important difference. Space as you think of it is, in your terms, filled with invisible particles. They are the unstated portion of physical reality, the unmanifest medium in which your world exists. In that regard, however, atoms and molecules are stated, though you cannot see them with your [unaided] eye. The smaller particles that make them up become "smaller and smaller," finally disappearing from the examination of any kind of physical instrument,

and these help bridge the gap between unmanifest and manifest reality.[1]

For the terms of this discussion of the beginning of [your] world, I will deal with known qualities for now—the atoms and molecules. In the beginning they imagined the myriad of forms that were physically possible. They imagined the numberless c-e-l-l-s *(spelled out)* that could arise from their own cooperative creation. Energy is boundless. It is exuberant. It knows no limits *(all intently)*. In those terms, the atoms dreamed the cells into physical being—and from that new threshold of physical activity cellular consciousness dreamed of the myriad organizations that could emerge from this indescribable venture.

Again, in actuality all of this took place at once, yet the depth of psychological experience contained therein can never be measured, for it involved a kind of value fulfillment with which each consciousness is involved. That characteristic of value fulfillment is perhaps the most important element in the being of All That Is, and it is a part of the heritage of all species.

Value fulfillment itself is most difficult to describe, for it combines *(pause)* the nature of a loving presence—a presence with the innate knowledge of its own divine complexity—with a creative ability of infinite proportions that seeks to bring to fulfillment even the slightest, most distant portion of its own inverted complexity. Translated into simpler terms, each portion of energy is endowed with an inbuilt reach of creativity that seeks to fulfill its own potentials in all possible variations—and in such a way that such a development also furthers the creative potentials of each other portion of reality *(all very emphatically)*.

In those terms, then, there was in the beginning an almost unimaginable time in which energized consciousness, using its own creative abilities, its own imagination (underlined), experimented with triumphant rambunctiousness, trying out one form after another. In the terms you are used to thinking of, nothing was stable. Consciousness as you think of it turned into matter, and then into pure energy and back again.

(Pause at 9:56.) Subjectivity still largely ruled. Like an adolescent leaving home for the first time, individualized consciousness was also somewhat homesick, and returned often to the family homestead—but gradually gained confidence and left finally to form a [universe].

Now because All That Is contains within itself such omnipotent, fertile, divine creative characteristics, all portions of its subjective experience attained dimensions of actuality impossible to describe. The thoughts, for example, of All that Is were not simply thoughts as you might have, but multidimensional mental events of superlative nature. Those events soon found that a transformation must occur *(pause)*, if they were to journey into objectivity—for no objectivity of itself could contain the entire reality of subjective events that existed within divine subjectivity. Only in that context could their relative (underlined) perfection be maintained. Yet they had yearned before the beginning for other experiences, and even for fulfillments of a different nature. They sensed a kind of value fulfillment that required of them the utilization of their own creative abilities. They yearned to create as they had been created, and All That Is, in a kind of divine perplexity, nevertheless realized that this had always been its own intent.

(Pause.) All That Is realized that such a separation would also allow you *(pause)* to bring about a different kind of divine art, in which the creators themselves created, and their creations created, bringing into actuality existences that were possible precisely because there would seem (underlined) to be a difference between the creator and the creations. All That Is is, therefore, within each smallest portion of consciousness.

Yet each smallest portion of consciousness can uniquely create, bring into being, eccentric[2] versions of All That Is, that in certain terms All That Is, without that separation, could not otherwise create. The loving support, the loving encouragement of the slightest probable consciousness and manifestation—that is the intent of All That Is.

(Long pause.) All That Is knows that even this purpose is a portion of a larger purpose. In terms of time, the realization of that purpose will emerge with another momentous explosion of subjective inspiration into objectivity, or into another form. In deeper terms, however, that purpose is also known now, and to one extent or another the entire universe dreams of it, as once cellular consciousness dreamed of the organs that it might "form."

(10:15.) I want to stress that I am speaking here not so much about a kind of spiritual evolution as I am about an expan-

sion.[3] We will for now, however, confine ourselves to a discussion of consciousness in the beginning of the world, stressing that the first basis of physical life was largely subjective, and that the state of dreaming not only helped shape the consciousness of your species, but also in those terms served to provide a steady source of information to man about his physical environment, and served as an inner web of communication among all species.

End of dictation.

(10:19.) Give us a moment. . . . Remind me, for our next session, to wind in a discussion of those subjective entities as they learned how to translate themselves into physical individuals.

(Heartily:) End of dictation, end of session, a fond good evening—

("Thank you.")

—and I enjoy the cozy specific nature of your den *(Jane's writing room)* in its hillside house, nestled in its physical nest, the specific streets and small city. Particularly when we are discussing issues of such complexity—issues seemingly so vast, and yet issues that are themselves responsible for your perception of a specific evening.

My fondest good wishes—a fond good evening.

("Thank you, Seth. Good night.")

(10:23 P.M. "I don't know whether it's going to last or not," Jane said, "but I'm enjoying this book more than any. I get into a certain state that's really nice. It's very rich and deep. Like I know the session wasn't too long, but I had that sense of completion when he went back incredibly far. It's satisfying as all shit."

I laughed. It was easy to tell that Jane was happy working on Seth's latest. I gladly told her the session was just as good, just as inspiring, as her last one—the 883rd: Once again her delivery had been intent, often impassioned, given with many gestures. She's been picking up from Seth on Dreams *quite often. Sometimes she tells me as soon as she's done this. At other times she may forget to mention it for a while, or the session material itself may remind her that she already knew what Seth was going to talk about.)*

Notes: Session 884

1. In Volume 1 of *"Unknown" Reality,* I wrote in Note 7 for Session 681 that atoms are "processes" rather than things. The clas-

sical conception of the typical atom as being composed of a neat nucleus of indivisible protons and neutrons circled by electrons is largely passé, although for convenience's sake we may still describe the atom that way. (In those terms, the one exception is the hydrogen atom, which evidently consists of but one proton and one electron cloud, or "smear.") For the simple purposes of this note, then, I'm leaving out considerations involving quantum mechanics, which concept repudiates the idea of "particles" to begin with. (And surely *that* notion involves more than a little of the psychic, or "irrational." What a heretical thought from the scientific viewpoint!) But each atom of whatever element is an amazingly complicated, finely balanced assemblage of forces and particles woven together in exquisite detail—one of the more basic examples of the unending and stupendous creativity, order, and design of nature, or consciousness, or All That Is.

Through their work with particle accelerators, or "atom smashers," physicists have discovered that protons and neutrons *themselves* are composed of forces and particles that in turn are almost certainly composed of forces and particles, and so on, in an ever-descending scale of smaller and smaller entities and concepts. Over 100 subatomic particles have been identified so far, and no one doubts now that many more will be found. The existence of a number of still-undiscovered specific particles has been predicted. All of which reminds me that almost 16 years ago, in only the 19th session he'd given us (on January 27, 1964), Seth remarked:

"Your scientists can count their elements. . . . That is, they will create more and discover more until they are ready to go out of their minds, because they will always create [physical] 'camouflages' of the real [nonphysical] thing. And while they create instruments to deal with smaller and smaller particles, they will actually see smaller and smaller particles, seemingly without end.

"As their instruments reach farther into the universe they will 'see'—and I suggest that you put the word 'see' into quotes —they will 'see' farther and farther, but they will automatically transform what they apparently 'see' into the camouflage patterns with which they are familiar. They are and they will be the prisoners of their own tools.

"Instruments calculated to measure the vibrations with which scientists are familiar will be designed and redesigned. All sorts finally of seemingly impossible phenomena will be discovered with these instruments, until the scientists realize that something is desperately wrong. The instruments will be planned to catch certain camouflages, and since they will be expertly thought out they will perform their function. I do not want to get too involved. However, by certain means the instruments themselves will transform data from terms that you cannot understand into terms that you can understand. Scientists do this all the time."

Some of the "particles" the theoretical physicists have discovered—and/or created—in their gigantic particle accelerators have unbelievably short life-spans in our terms, vanishing, it seems, almost before they're born. I like to think of such research from the particle's point of view, though, a consideration I haven't seen mentioned in the few scientific journals I read. Keep in mind that according to the Seth material the merest particle is basically conscious in its own way. Mesons are classes of particles produced from the collisions of protons. Did a meson, for example, *choose* to participate in an atom-smashing experiment in order to merely peek in on our gross physical reality for much less than the *billionth* of a second it exists *with that identity*, before it decays into electrons and photons? From its viewpoint, our reality might be an incomprehensible to it as its reality is to us—yet the two inevitably go together.

In its way the meson may have all of the "time" it needs, or wants. It may look upon our world as one frozen or motionless, upon other subatomic particles as very slow-moving indeed, or even faster than it is. (As far as "time" goes, some particles live for far less than a trillionth of a second.) I'm quite sure, however, that the meson, or any short-lived particle, searches out its own kind of value fulfillment while here with us. Probable realities, which I haven't even mentioned, must be deeply involved also.

And of course there are all sorts of motion, some of them very stable, if still incomprehensible to us. But whereas the meson vanishes from our view after its exceedingly brief existence, the electron has an "infinite" life-span. Think of the unending varieties of value fulfillment it explores in just our world alone! Talk about motion: The average electron orbits its atomic nucleus about a million times each billionth of a second (or nanosecond)!

At this point in my speculations I'm usually led back to Seth's

EE (or electromagnetic energy) units, and his CU's (or units of consciousness). These nonphysical entities—and many others of a like nature—are emanations of consciousness, or All That Is, and in "size" rank far below the tiniest particles ever observed in an atom smasher. According to Seth, each unit of consciousness "contains within itself innately infinite properties of expansion, development and organization; yet within itself always maintains the kernel of its own individuality. . . . It is aware energy . . . not 'personified' but awareized." See Session 682 for Volume 1 of "*Unknown*" *Reality.*

Seth came through with that session on February 13, 1974. Now let me close this note with an excerpt from a private session he gave on July 3, 1978:

"The varieties of consciousness—the inner 'psychological particles,' the equivalent, say, of the atom or molecule, or proton, neutron or quark—those nonphysical, 'charmed,' 'strange,' forms of consciousness that make experience go up or down *(all with amusement)*, and around and around—are never of course dealt with *(by science)*.

"If physical form is made up of such multitudinous, invisible particles, how much more highly organized must be the inner components of consciousness, without whose perceptions matter itself would be meaningless. The alliances of consciousness, then, are far more vast than those of particles in any form."

2. I've always liked the way Jane uses the word "eccentric" in relation to the abilities of any portion of consciousness to create new versions of itself; she's added her own original interpretation of the word to the dictionary version of "eccentric" as meaning out of the ordinary, or odd, or unconventional.

She began to refer to the eccentricities of consciousness in October 1974, following her first conscious experience with her "psychic library," and a subsequent transcendental experience in which she suddenly began to see, with an astonishing clear vision, the great "model" of each portion of the world about her —each person, each building, each blade of grass, each bird, for example; our ordinary world suddenly appeared quite shabby by contrast. Jane wrote that "everyone was a classic model, yet each was also a fantastic eccentric. . . . I saw that each of us is a beloved eccentric not only because we have inner models of the self, but also the freedom to deviate from them, all of which makes the model living and creative in our time."

In *Psychic Politics*, see chapters 2 and 3.

3. Now what, I wondered, as I typed this session from my notes, does Seth mean here, and in the paragraph above? Sometimes it's difficult to pinpoint just what he's saying. His material usually generates more questions than answers, but this time he'd outdone himself. I try to avoid reading too much into such brief passages, but I felt that if Seth answered all of the questions I could ask based upon this session, a book would result. Was he referring to another big-bang type of "momentous explosion"? I doubted it. Without going into a lot of speculative detail, such an event would imply the obliteration of our probable physical universe as we know it. Instead, I thought, by "another form" he may mean an explosion of *ideas* or *knowledge* in our reality, with the tremendous objective results that would follow. Such results would stem even from "just" a spiritual explosion. (I could also see correlations here between Seth's ideas about the primary nature of All That Is and the inflationary model of the universe. See Note 2 for Session 883.)

Since it's sometimes difficult to be sure of just what Seth *is* saying, in retrospect I wished that either he'd volunteered more information about his explosion-expansion, or that I'd been quick enough to ask him to do so. But if words are often necessarily limited and stereotyped, they can also be quite elusive— and this is an excellent thing, for it shows they're still alive, charged with meanings that change. Basically, those meanings can never really be "put into words."

SESSION 885, OCTOBER 24, 1979
9:20 P.M. WEDNESDAY

(Five scheduled session dates have passed since we held the 884th session three weeks ago; we missed four of those, but did hold a private, or deleted, session on October 10. We've been busy. Jane has been working hard on her God of Jane. He's also written a number of poems. [Some of them are on reincarnation, and I plan to present them when Seth gets

into that subject in Dreams.*] On October 7, a Sunday, Jane saw for the first time the work Sue Watkins has done on* Conversations With Seth, *the book she's writing about the ESP classes Jane used to hold. The project is turning out to be much longer than Sue had thought it would be, and she still has a few chapters to go. The two women spent the day going over the manuscript, and I had a chance to read some of it also. Later Sue laughingly admitted that she'd been nervous at first, imagining all kinds of adverse reactions either Jane or I might have—but she's doing a fine job. She has complete freedom to do* Conversations *in her own way. The next day Jane began making notes for the introduction she's to write for the book.*

Four days after Sue's visit we received an enthusiastic letter from an independent motion-picture producer and director in Hollywood, informing us that he's finally succeeding in his quest for an option to the film rights to Jane's novel, The Education of Oversoul Seven. *This event marks the latest step in a rather complicated affair that began 18 months ago. It means only that our friends in Hollywood and in the subsidiary rights department at Prentice-Hall have agreed upon the terms of the option; a contract has yet to be signed by all of us. We've never asked Seth to comment upon either this project itself or anyone involved with it—nor has he volunteered such information, even in private sessions.*

During this session hiatus I've been spending much time upon a series of letters to the publishers of Seth Speaks *in Switzerland and in the Netherlands, as well as to those in charge at Prentice-Hall.[1] Last Saturday night we had a very interesting meeting with a psychologist from New York City. Our visitor taped Seth's copious material, and is to send us a transcript of it.*

Today, Jane wrote three more excellent little poems, all of which I hope to eventually see published.[2] I think she grumbled the whole time she was doing them, though, since she kept at herself because she wasn't working on God of Jane.

Then tonight she began writing "a fun thing" about our cats, Billy and Mitzi, who are brother and sister just 10 months old now: "In the beginning, Billy and Mitzi weren't even kittens yet, but only bits of sky and cloud that wanted to be pussycats. Not that anyone knew what cats were, because God hadn't created any yet. If it hadn't been for Billy and Mitzi, cats might not exist at all. . . ." The story sprang out of the hilarious way she's taken to addressing Mitzi in regard to that cat's gifts from heaven; I've been telling her that the affair would make a great children's book.[3] *In the several pages she wrote this evening Jane presented her material quite humorously, in a manner reminiscent of, yet different from, her second Seven novel,* The Further Education of Oversoul Seven, *and her* Emir.[4]

Jane surprised me at the last moment by asking if I wanted the session; I'd thought she was going to pass it up because of her general discontent with herself. Seth didn't call this one book dictation, but it certainly applies to Dreams. *And in his opening delivery he referred to the creative freedoms that—seemingly in spite of her conscious fussing—Jane* had *allowed herself today.)*

(Whispering:) Good evening.

("Good evening, Seth.")

A few notes. When Ruburt forgot to worry because "he wasn't working," his natural playful creativity bubbled to the surface, and today he wrote poetry. Poetry, however, did not fit into his current ideas about work, and so that excellent creativity was hardly counted at all.

In a fashion—in a fashion—the [universe] began in the same way that Ruburt's story this evening began: with the desire to create—out of joy, not from a sense of responsibility.

Many of the ideas in our current book will be accepted by scientists most dubiously, though some, of course, will grasp what I will be saying. It is of course very difficult for you, because *(pause)* the deepest truths cannot be physically proven. *(Pause.)* Science is used to asking quite specific questions, and as Ruburt wrote recently *(in* God of Jane*)* it usually comes up with very specific answers—even if those answers are wrong *(with some humor).*

"Wrong" answers can fit together, however, to present a perfect picture, an excellent construct of its own—and why not? For any answers that do not fit the construct are simply thrown away and never appear. So in a fashion we are dealing with what science has thrown away. The picture we will end up presenting, then, will certainly not fit that of established science.

However, if objective proof of that nature is considered the priority for facts, then as you know science cannot prove its version of the [universe's] origin either. It only sets up an hypothesis, which collects about it all data that agree, and again ignores what does not fit. Moreover, science's thesis meets with no answering affirmation in the human heart—and in fact arouses the deepest antipathy, for in his heart man well knows his own worth, and realizes that his own consciousness is no accident.[5] The psyche, then, possesses within itself an inner affirmation, an affirmation that provides the impetus for physical emergence, an affirmation that keeps man from being completely blinded by his own mental edifices *(all with much emphasis and fast delivery.*

(9:33.) There is furthermore a deep, subjective, immaculately knowledgeable standard within man's consciousness by which he ultimately judges all of the theories and the beliefs of his time, and even if his intellect is momentarily swamped by ignoble doctrines, still that point of integrity within him is never fooled.

There is a part of man that Knows, with a capital K. That is the portion of him, of course, that is born and grows to maturity even while the lungs or digestive processes do not read learned treatises on the body's "machinery,"[6] so in our book we will hope to arouse within the reader, of whatever persuasion, a kind of subjective evidence, a resonance between ideas and being. Many people write, saying that they feel as if somehow they have always been acquainted with our material—and of course they have, for it represents the inner knowing within each individual. *(Pause.)* In a fashion, creative play is your human version of far greater characteristics from which your universe itself was formed. There are all kinds of definite, even specific, subjective evidence for the nature of your own reality—evidence that is readily apparent once you really begin to look for it, particularly by comparing the world of your dreams with your daily life.

In other words, subjective play is the basis for all creativity, of course—but far more, it is responsible for the great inner play of subjective and objective reality.

With all due respect, your friend [the psychologist] is, with the best of intentions, barking up the wrong psychological tree. He is very enthusiastic about his value tests, and his enthusiasm is what is important. The nature of the subjective mind, however, will never open itself to such tests, which represent, more than anything else, a kind of mechanical psychology, as if you could break down human values to a kind of logical alphabet of psychic atoms and molecules. A good try *(with humor)*, but representative of psychology's best attempt to make sense of a poor hypothesis.

You may do what you wish yourselves *(about taking the tests)*, of course, but our main purpose is to drive beyond psychology's boundaries, and not play pussyfoot among the current psychological lilies of the field.

As for Ruburt, he became overconcerned about work because of the contracts *(for* Mass Events *and* God of Jane, *which we have yet to sign with Prentice-Hall),* and the foreign hassles. It would be nice if you took it for granted that all of those issues were also being creatively worked out to your advantage. He is still somewhat afraid of relaxing. It makes him feel guilty. His body is responding, however, so let him remember that creativity is playful, and that it <u>always</u> surfaces when he allows his mind to drop its worries.

Do you have questions?

("No, I guess not.")

You are doing well, and your notes *(for* Mass Events) are coming together in their own order, so let them.

I bid you a fond good evening.

("Thank you, Seth. The same to you.")

(9:57 P.M. "He was right there," Jane said with a smile. "That's nice."

Our visiting psychologist left us a couple sets of the tests Seth referred to. Jane had resisted filling them out during our meeting with him, and has little intention of doing so now. Even our guest said the tests were very experimental; I believe that actually a colleague of his had devised them in large part. I thought they'd been [perhaps unwittingly] oriented in certain negative directions—that is, the one taking the test has to choose from a series of more or less negative possibilities, listing specific choices in an order that depends upon his or her personal belief systems —I think.

Obviously, Seth didn't follow through on the statement he'd made near the end of the last book session, which we held much earlier this month: "Remind me, for our next session, to wind in a discussion of those subjective entities as they learned how to translate themselves into physical individuals." However, I didn't ask him for the material tonight, either. Jane hasn't mentioned it. Such omissions can easily result when the session routine is interrupted—we simply may not keep a particular session that closely in mind as we become involved in other matters during a break. The information in question will be most interesting when Seth does come through with it.)

NOTES: SESSION 885

1. Some of my letters were triggered on October 9 (this month), when Jane and I received our first copies of *Seth Spreekt,* the Dutch-language edition of *Seth Speaks.* We saw at once that the people at Ankh-Hermes, the publishing company in the Netherlands, had cut the book considerably. As I wrote in the notes for the private session we held the next evening: "Our first reactions were ones of such stunned surprise that we didn't even get mad."

In effect, Ankh-Hermes has published not only a translation but a condensation. Considering the eagerness with which we've looked forward to having the Seth material published in other languages, and the long waiting periods involved, this situation is frustrating indeed. Many of my notes, some of which contain excerpts of Seth material, have been eliminated. So have large portions of a number of the sessions themselves. The Appendix in *Seth Spreekt* is only 11 pages long, chopped down from 67 pages.

"My own position cannot be as immediate as your own," Seth said on October 10. "I respect your emotional reactions, whatever they are, and your right to them. *(Loudly and amused:)* Seth, it seems, speaks a bit more briefly in Dutch than he does in English—but the material is there, and if the Dutch have cut it, or your notes, it is, in the most basic of terms, now, their loss. Agreements of a legal order should, however, always be honored, and each society has been built upon that precept. . . ."

"Whenever a book is translated, it is almost impossible, of course, to say the same thing in the same way. Such a book will always be expressed through those invisible national characteristics that are so intimately involved with language—and obviously, were that not so, no book could be understood by someone of a foreign language. There are bound to be distortions, but the distortions themselves are meaningful."

Our editor, Tam Mossman, has verified for us that the contract between Prentice-Hall and Ankh-Hermes contains a clause prohibiting cutting, unless Jane's and my permission is given. Already those at Ankh-Hermes have been asked to withdraw from sale their shortened version of *Seth Spreekt,* and to publish a full-length one instead—a very expensive proposition indeed. Jane and I regret this, now that our first anger has passed. We're caught between the economic realities of the situation as far as Ankh-Hermes is concerned, and our own intense desires that translations of the Seth books match the original versions as closely as possible. We fully agree with Seth that changes and distortions are inevitable as the Seth material is moved from English into other languages; we just want those alterations kept to a minimum. It appears that language difficulties involving publishers and agents led to the whole mix-up to begin with. Tam has begun work on a contractual amendment designed to prevent more such confusions. And all concerned must wait at least another year before a full-length version of *Seth Speaks* will be published in the Dutch language.

For a number of reasons, hardcover books especially are much more expensive in Europe than they are in the United States. In Europe a book can be priced at more than double its comparative cost in this country.

2. Jane hasn't given titles to any of her poems of the day. In all three of them she celebrated, in a deceptively simple, almost innocently mystical way, the changing look of autumn. For example:

> When all of summer's
> splendid leafery is gone
> then space seems to surround
> us everywhere, far and close.
> The immense vault of the universe
> turns intimate,
> reaches to our chimneytops
> in shining swirls of sudden openness
> just outside of our back doors.
> Space from the galaxies
> rushes in to fill the new emptiness
> where a million million leaves were,
> and the valleys hold
> natural cupfuls of space,
> filled to their transparent brims.

Jane has been doing 3" x 6" sketches in concert with her poetry about nature. She works in brilliant simple colors, obtaining her effects with porous pens whose inks she can partially blend with water. I'd like to frame some of those little pieces, for visually they present the same qualities her poetry does verbally. We usually keep her sketches covered, however, since their colors begin to fade after a few weeks' exposure to light.

3. I've also suggested to Jane that she might be able to incorporate into her story about Billy and Mitzi the little poem below. It's from a number of sketches and untitled poems she did as a birthday book for me last June:

> *There* seems *to be*
> *no unexpressed self*
> *in animals,*
> *as if they are*
> *as fully themselves*
> *in flesh as possible,*
> *with no lag*
> *of consciousness*
> *to fill up,*
> *while we keep*
> *trying to grow*
> *into something*
> *else.*

4. *Seven Two*, as we call it, was published by Prentice-Hall in May —five months ago. Delacorte Press published *Emir* just last month.

5. By now, a number of the world's leading scientists in the physical disciplines have publicly stated their beliefs that basically consciousness plays the primary role in our world and/or universe. For reasons too complicated to go into here, this attitude prevails even with some mathematicians who seek to penetrate to the core of our reality as they understand it.

However, for every scientist bold enough to think this way, there are scores of others who vehemently disagree. For most scientific materialists only physical matter is real. For them consciousness is nothing more than an epiphenomenon, the passive by-product of the brain's physiology and chemical events. They believe that physical death is the end of everything, that ultimately all is pointless. They derisively call their rebellious colleagues "animists"—those who believe that all life forms and natural phenomena have a spiritual origin independent of physical matter. (Such heretics are also called "vitalists," a term related to animism, and one which also has a long history of scientific contempt behind it.)

Jane and I have often been most intrigued by the obvious contradictions involved here, for what can the materialistic scientists use *other than* mind—or consciousness, that poor epiphenomenon—to study and dissect matter? (Not to mention that innumerable experiments have proven that "physical matter" isn't solid or objective at all, but "only" energy!) We have, then, the paradox of mind denying its own reality, let alone its importance. As far as we know, human beings are the only creatures on earth who would seriously engage in such learned, futile behavior. It's also very ironic, I think, that the materialists spend years acquiring their specialized educations, and prestige, both of which they then use to inform us of the ultimate futility of all of our endeavors (including their own, of course). But for the materialists, the mind-brain duality isn't scientific in the orthodox sense. It isn't falsifiable; that is, it cannot be stated under what precise conditions the mind-brain duality could be proven false. To which, understandably enough, those scientists who do accept the reality of mind reply that neither can the idea be falsified that only what is "physical" is real.

Aside from anything Seth has said or ever may say about other probable realities, or even about human origins here on earth, I think it most risky at this stage in history for anyone— scientist or not—to dogmatically state that life has no meaning, or is a farce, or that attributes of our reality of which we can only mentally conceive at this time do not really exist. Discoveries in the "future" are quite apt to prove such limited viewpoints wrong. The history of science itself contains many examples of theories and "facts" gone awry. Moreover, why would our species want to depend upon as fragile a conception as epiphenomenalism through which to comprehend our reality? Or better yet, *why does it* in large part? Truly, our individual and collective ignorance of just our own probable reality is most profound at this time in our linear history (in those terms). Jane and I wouldn't be surprised if ultimately, as a result of mankind's restless search for meaning, we didn't end up returning in a new official way to our ancient concepts of spirit within everything, animate and inanimate. Such an updated animistic/vitalistic view would take into account discoveries ranging from subnuclear events to the largest imaginable astronomical processes in our observable universe. Human beings *do* know their own worth, as Seth stated in this session.

Jane herself commented on these questions in her own way recently (as Seth indicated a bit earlier this evening). Her notes will end up in one of the later chapters of *God of Jane*, which she's still roughing out:

"There is no doubt that we need to believe that life has meaning. That belief may well be a biological imperative. If we were as science maintains—only creatures formed by elements combining mindlessly in a universe itself created by chance, surrounded everywhere by chaos—then how could we even conceive of the idea of meaning or order?

"Science would say that the idea of meaning itself is simply a reflection of the state of the brain, as is the illusion of our consciousness. But a science that disregards consciousness must necessarily end up creating its own illusion. It ignores the reality of experience, the evidence of being, and in so doing it denies rather than reinforces life's values."

6. Seth's passage reminded both of us of "If Toes Had Eyes," a poem Jane wrote some four months ago, which she's using in an earlier chapter of *God of Jane*. Here's the first verse:

> *If toes had eyes,*
> *then I could see*
> *how my feet know where to go,*
> *but toes are blind.*
> *And how is it that my tongue*
> *speaks words it cannot hear?*
> *Because for all its eloquence,*
> *the tongue itself is deaf,*
> *and flaps in soundlessness.*

SESSION 886, DECEMBER 3, 1979
9:20 P.M. MONDAY

(We've held only three private, or deleted, sessions since Seth came through with the last regular one [the 885th] almost six weeks ago. I just wish I could present those sessions here, for in them Seth gave us much valuable information—not only about ourselves [including Jane's somewhat impaired physical condition, her "stiffness"], but about the myriad interchanges occurring constantly between our inner and outer realities, or Frameworks 1 and 2, as he calls them. Some of that framework material is personal, but much more of it is general.

In the Preface for Dreams *I mentioned Jane's idea for a second book of poetry. She's progressed with the subject matter for it to the point where Seth could remark on November 21: "The book of love poetry is an excellent idea." For now Jane wants the volume to contain some of the poetry she's dedicated to me over the years since we met in February 1954. She called Tam Mossman last month about the book, and they discussed possible titles for it. But Jane doesn't yet have one she likes.*

In the Preface I also wrote about how I thought the great blossomings of religious consciousness and scientific consciousness engendered by the events at Three Mile Island and Jonestown/Iran would continue to grow, once born, seemingly with lives of their own. Jane and I have watched these effects steadily increase since we held the 885th session. Now, our country's initial concern over the accident at TMI has grown to include deep questions about why we've built so many nuclear energy generating plants near large population centers; carrying out a mass evacuation in case of a serious accident at any of those sites seems to present a series of insurmountable challenges.

As for Iran, I described how last February [1979] a mob of Marxist-led Iranian guerrillas overran the United States Embassy in that country's capital, Tehran, and temporarily held prisoner some 70 Americans. I noted that such a situation could happen again—and it did: On November 4, Iranian students assaulted our embassy compound and took 63 Americans hostage; 3 others were imprisoned at Iran's Foreign Ministry. Day 1 began of a countdown toward the release of the hostages (it's day 30 as I write this note). The Moslem militants released 13 of our citizens—5 white women and 8 black men—who returned home by Thanksgiving Day, but this time they kept in bondage the remaining 53 Americans. Iran holds our entire country in contempt.

This may hardly be original thinking here, but these proliferations of consciousness imply some pretty fantastic abilities on the part of we humans—for such developments show that even though we live as small creatures within the incredible richness of an overall consciousness, or All That Is, still our actions can result in that great consciousness exploring new areas of itself. Quite awesome creative abilities on our part, I'd say, and ones that unknowingly we take for granted. We do this all of the time, of course, individually and collectively.

Earlier today Jane and I had talked about Seth's resuming work on Dreams. *I was still surprised when he did so. Jane had also expressed a strong desire for some personal information in the session.)*

(Rather slowly and deliberately to start:)

Now: In the beginning, there was not God the Father, Allah, Zoroaster, Zeus, or Buddha.[1]

In the beginning there was instead, once more, a divine psychological gestalt—and by that I mean a being whose reality escapes the definition of the word "being," since it is the source from which all being emerges. That being exists in a psychological dimension *(long pause)*, a spacious present, in which everything that was or is or will be (in your terms) is kept in immediate attention, poised in a divine context that is characterized *(long pause, eyes closed)* by such a brilliant concentration that the grandest and the lowliest, the largest and the smallest, are equally held in a multiloving constant focus.

Your conceptions of beginnings and endings make an explanation of such a situation most difficult, for in your terms the beginning of the [universe] is meaningless—that is, <u>in those terms</u> (underlined) there was no beginning *(intently)*.

The [universe] is, as I explained, always coming into existence, and each present moment bring its own built-in past along with it. You agree on accepting as fact only a small portion of the large available data that compose any moment individually or globally. You accept only those data that fit in with your ideas of motion in time. As a result, for example, your archeological evidence usually presents a picture quite in keeping with your ideas of history, geological eras, and so forth.

(9:34.) The conscious mind sees with a spectacular but limited scope. It lacks all peripheral vision. I use the term "conscious mind" as you define it, for you allow it to accept as evidence only those physical data available for the five senses—while the five

senses, of course, represent only a relatively flat[2] view of reality, that deals with the most apparent surface.

The physical senses are the <u>extensions</u> of inner senses[3] that are, in one way or another, a part of each physical species regardless of its degree. The inner senses provide all species with an inner method of communication. The c-e-l-l-s *(spelled out)*, then, possess inner senses.

Atoms perceive their own positions, their velocities, motions, the nature of their surroundings, the material that they compose. [Your] world did not just come together, mindless atoms forming here and there, elements coalescing from brainless gases—nor was the world, again, created by some distant objectified God who created it part by part as in some cosmic assembly line. With defects built in, mind you *(with some humor)*, and better models coming every geological season.

The universe formed out of what God is.

The universe is the natural extension of divine creativity and intent, lovingly formed <u>from the inside out</u> (underlined)—so there was consciousness before there was matter, and not the other way around.

In certain basic and vital ways, your own consciousness is a portion of that divine gestalt. In the terms of your earthly experience, it is a metaphysical, a scientific, and a creative error to separate matter from consciousness, for consciousness materializes itself as matter in physical life.

(Long pause.) Your consciousness will survive your body's death, but it will also take on another kind of form—a form that is itself composed of "units of consciousness." You have a propensity for wanting to think in terms of hierarchies of consciousness, with humanity at the top of the list, in global terms. The Bible, for example, says that man is put in dominion over the animals, and it seems as if upgrading the consciousnesses of animals must somehow degrade your own. The divine gestalt, however, is expressed in such a way that its <u>quality</u> *(pause)* is undiluted. It cannot be watered down, so that in basic terms one portion of existence is somehow up or down the scale from another. It is all Grade A *(with amusement)*.

You limit the capacity of your conscious mind by refusing to allow it to use a larger scope of attention, so that you have remained closed and ignorant about the different, varied, but rich experiences of other species: They do appear beneath you. You have allowed a certain stubborn literal-mindedness to provide you with definitions that served to categorize rather than illuminate other realities beside your own.

(*Long pause at 9:55.*) In the beginning, then, there was a subjective world that became objective. Matter was not yet permanent, in your terms, for consciousness was not yet as stable there. In the beginning, then, there was a dream world, in which consciousness formed a dream of physical reality, and gradually became awake within that world.

Mountains rose and tumbled. Oceans filled. Tidal waves thundered. Islands appeared. The seasons themselves were not stable. In your terms the magnetic fields themselves fluctuated—but all of the species were there at the beginning, though in the same fashion, for as the dream world broke through into physical reality there was all of the tumultuous excitement and confusion with which a mass creative event is achieved. There was much greater plasticity, motion, variety, give-and-take, as consciousness experimented with its own forms. The species and environment together formed themselves in concert, in glorious combination, so that each fulfilled the requirements of its own existence while adding to the fulfillment of all other portions of physical reality (*all very intently, and with many gestures*).

That kind of an event simply cannot fit into your concepts of "the beginning of the world," with consciousness arising out of matter almost as a second thought, or with an exteriorized God initiating a divine but mechanistic natural world.

(*Pause.*) Nor can this concept fit into your versions of good and evil, as I will explain later in this book. God, or All That Is, is in the deepest sense completed, and yet uncompleted. Again, I am aware of the contradiction that seems to be presented to your minds. In a sense, however (underlined), a creative product, say, helps complete an artist, while of course the artist can never be completed. All That is, or God, in a certain fashion, now (underlined)—and this is qualified—learns as you learn, and makes adjustments according to your knowledge. We must be very careful here, for delusions of divinity come sometimes too easily, but in a basic sense you all carry within yourselves the undeniable mark of All That Is—and an inbuilt capacity—capacity—to glimpse in your own terms undeniable evidence of your own greater existence. You are as close to the beginning of [your] world as Adam and Eve were, or as the Romans, or as the Egyptians or Sumerians. The beginning of the world is just a step outside the moment.

I have a purpose in this book—for this is dictation—and that purpose is to change your ideas of yourselves, by showing you a truer picture of your history both in terms of your immortal consciousness and your physical heritage.

End of dictation.

(10:13. After giving some material for Jane, Seth ended the session at 10:32 P.M. "I had no idea he was going to do it that way," Jane said. "I'm so glad to be back on the book.")

NOTES: SESSION 886

1. Since according to Seth something like a basic religious awareness has always been with mankind, Seth here indicates a few historical and mythological signposts of that intuitive understanding.

A. God the Father. There's no way to assign any reasonably accurate date to when God the Father created all things, as described in Genesis, the first book of the Bible. (The Biblical account of Creation makes evolution an impossibility.) Nor can the date of Creation be arrived at by counting the Bible's lists of generations, as given in the Old Testament, since these may well be incomplete.

B. Mohammed (A.D. 570?–632), the Prophet of Islam, stressed the uniqueness of the god Allah, whose name was already well known in pre-Islamic Arabia.

C. Zoroaster (628?–551? B.C.) was a Persian religious teacher and prophet.

D. Zeus was the supreme god of the ancient Greeks, who worshipped him in connection with almost every facet of daily life. He was the son of Cronus and Rhea, and the husband of his sister Hera. The Romans identified Zeus with their own supreme god, Jupiter, or Jove.

E. Buddha. This is the title given to Siddhartha Gautama, the founder of Buddhism. He was a religious teacher and philosopher who lived in India, probably from 563 to 483 B.C.

2. I see correlations between the "flat view of reality" given to us by our physical senses, as Seth maintains, and the "flat" view of the universe that cosmologists perceive when they look way out into space. In his general theory of relativity, Einstein postulated that space can curve, and this has been shown to happen near our sun. Yet when scientists examine our universe of galaxies and clusters of galaxies, they see space as essentially flat, instead of curving in upon itself as it should over those enormous distances. Nor can the big-bang theory of the origin of the universe account for the homogeneity of a flat universe. The inflationary model *can* explain both the appearance of flatness and homogeneity—but, like all theories, it poses other problems that have yet to be resolved.

3. Jane gave Seth's partial list of the inner senses in Chapter Nineteen of *The Seth Material*, which was published back in 1970.

SESSION 887, DECEMBER 5, 1979
9:17 P.M. WEDNESDAY

(This noon Jane and I signed our wills, with our attorney and his wife serving as witnesses. Jane had been somewhat depressed this morning, and her writing hadn't gone well. The obvious implications posed by the wills did nothing to cheer her up.[1] Still, trusting her impulses, she slept for a couple of hours this afternoon—then, perversely, wasn't happy with herself for doing so when she woke up. She was quieter than usual through supper, although she said she wanted to hold the session.

Her delivery as Seth was for the most part comparatively subdued.)

(Whispering:) Good evening.

("Good evening, Seth.")

Now: Dictation. *(With many pauses:)* When I speak of the dream world, I am not referring to some imaginary realm, but to the kind of world of ideas, of thoughts, of mental actions, out of which all form as you think of it emerges. In actuality this is an inner universe rather than an inner world. Your physical reality is but one materialization of that inner organization. All possible civilizations exist first in that realm of inner mind.

(Long pause.) In the beginning, then, the species did not have

the kinds of forms they do now. They had pseudoforms—
dream bodies, if you prefer—and they could not physically
reproduce themselves. Their experience of time was entirely
different, and in the beginning the entire earth operated in a
kind of dream time. In your terms, this meant that time could
be quickened, or lengthened. It was a kind of psychological
time.

Again, forms appeared and disappeared. *(Pause.)* In your
terms of time, however, the dream bodies took on physical
forms. Physical reproduction was impossible. That did not happen to all of the species at once, however. For a while, then, the
earth had a mixed population of species who had completely
taken on physical forms, and species who had not. The forms,
however, whether physical or not, were complete in themselves.
Birds were birds, and fish fish.

(9:30.) In the beginning there were also species of various
other kinds: combinations of man-animal and animal-man, and
many other "crossbreed" species, some of fairly long duration in
your terms. This applies to all areas. There were dream trees,
with dream foliage, that gradually became aware within that
dream *(with gentle emphasis)*, turning physical, focusing more and
more in physical reality, until their dream seeds finally brought
forth physical trees.

There may be other terms I could use, in some ways more
advantageous than the term, "the dream world." I am emphasizing this dream connection, however, because the dream state is
one familiar to each reader, and it represents your closest touch-
stone to the kind of subjective reality from which your physical
world emerges. The dream state appears chaotic, shadowy, sus-
picious, or even meaningless, precisely because in life you are so
brilliantly focused in daily reality that dreams appear to be sta-
ticky objective background noise, left over from when you sleep.
But that is how physical experience would seem to someone not
focused in it, or inexperienced with its organization.

(Pause.) Again, the world came into being in the same way
that any idea does. The physical world expands in the same way
that any idea does. I am speaking for your edification of the
world you recognize, of the earth you know, but there are probable earths, of course, as real as your own. They coexist with
your own, and they are all in one way or another connected.

Each one carries hints and clues about the others. In the terms used by science, there was no evolution in linear terms, but vast *(long pause)* explosions of consciousness, expansions of capacities, unfoldings on the parts of all species, and these still continue. They are the inner manipulations with which consciousness presents itself.

Later in the book I will discuss some of these, but they represent intuitive leaps of new understandings. The pattern of animal behavior, for example, is not at all as set and finished as you suppose. Your physical experience is a combination of dream events interlaced with what you call objective acts.

Were it not for your myths, you would have discovered no "facts."

Give us a moment. . . . End of dictation.

(9:48. Now Seth came through with a rather long dissertation concerning the psychological manipulations Jane and I make between Frameworks 1 and 2, and how we can help each other during those transitions. End at 10:13 P.M.)

NOTE: SESSION 887

1. In this note I describe events that are of great importance to Jane and me.

Even though making our wills led us to think of our deaths, in ordinary terms, still that making implies both order and things accomplished during our lifetimes. We have achieved a situation beneficial to all—for Jane's will and my own each declares that upon the death of the survivor of the two of us, our estate is to be donated to the Manuscripts and Archives division of Yale University Library, in New Haven, Connecticut. Our physical effects, even including the hill house and the car, are few. But our creative work is everything, and so it, and whatever pertains to it, go to a place where all will be preserved and protected, yet made available for study by researchers and lay people alike as it is transmitted there.

The collection will include our family trees; my father's journals and photographs; Jane's and my own grade-school, high-school, college, and family data; our youthful creative efforts in writing and painting; the comic books and other commercial artwork I produced; our early published and unpublished short stories; my original notes for the sessions; session transcripts, whether published or unpublished, "regular," private, or from ESP class; tapes, including those made in class of Jane speaking for Seth and/or singing in Sumari; our notes, dream records, journals, and manuscripts; our sketches and paintings; Jane's extensive poetry; our business correspondence; books, contracts, and files; newsletters about the Seth material, published in the United States and abroad (independently of Jane and me); the greater number of letters from readers—in short, a mass of material showing how our separate beginnings flowed together and resulted in the production of a joint lifework.

At first we thought of keeping the collection closed until after our deaths, as donors usually request to be done, but we've decided to make everything accessible as soon as we can, both for scholarship and for study by the public. To make this possible, we'll be transferring copies of many of our papers and tapes to the library while keeping the originals with us to work with during our lifetimes. This decision is especially apropos where we have but one copy of the material in question: We like knowing that "security copies" will be on file elsewhere—as with Jane's journals, for example, and many of my own notes.

To make the copies I plan to install equipment here in the house, so that I can work at the job whenever I have a minute. The task will take lots of time—perhaps several years—and I may have to hire help; it will cost us something to copy the many thousands of papers for the library. Others arc to duplicate tapes and photographs for us.

Jane's editor, Tam Mossman, who graduated from Yale, helped us contact officials at Sterling Memorial a year ago (in December 1978). Jane and I completed arrangements after that, when those at the library explained how our collection would complement others already there. An archivist from Manuscripts and Archives has visited us to get a rough idea of the amount of material we have to offer. We don't know when our work will actually be ready for study: First we must get it to the library, and then the staff must see to its processing—which will be quite a project in itself. Jane and I are most pleased that the Seth material and everything connected with it are to be preserved.

SESSION 888, DECEMBER 10, 1979
9:04 P.M. MONDAY

(Last Saturday evening we were visited by Dr. LeRoy Guy [I'll call him], a professor of psychology at a well-known nearby university. He'd written Jane on November 16. When Jane called Dr. Guy in return, he told her that he'd contacted her at the behest of a Dr. Camper [another pseud-onym].[1] Dr. Camper, a professor of sociology at a midwestern university, had asked Dr. Guy to ask Jane to be tested for her psychic ability. [The two scientists haven't met personally, by the way.]

The evening had been very pleasant. Dr. Guy knows a number of people who are prominent in parapsychology. Both Dr. Guy and Dr. Camper have a strong interest in magic. Seth came through several times, delivering beautifully organized little dissertations to Dr. Guy on how he might relax enough to allow the psychic signs that he's so interested in to come through. Strangely enough, Dr. Guy didn't bring a tape recorder with him. We didn't use one either, and so for the first time in a long while Seth's material disappeared as rapidly as it was given—an odd experience for us. Seth also discussed with Dr. Guy the practice of, and the motivations behind, the art of magic. And in return for Seth speaking, Dr. Guy staged his own little magic show for Jane and me—to our amazement and intense interest—as the three of us sat around the living-room table.

As Jane commented afterward, LeRoy Guy said not a single word to us about his reaction to Seth, although I'd watched him pay the same rapt attention to that personality as had many others. "I suppose he'll write to Camper now," Jane said. We hadn't asked Dr. Guy what he intended to do. For that matter, we hadn't even asked him exactly what Dr. Camper wanted him to find out about Jane and Seth—or even me. Dr. Guy left us a book written by a scientist about a famous medium, and I'll be mailing it back to him as soon as we've read it.)

(With a smile:) Good evening.

("Good evening, Seth.")

Dictation: You can only locate or pinpoint an event that falls one way or another into the range of your perception.

You cannot really locate or pinpoint microscopic or macroscopic events with any precision. You cannot pinpoint "invisible" events, for even as your sophisticated instruments perceive them, they have not met them in the same time scheme. I want to deal briefly with such ideas, so that later we can discuss the location of the universe.

Any event that you perceive is only a portion of the true dimensionality of that event. The observer and the object perceived are a part of the same event, each <u>changing</u> the other. This interrelationship always exists in any system of reality and at any level of activity. In certain terms, for example, even an electron "knows" it is being observed through your instrument. The electrons within the instrument itself have a relationship with the electron that scientists may be trying to "isolate" for examination.

Quite apart from that, however, there is what we will call for now the collective unconscious of all of the electrons that compose the entire seemingly separate event of the scientists observing the electron. In your range of activity you can adequately identify events, project them in time and space, only by isolating certain portions of much larger and much smaller events, and recognizing a highly specific order of events as real.

(Pause, one of many.) Light can be defined as a wave or as a particle,[2] and the same is true in many other instances. Consciousness, for example, can be defined as a wave or as a particle, for it can <u>operate</u> as either, and <u>appear</u> as either, even though its true definition would have to include the creative capacity to shape itself into such forms.

You cannot pinpoint the beginning of the universe—for *(suddenly louder)* that beginning is simultaneously too vast and too small to be contained in any of your specifications. While everything seems neat and tidy within those specifications, and whole, you operate with brilliant nonchalance in the theater of time and space. Time and space are each the result of psychological properties. *(Pause.)* When you ask how old is the universe, or how old is the world, then you are taking it for granted that time and space are somehow or other almost absolute qualities. You are asking for answers that can only be found by going outside of the context of usual experience—for within that experience you are always led back to beginnings and endings, consecutive moments, and a world that seems to have within it no evidences of any other source.

(Pause at 9:23.) The physical world as you know it is unique, vital to the importance of the universe itself. It is an integral part

of that universe, and yet it is also quite its own reality. That reality is dependent upon the perceptions of each kind of life that composes it. It is a creation of consciousness, rising into one unique kind of expression from that divine gestalt of being— and that divine gestalt of being is of such unimaginable dimensions that its entire reality cannot appear within any one of its own realities, its own worlds.

Space, again, is a psychological property. So is time. The universe did not, then, begin at some specified point in time, or at any particular location in space—for *(louder)* it is true to say that all of space and all of time appeared simultaneously, and appear simultaneously.

You cannot pinpoint the location of consciousness.

(Long pause.) When you are dreaming you cannot pinpoint your dream location in the same way that you can determine, say, the chair or the bureau that may sit on the floor by the bed in which you dream. That inner location is real, however, and meaningful activity can take place within it. Physical space exists in the same manner, except that it is a mass psychologically shared property—but at one "time" in the beginning this was not so.

In the beginning, physical space had the qualities that dream space has to you now. It seemed to have a more private nature, and only gradually, in those terms, did it become publicly shared.

(Pause.) What was such a world like, and how can you possibly relate it to the world that you know?

End of chapter.

CHAPTER 3

SLEEPWALKERS.
THE WORLD IN EARLY TRANCE.
THE AWAKENING OF THE SPECIES

(9:36.) Chapter Three.

("Three?")

Three: "Sleepwalkers. The World in Early Trance. The Awakening of the Species." Those are the headings.

(Pause.) Give us a moment. . . . You have taught yourselves to respond to certain neural patterns, and to ignore alternate ones that now simply operate as background activity. That background activity, however, supports a million forces: the neural stimuli that you accept as biologically real. Those other background stimuli are now quite difficult for you to identify, but they are always there in the [hinterland] of your waking consciousness, like dream chatter way beneath your usual associations.

Neurologically, you tune into only a portion of your body's reality and are ignorant of the great, tiny but tumultuous communications that are ever flying back and forth in the microscopic but vital cellular world.

166

Electrons in your terms are precognitive, and so is your cellular consciousness. Your body's relative permanence in time is dependent upon the electron's magnificent behavior as it deals with probabilities. *(Pause.)* The cell's stability, and its reliability in the bodily environment, is dependent upon its innate properties of instant communication and instant decision, for each cell is in communication with all others and is united with all others through fields of consciousness,[3] in which each entity of whatever degree plays a part.

At one level your cells obey the rules of time, but on other levels they defy it. All of these communications are a part of the human parcel of reality, and they all exist beneath what you think of as normal consciousness. Events are not built up initially from physical particles. They are the result of psychological activity.

(9:51.) Give us a moment. . . . "In the beginning" you were only aware of that psychological activity. It had not "as yet" thickened itself into form. The form was there, but it was not manifest *(intently)*. I do not particularly like the analogy, but it is useful: Instead of small particles *(long pause)*, you had small units of consciousness gradually building themselves into large ones —but a smaller unit of consciousness, you see, is not "less than" a larger unit, for each unit of consciousness contains within itself the innate (underlined) heritage of All That Is.

You think of the conscious mind, as you know it, as the only kind of consciousness with a deliberate intent, awareness of itself as itself, and with a capacity for logic and the appreciation of symbolism. That only seems true because of your particular range of activity, and because you can only pinpoint events within a particular psychological spectrum.

End of dictation. For our friend:

(10:01. Now Seth gave a few paragraphs for Jane, then said good night at 10:10 p.m. Even with the many pauses she'd used this evening —most of which I didn't indicate—Jane's delivery had often been quite intent and meaningful. In their own way the pauses served as additional punctuation and emphasis for some of Seth's information.)

NOTES: SESSION 888

1. Last summer, through the mail, Jane and I had our own encounters with Dr. Camper. Those events are too complicated to go into here, but Jane is devoting considerable space to them in her own *God of Jane*.

2. Seth should have said that light can be defined as *being made up of* waves or particles, but he didn't put it quite that way, and I let stand what he did say. He gave me a knowing, half-smiling look while delivering this paragraph, for it was obvious that his material was related to a note I'd shown Jane today—one I'm finishing for *Mass Events*. In it, I'm trying to deal very simply with both the uncertainty principle and the complementarity of light, among other tenets of physics. (It will be Note 2 for Session 823.)

In fact, I believe that a good amount of Seth's material this evening was inspired by my struggles with that note. Such interchanges among Jane, Seth, and me—and among books—often take place.

3. Seth's "fields of consciousness" sounds like an elaboration of field theory in physics. In physics, however, the field is called "energy and momentum," not consciousness.

SESSION 889, DECEMBER 17, 1979
8:45 P.M. MONDAY

(On December 13 Jane came up with her best title yet for the book of poetry she's putting together: If We Live Again: Love's Lives and Probable Selves. *She's writing some excellent new poems for the book, besides working on* God of Jane. *My wife is also doing some poetry as a Christmas present for me—though she's very secretive about this activity; I'm not supposed to know what she's up to.*

Last night was our coldest of the winter, I believe—about 9°—and this evening wasn't much warmer as we sat for the session. However, the season has been exceptionally mild in our area. The ground has been bare of snow most of the time—so far!

Jane called me at 8:30 to say that she was ready for the session. "I'd better get started," she said. "Otherwise I might put it off, I'm getting so relaxed. I've been picking up some great stuff from Seth on the book, too. . . ." And that's why we missed the regularly scheduled session for last Wednesday evening: She became so relaxed she didn't care to focus on going into trance.)

Dictation.

Now: I call the building blocks of matter CU's—units of consciousness. They form physical matter as it exists in your understanding and experience. Units of consciousness also form other kinds of matter that you do not perceive.[1]

CU's can also operate as "particles" or as "waves." Whichever way they operate, they are aware of their own existences. When CU's operate as particles, in your terms, they build up a continuity in time. They take on the characteristics of particularity. They identify themselves by the establishment of specific boundaries.

(Long pause.) They take certain forms, then, when they operate as particles, and experience their reality from "the center of" those forms. They concentrate upon, or focus upon, their unique specificiations. They become in your terms (underlined) individual.

When CU's operate as waves, however, they do not set up any boundaries about their own self-awareness—and when operating as waves CU's can indeed be in more than one place at one time.

I understand that this is somewhat difficult material to comprehend. However *(pause)*, in its purest form a unit of consciousness can be in all places at the same time *(forcefully)*. It becomes beside the point, then, to say that when it operates as a wave a unit of consciousness is precognitive, or clairvoyant, since it has the capacity to be in all places and all times simultaneously.

Those units of consciousness are the building blocks for the physical material of your body, for the trees and rocks, the oceans, the continents, and the very manifestation of space itself as you understand it.

(Seth repeated the last phrase very loudly when I failed to understand him the first time.)

These CU's can operate as separate entities, as identities, or they can flow together in a vast, harmonious wave of activity, as a force. Period. Actually, units of consciousness operate in both ways all of the time. No identity, once "formed," is ever annihilated, for its existence is indelibly a part of "the entire wave of consciousness to which it belongs."

(Pause at 9:04, one of many.) Each "particleized" unit, however, rides the continual thrust set up by fields of consciousness, in which wave and particle both belong. Each particleized unit of consciousness contains within it inherently the knowledge of all other such particles—for at other levels, again, the units are operating as waves. Basically the units move faster than light,[2] slowing down, in your terms, to form matter. *(Pause.)* These units can be considered, again, as entities or as forces, and they can operate as either. Metaphysically, they can be thought of as the point at which All That Is acts to form [your] world—the immediate contact of a never-ending creative inspiration, coming into mental focus, the metamorphosis of certainly divine origin that brings the physical world into existence from the greater reality of divine fact. Scientifically, again, the units can be thought of as building blocks of matter. Ethically, the CU's represent the spectacular foundations of the world in value fulfillment, for each unit of consciousness is related to each other, a part of the other, each participating in the entire gestalt of mortal experience. And we will see how this applies to your attitudes toward specieshood, and man's relationship with other conscious entities and the planet he shares with them.

(Pause at 9:17. Once again, as it often has since she began dictating this book, Jane's delivery for Seth had taken on a charged and inspired cast. The words in paragraphs like the one above rolled out of her in a strong and almost grand manner. It was easy to tell that she enjoyed working on Dreams—*that she gave permission to be carried away if need be. Perhaps her method of presentation was in keeping with Seth's own pronouncement at the beginning of his Preface, almost three months ago: "This book will be my most ambitious project thus far. Period.")*

In the beginning CU's, then, units of consciousness, existing within a divine psychological gestalt, endowed with the unimaginable creativity of that sublime identity, began themselves to create, to explore, and to fulfill those innate values by which they were characterized. Operating both as waves and particles, directed in part by their own creative restlessness, and directed in part by the unquenchable creativity of All That Is, they embarked upon the project that brought time and space and your entire [universe] into being. They were the first entities, then.

I want you to try and imagine a situation in which *(long pause)* there exists a psychological force that includes within its capabilities the ability to act simultaneously on the most microscopic and the most macroscopic levels; that can form within itself *(long pause, eyes closed)* a million separate inviolate unique identities, and that can still operate as a part of those identities, and as a larger unit that is their source—in which case it is a wave from which the particles emerge. That description fits our units of consciousness.

(9:26.) They built your world from the inside out. As physical creatures, they focused upon what you think of as physical identities: separate, individual differences, endowing each physical consciousness with its own original variations and creative potentials, its own opportunity for completely original experience, and a viewpoint or platform from which to participate in reality —one that at that level could not be experienced in the same way by any other individual *(all very intently)*. This is [the] privileged, always new, private and immediate, direct experience of any individual of any species, or of any degree, as it encounters the objective universe.

At other levels, while each individuality is maintained, it rides the wavelike formations of consciousness. It is everywhere at once, and the units of consciousness that make up your cells know the positions of all other such units, both in time and in space.

In the beginning, then, these units operated both as identities or particles, and as waves. The main concentration was not yet physical in your terms. What you now think of as the dream state was the waking one, for it was still the recognized form of purposeful activity, creativity, and power. The dream state continues to be a connective between the two realities, and as a species you literally learned to walk by first being sleepwalkers. You walked in your sleep. You dreamed your languages. You spoke in your dreams and later wrote down the alphabets—and your knowledge and your intellect have always been fired, sharpened, propelled by the great inner reality from which your minds emerged.

Physical matter by itself could never produce consciousness.

One mind alone could not come into being from chance alone; one thought could not leap from an infinite number of nerve ends, if matter itself was not initially alive with consciousness, packed with the intent to be. A man who believes life has little meaning quickly leaves life—and a meaningless existence could never produce life *(intently)*. Nor was the universe created for one species alone, by a God who is simply a supervision of the same species—as willful and destructive as man at his worst.

(9:45.) Instead, you have an inner dimension of activity, a vast field of multidimensional creativity, a Creator that becomes a portion of each of its creations, and yet a Creator that is greater than the sum of its parts: a Creator that can know itself as a mouse in a field, or as the field, or as the continent upon which the field rests, or as the planet that holds the continent, or as the universe that holds the world—a force that is whole yet divisible, that is one and the inconceivably many, a force that is eternal and mortal at once, a force that plunges headlong into its own creativity, forming the seasons and experiencing them as well, glorifying in individuation, and yet always aware of the great unity that is within and behind and through all experiences of individuality: a force from [which] each moment pasts and futures flow out in every conceivable direction.

(Jane delivered that whole paragraph with great flowing intensity, and I've punctuated it to the best of my ability just as it came through her. I don't think I've ever heard her speak more eloquently for Seth, and with more certainty. This book has turned her on.)

(Long pause.) In your terms of time, however, we will speak of a beginning, and in that beginning it was early man's dreams that allowed him to cope with physical reality. The dream world was his original learning ground. In times of drought he would dream of the location of water. In times of famine he would dream of the location of food. That is, his dreaming allowed him to clairvoyantly view the body of land. He would not waste time in the trial-and-error procedures that you now take for granted. In dreams his consciousness operated as a wave.

In those early times all species shared their dreams in a way that is now quite unconscious for your kind, so that in dreams man inquired of the animals also—long before he learned to follow the animal tracks, for example. Where is there food or water? What is the lay of the land? Man explored the planet because his dreams told him that the land was there.

People were not nearly as isolated as it now appears, for in their dreams early men communicated their various locations, the symbols of their cultures and understanding, the nature of their arts. All of the inventions that you often think now happened quite by chance—the discovery of anything from the first tool to the importance of fire, or the coming of the Iron Age or whatever—all of that inventiveness was the result of the inspiration and communication of the dream world. Man dreamed his world and then created it, and the units of consciousness first dreamed man and all of the other species that you know.

(Pause at 10:02.) There is a point here that I want to emphasize before we go too far, and it is this: The dream world is not an aimless, nonlogical, unintellectual field of activity. It is only that your own perspective closes out much of its vast reality, for the dreaming intellect can put your computers to shame. I am not, therefore, putting the intellectual capacities in the background —but I am saying that they emerge as you know them because of the dreaming self's uninterrupted use of the full power of the united intellect and intuitions.

The intellectual abilities as you know them *(pause)* cannot compare to those greater capacities that are a part of your own inner reality.

End of dictation.

("Okay.")

(10:08. Now Seth came through with a paragraph—here deleted—for Jane and me. Then:)

Do you have questions?

("What do you think of my remarks about watching the news on television every day?"[3])

It makes little difference whether you watch the news or not —but it makes all the difference in the world what you <u>think</u> of world events.

The perspective from which you watch world events is vital, and it is true that communication now brings to the conscious mind a far greater barrage than before. But it is also a barrage that makes man see his own activities, and even with the growth of the new nationalism in the Third World, those nations begin from a new perspective, in which the eyes of the world are indeed upon them.

Your country faces the results of its own policies—its greed as well as its good intent, but it is out in the open in a new way. The world will be seen as one, but there may be changes in the overall tax assessments along the way, as those who have not paid much, pay more.

The results of fanaticism are also out in the open. Never before, in your terms, has the private person been able to see a picture of the mass world in such a way, or been forced to identify with the policies of his or her government. That in itself is a creative achievement, and means that man is not closing his eyes to the inequities of his world.

End of session. A fond good evening.

("The same to you, Seth. Thank you very much.")

(10:18 P.M. "Talk about energy!" Jane exclaimed as soon as she was out of her excellent trance state. "I just had the feeling we were getting some great stuff—I just had the feeling. I don't remember what he said that well, but I just felt that terrific conviction. You know what I mean?"

I certainly did. I congratulated her upon the session.)

NOTES: SESSION 889

1. Later, I asked Seth to comment upon his most intriguing statement. His answer was brief, for insertion here, and as much as I wanted to I didn't ask him to enlarge upon it. However, I'm sure that the subject of "other kinds of matter" is one with almost endless ramifications. Seth:

"Units of consciousness do help form different kinds of physical realities—as indeed Ruburt has himself hinted in some of his poetry. There are many dimensions that are as physical, so to speak, as your own world, but if you are not focused in them you would not at all be aware of their existence, but perceive only empty space.

"Nothing in the universe is ever lost, or mislaid, or wasted, so the energy of your own thoughts, while they are still your own thoughts, helps to form the natural attributes of physical realities that you do not perceive. So is your own world formed by units of consciousness. Its natural elements are the glistening remnants of other units of consciousness that you do not see."

2. According to Albert Einstein, no material particle in our universe can be accelerated from rest to quite the speed of light,

which is about 186,000 miles per second in a vacuum. However, as I wrote in Note 1 for Session 709, in Volume 2 of *"Unknown" Reality*, "supposed faster-than-light particles are thought to be possible within the context of Einstein's special theory of relativity."

Seth gave excellent material on the units of consciousness in both volumes of *"Unknown" Reality*. In Volume 1, for example, see Session 682 for February 13, 1974.

3. Earlier this evening I'd wondered to Jane why we keep dosing ourselves with the endless barrage of bad news the TV networks offer us as we eat supper each day. The hostage crisis in Iran is a case in point. I remarked that most of our world's problems seem to result from Framework-1 thinking, that our species is so steeped in such conscious-mind behavior—locally, nationally, and worldwide—that there seems little chance of our ever breaking out of that iron pattern. I further told Jane that our history reflects our stubborn refusal to modify to any significant degree our great reliance upon Framework-1 manipulations, even though I grant that there are many complicated reasons for such long-term mass behavior.

I also felt that my question grew out of Jane's and my own recent efforts to improve our habitual thinking patterns, to draw from Framework 2 more of those elements that will help us create the daily results we really want. As an aid, I use a set of resolutions Seth gave us last January 1—although, oddly, Jane doesn't pay that much attention to them. However, both of us have noticed definite improvements lately in attitude and peace of mind.

SESSION 890, DECEMBER 19, 1979
9:17 P.M. WEDNESDAY

(Jane was in a "bitchy" mood as session time approached. Her manner was both funny and understandably sharp when I asked her if she had any questions for Seth tonight. She'd wanted to start the session at 8 o'clock, but it hadn't worked out. "But now I'm beginning to feel him around," she said at 9:10. Her delivery was quite slow as the session opened.)

Now: Good evening.

("Good evening, Seth.")

Dictation: This inner universe *(pause)* is a gestalt formed by fields of awareized energy that contains what we will call "information" for now—but we will have some comments later, for this is not the kind of information you are used to.

Each unit of consciousness inherently possesses within itself all of the information available to the whole, and its specific nature when it operates as a particle rests upon that great "body" of inner knowledge. Any one such particle can be where it "is," be what it is, and be when it is only because the positions, relative positions, and situations of all other such particles are known.

(Long pause at 9:23.) In the deepest terms, again, your physical world is beginning at each point at which these units of consciousness assert themselves to form physical reality. Otherwise, life would not be "handed down" through the generations. Each unit of consciousness *(or CU)* intensifies, magnifies its own intent to be—and, you might say, works up from within itself an explosive spark of primal desire that "explodes" into a process that causes physical materialization. It turns into what I have called [an] EE unit,[1] in which case it is embarked upon its own kind of physical experience.

These EE units also operate as fields, as waves, or as particles, as the units of consciousness do—but in your terms they are closer to physical orientation. Their die is cast, so to speak: They have already begun the special kind of screening process necessary that will bring about physical form. They begin to deal with the kinds of information that will help form your world. There are literally numberless steps taken before EE units combine in their own fashion to form the most microscopic physical particles, and even here the greatest, gentlest sorting-out process takes place as these units disentangle themselves at certain operational levels (underlined) from their own greater fields of "information," to specialize in the various elements that will allow for the production of atoms and molecules impeccably suited to your kind of world.

(By now Jane was moving into a more subdued form of that rolling, resonant delivery for Seth that she'd used in the last session.)

First, again, you have various stages of, say, pseudomatter, of dream images, that only gradually—in those terms—coalesce and become physically viable, for there are endless varieties of "matter" between the matter that you recognize and the anti-matter of physicists' theories.

Form exists at many other levels than those you recognize, in other words. Your dream forms are quite as real as your physical ones. They simply fit into their own environment at another level of activity, and they are quite reminiscent of the kinds of forms that you had in the beginning of [your] world.

While you and all of the other species were what I have called sleepwalkers, your bodies by then were physically capable. In a manner of speaking, you did not know how to use them properly as yet. Now, from a waking state, you do not understand how your dream bodies can seem to fly through the air, defy space and even time, converse with strangers and so forth. In the same way, however, once, you had to learn to deal with gravity, to deal with space and time, to manipulate in a world of objects, to simply breathe, to digest your food, and to perform all of the biological manipulations that now you take for granted *(all most emphatically)*.

You could not afford to identify too completely with such bodies until you learned how to survive within them, so in the dream state *(pause)* the true processes of life began as these new bodies and earth-tuned consciousnesses saw themselves mentally exercising all portions of the body. Behind all that was the brilliant comprehension and cooperation of all of the units of consciousness that go to compose the body, each adding its own information and specific knowledge to the overall bodily organizations, and each involved in the most intricate fields of relationships, for the miracle of the body's efficiency is the result of relationships that exist among all of its parts, connecting it to other levels of existence that do not physically appear.

(9:48.) Units of consciousness *(CU's)*, transforming themselves into EE units, formed the environment and all of its inhabitants in the same process, in what you might call a circular manner rather than a serial one. And in those terms, of course, there are only various physical manifestations of consciousness, not a planet and its inhabitants, but an entire gestalt of awareized consciousness. In those terms (underlined), each portion of

physically oriented consciousness sees reality and experience from its own privileged viewpoint, about which it seems all else revolves, even though this may involve a larger generalized field than your own, or a smaller one.

So to rocks, say, you can be considered a portion of their environment, while you may consider them merely a portion of your environment. You simply do not tune into the range of rock consciousness. Actually *(pause)*, many other kinds of consciousness, while focused in their own specific ways, are more aware than man is of earth's unified nature—but man, in following his own ways, also adds to the value fulfillment of all other consciousnesses in ways that are quite outside of usual systems of knowledge.

If you remember that beneath all, each unit of consciousness is aware of the position of each other unit, and that these units form all physical matter, then perhaps you can intuitively follow what I mean, for whatever knowledge man attains, whatever experience any one person accumulates, whatever arts or sciences you produce, all such information is instantly perceived at other levels of activity by each of the other units of consciousness that compose physical reality—whether those units form the shape of a rock, a raindrop, an apple, a cat, a frog or a shoe. Manufactured products are also composed of atoms and molecules that ride upon units of consciousness transformed into EE units, and hence into physical elements.

What you have, really, is a manifested and an unmanifested consciousness, but only relatively speaking. You do not perceive the consciousness of objects. It is not manifest to you because your range of activities requires boundaries to frame your picture of reality.

All of your manufactured objects also originated in the realm of dreams, first obviously being conceived of mentally, and in the same way man produced his first tools. He was born with *(long pause)* all of those abilities—abilities by which he is now characterized—and with other abilities that in your terms still wait for development. Not that he has not used them so far, but that he has not focused upon them in what you consider the main lines of civilized continuity. Hints of those abilities are always present in the dream state, and in the arts, in the religions, and even in the sciences. They appear in politics and business, but as the largely unmanifest intuitive background, which is largely ignored. We will return to these later in the book.

(10:12.) Man's dreams have always provided him with a sense of impetus, purpose, meaning, and given him the raw material from which to form his civilizations. The true history of the world is the history of man's dreams, for they have been responsible in one way or another for all historic developments.

They were responsible for the birth of agriculture, as well as industry, the rise and fall of nations, the "glory" that was Rome, and Rome's destruction. *(Pause.)* Your present technological advances can almost be dated from the [invention of] the printing press, to Edison's inventions, which were flashes of intuition, dream-inspired. But if what I am telling you is true, then it is obvious that when I say that your physical world originated in the world of dreams, I must mean something far different from the usual definition of dream reality. Again, I could choose another term, but I want to emphasize each person's intimate contact with that other reality that does occur in what you think of as the state of dreaming *(all very intently).*

That analogy will help you at least intuitively understand the existence of situations such as suffering, and poverty, that otherwise seem to have no adequate explanations *(as Jane and I were discussing today)*. I hope also to account for behavior on the part of nature that certainly seems to imply the survival of the fittest in a tooth-and-claw fashion, or the punishing acts of a vengeful God on the one hand and the triumph of an evil force on the other.

For now in our tale of beginnings, however, we still have a spasmodic universe that appears and disappears—that gradually, in those terms, manifests for longer periods of time. What you really had in the beginning were images without form, slowly adopting form, blinking on and off, then stabilizing into forms that were as yet not completely physical. These then took on all of the characteristics that you now consider formed physical matter.

As all of this occurred, consciousness took on more and more specific orientations, greater organizations at your end. At the "other end," it disentangled itself from vaster fields of activity to allow for this specific behavior. All of these units of consciousness, again, operate as entities (or particles, or as waves or forces). In those terms, consciousness formed the experience of time—and not, of course, the other way around.

(Quietly at 10:29:) End of dictation. A small note:

(Seth came through with a couple of sentences for Jane. Then:)

I bid you a fond good evening. And we will have a session on anything you want, at any time.

("Thank you, Seth. Good night.")

(10:31 P.M. Seth's last remark, which I took to be rather humorous, reflected one of the reasons for Jane's upset before the session: the conflict she feels between having just book sessions versus obtaining Seth material on at least a few of the other subjects we always have in mind. Currently these include topics like Jonestown, Iran, Frameworks 1 and 2—and one I initiated earlier this year about human reproduction, called "the community of sperm." In a couple of essays I discussed, and asked questions about, the roles played by the 200 million to 500 million sperm that don't make contact with the female egg at the time of conception. I also wanted to know about the deep biological communication that must go on among all of the sperm in a man's body at any given time, and why one of the "fittest" sperm in a particular ejaculate evidently doesn't always fertilize the egg. Seth has given some answers in a couple of sessions, and we want more. Originally I'd planned to present excerpts here from our joint material—but I see now that I have no space in which to do so.

Jane's delivery had turned out to be excellent this evening, her manner steady and with fewer pauses than she'd used in Monday night's session. Although she didn't reach the peaks of soaring eloquence she'd touched upon in that last session, elements of that state were present tonight.)

NOTE: SESSION 890

1. Seth's earliest material on EE (electromagnetic energy) units came through in September and October of 1967; in the Appendix of *The Seth Material*, see the excerpts Jane presented from sessions 504 through 506. Then in Chapter 20 of *Seth Speaks*, see Session 581 for April 14, 1971.

SESSION 891, DECEMBER 26, 1979
9:07 P.M. WEDNESDAY

(No session was held last Monday evening, Christmas Eve. Instead, we had a few close friends in; all of us exchanged gifts. After the party was over Jane and I gave each other our own presents. My high point was receiving the little book of poems and sketches she'd made for me. [I hadn't created anything like that for her, though.] When Jane read her poetry to me I strongly felt once again her innocence and perception: "The universe keeps turning into us. . . ." We had a quiet but very enjoyable Christmas day.

Tonight's session may not be formal book dictation, but it contains many connections to Dreams. *"I don't care whether we have a book session or one on something else," Jane said as we sat for the session at 8:50. "I'm just waiting. I don't even feel him around. . . ." She thought this was strange, since during the last couple of days she'd picked up quite a few insights from Seth on various subjects. We'd discussed all of them, but without making any notes.*

At 9:06: "I guess I'm ready. It doesn't sound like the book, though. Sometimes I get a first line. . . .")

(Softly, eyes dark and luminous:) Good evening.

("Good evening, Seth.")

(With humor:) Tonight's subject matter: "Great Expectations" —for I am here referring to the book by *(Charles)* Dickens.

Now: The year 1980 exists in all of its <u>potential</u> versions, now in this moment. Because mass events are concerned there is not a completely different year, of course, for each individual on the face of the planet—but there are literally an endless number of mass-shared worlds of 1980 "in the wings," so to speak.

It is not quite as simple a matter as just deciding what events you want to materialize as reality, since you have, in your terms, a body of probabilities of one kind or another already established as the raw materials for the coming year. It would be quite improbable for you, Joseph *(as Seth calls me)*, to suddenly turn into a tailor, for example, for none of your choices with probabilities have led toward such an action.

In like manner, England in all probability next year will not suddenly turn into a Mohammedan nation. But within the range of workable probabilities, private and mass choices, the people of the world are choosing their probable 1980s.

(Long pause.) I am taking my time here, for there are some issues that I would like to clear up, that are difficult to explain.

Any of the probable actions that a person considers are a part of that person's conscious thought. Just underneath, however, people also consider other sets of probabilities that may or may not reach conscious level, simply because they are shunted aside, or because they seem to meet with no conscious recognition. I want you to try and imagine actual events, as you think of them, to be *(pause)* the vitalized representations of probabilities—that is, as the physical versions of mental probabilities. The probabilities with which you are not consciously concerned remain psychologically peripheral: They are there but not there, so to speak.

Your conscious mind can only accept a certain sequence of probabilities as recognized experience. As I have said, the choices among probabilities go on constantly, both on conscious and unconscious levels. Events that you do not perceive as conscious experience are *(pause)* a part of your unconscious experience, however, to some extent. This applies to the individual, and of course en masse the same applies to world events. Each action seeks all of its own possible fulfillments. All That Is seeks all possible experience, but in such a larger framework in this case that questions of, say, pain or death simply do not apply, though [certainly] they do on the physical level *(all quite forcefully)*.

(9:25.) Great expectations, basically, have nothing to do with degree, for a grass blade is filled with great expectations. Great expectations are built upon a faith in the nature of reality, a faith in nature itself, a faith in the life you are given, whatever its degree—and all children, for example, are born with those expectations. Fairy tales are indeed often—though not always—carriers of a kind of underground knowledge, as per your discussion about Cinderella *(also see the 824th session for* Mass Events*)*, and the greatest fairy tales are always those in which the greatest expectations win out: The elements of the physical world that are unfortunate can be changed in the twinkling of an eye through great expectations.

Your education tells you that all of that is nonsense, that the world is defined by its physical aspects alone. When you think of power you think of, say, nuclear energy, or solar energy—but power is the creative energy within men's minds that allows them to use such powers, such energies, such forces.

The true power is in the imagination which dares to speculate upon that which is not yet *(intently)*. The imagination, backed by great expectations, can bring about almost any reality within the range of probabilities. All of the possible versions of 1980 will happen. Except for those you settle upon, all of the others will remain psychologically peripheral, in the background of your conscious experience—but all of those possible versions will be connected in one way or another.

The important lessons have never really appeared in your societies: the most beneficial use of the directed will, with great expectations, and that coupled with the knowledge of Framework 1 and 2 activities. Very simply: You want something, you dwell upon it consciously for a while, you consciously imagine it coming to the forefront of probabilities, closer to your actuality. Then you drop it like a pebble into Framework 2, forget about it as much as possible for a fortnight, and do this in a certain rhythm.

I gave you some New Year's resolutions last year, and it seems to me *(with some irony)* that they could be resurrected.

("I read them several times a week," I told Seth. Actually, he gave us his resolutions this year—on January 1.[1])

They are as good, tell Ruburt, who does not read them now, as they were then. They help focus both mind and imagination. That focusing helps you to act, to be. Now give us a moment. . . .

(9:37. Seth came through with two short paragraphs for Jane. Then:)

Now: In our book, I will be doing my best to explain the origin of your universe, and in such a way that most of the pertinent questions are answered, but man's present concept of reality is so limited that I must often resort to analogies.

In the most basic of terms, as 1980 happens the energy that comes into your universe is as new as if (in your terms) the world were created yesterday—a point that will be rather difficult to explain. All of the probable versions of 1980 spin off their own probable pasts as well as their own probable futures, and any consciousness that exists in 1980 was (again in those terms) a part of what you think of as the beginning of the world.

(To me:) Your mother did not simply choose to believe, in her old age, in a different past than the one that was accepted by the family—she effectively changed probabilities. She was not deluded or obsessed. Her memory in that regard, now, was not defective: It was the memory of the probable woman that she became.[2]

Like the entire American hostage affair *(in Iran)*, any physical event serves as a focus that attracts all of its probable versions and outcomes. The hostage situation *(now in day 53)* is a materialized mass dream, meant to be important and vital on political and religious platforms of reality, meant to dramatize a conflict of beliefs, and to project that conflict outward into the realm of public knowledge. Everyone involved was consciously and unconsciously a willing participant at the most basic levels of human behavior, and it is of course no coincidence that 1980 is immediately foreshadowed by that event. What will the world do with it?

Your TV and news systems of communication are a part of the event itself, of course. It is in a way far better that these events occurred now, and in the way that they have, so that the problems appear clearly in the world arena. They are actually thus of a far less violent nature than they might otherwise have been.

Religious beliefs will be examined as they have not been before, and their connections and political affiliations. The Arab world still needs the West, and again, it is better that those issues come to light now, while they must to some extent consider the rest of the world.

Do not personally give any more conscious consideration, either of you, to events that you do not want to happen. *(Long pause.)* Any such concentration, to whatever degree, ties you in with those probabilities, so concentrate upon what you want, and as far as public events are concerned, take it for granted that sometimes even men are wiser than they know.

Do you have questions?

(Only a million of them, I thought. "No, I guess not," I said to Seth.)

Then I wish you a happy anniversary—

("Thank you.")

—and the most auspicious of 1980's. A fond good evening.

("Thank you, Seth. Good night.")

(9:58 P.M. Jane and I celebrate our 25th wedding anniversary tomorrow.)

NOTES: SESSION 891

1. I referred to Seth's resolutions at the end of the 889th session. I think they're very effective; I try to keep them constantly in mind:

"One: I will approve of myself, my characteristics, my abilities, my likes and dislikes, my inclinations and disinclinations, realizing that these form my unique individuality. They are given me for a reason.

"Two: I will approve of and rejoice in my accomplishments, and I will be as vigorous in listing these—as rigorous in remembering them—as I have ever been in remembering and enumerating my failures or lacks of accomplishment.

"Three: I will remember the creative framework of existence, in which I have my being. Therefore the possibilities, potentials, seeming miracles, and joyful spontaneity of Framework 2 will be in my mind, so that the doors to creative living are open.

"Four: I will realize that the future is a probability. In terms of ordinary experience, nothing exists there yet. It is virgin territory, planted by my feelings and thoughts in the present. Therefore I will plant accomplishments and successes, and I will do this by remembering that nothing can exist in the future that I do not want to be there."

2. Here Seth referred to the striking way in which my mother, Stella Butts, had recreated for the better her "memories" of her husband (my father). Robert Butts, Sr., died in February 1971, 34 months before she did. All of the members of the Butts family observed the pronounced changes in Stella's thinking about her husband, although Jane and I were the only ones who ascribed those changes to her moving into another probable reality.

SESSION 892, JANUARY 2, 1980
8:47 P.M. WEDNESDAY

(On December 27, the night of our anniversary, Jane held an unplanned session for young married friends of ours. Although she seldom does this anymore because of the work load involved, such spontaneous expressions of her creativity help my wife as well as the others involved. I taped the session on the recorder I'd given Jane for Christmas; our friends are to send us a transcript of the tape.

Seth didn't come through last Monday evening, New Year's Eve. Instead, Jane and I gave a party for a change. The next day we were ready to get back to our writing and painting, but first I cleared the house of holiday paraphernalia—including our beautiful Christmas tree. I carefully propped up the tree, a balsam fir, in the woods at the back of the hill house. I told myself that next summer the tree's skeleton would remind me of the days that had passed since 1980 began, in our terms; I knew I'd be grateful for having physically experienced every one of them. [And as an artist, I'd be as much intrigued by the tree's naked structure as I had been when it bore its dense greenery.]

Over the weekend we'd signed the contracts with our publisher, Prentice-Hall, for Mass Events *and* God of Jane, *and I mailed them this morning. We're progressing well on both projects. In their unique ways, I told Jane, my notes for* Mass Events *are the most challenging writing I've done. We're getting up at 6:00 again, so that we can get in a good morning's "work" before lunchtime.)*

(Whispering:) Good evening.

("Good evening, Seth.")

Happy New Year.

("Thank you. The same to you," I said, knowing that Seth's understanding of "time" was certainly much different than ours.)

Dictation. You were *(pause)* each present at the beginning of the world, then, though you may be present in the world now in a somewhat different fashion.

Remember that each unit of consciousness is a fragment of All That Is, a divine portion. Then perhaps what I am about to explain will make more sense.

For some time, in your terms, the sleepwalkers remained more or less at that level of activity, and for many centuries they used the surface of the earth as a kind of background for other activity. Their real life was what you would now call the dreaming one. They worked mentally while asleep, constructing in their individual minds and in their joint mental endeavors *(long pause)* all of the dazzling images that would later become a mental reservoir from which men could draw. In that multidimensional array, consciousness mentally learned to form itself into EE units, atoms and molecules, electrons and chromosomes. It mentally formed the patterns through which all physical life could flow. The world then came into physical existence. Those units of consciousness are indestructible and vitalized, regardless of the forms they take, and while men's forms were dream images, consciousness spun forms into physical material.

Consciousness possesses the most unimaginable agility without ever losing any potency. Those units of consciousness, for example, can mix and combine with others to form a million different sequences of memory and desire, of neural achievement and recognition, [of] structure and design.

You read your own consciousness now in a kind of vertical fashion, identifying only with certain portions of it, and it seems to you that any other organization of perception, any other recognition of identity, would quite necessarily negate your own or render it inoperable. In the beginning of the world there were numberless groupings, however, and affiliations of consciousness, many other organizations of identity that were recognized, as well as the kind of psychological orientation you have now— but [your] kind of orientation was not the paramount one. While, generally speaking, earth's species existed from the beginning in the forms by which you now know them, consciousness of species was quite different, and all species were much more intimately related through various kinds of identification that have since gone into the underground of awareness.

(9:05.) Initially, then, the world was a dream, and what you think of as waking consciousness was the dreaming consciousness. In that regard the earth's entire environment was built mentally, atom by conscious atom—each atom, again, being initially formed by units of consciousness. I said that these units could operate as entities, and as forces, so we are not speaking of a mental mechanics but of entities in the true meaning of the word: entities of unimaginable creative and psychic properties, purposeful fragments propelled from the infinite mind as that

mind was filled with the inspiration that gave light to the world. Those entities, in your terms so ancient, left fragments of themselves in trance (underlined), so to speak, that form the rocks and hills, the mountains, the air and the water, and all of the elements that exist on the face of the earth.

(A one-minute pause at 9:13.) Those entities are in trance, in those terms, but their potency is not diminished, and there is constant communication among them always.

(Long pause.) There is also constant communication between them and you at other levels than those you recognize, so that there is an unending interplay between each species and its environment.

(Long pause.) There is no place where consciousness stops and the environment begins, or vice versa. Each form of life is created along with each other form—environment and organism in those terms creating each other. After forms were fully physical, however, all species operated as sleepwalkers for many centuries, though on the scale that existed then the passage of time was not considered in the same fashion. During that period the work of wedding nonphysical consciousness to matter was accomplished. Effects of gravity, for example, were stabilized. The seasons took on the rhythms best suited to the creatures in various locations. The environment and the creatures accommodated each other.

Up until then, the main communications had followed the characteristic patterns of units of consciousness *(long pause)*, each unit knowing its relationship to all others upon the planet. Creatures relied upon inner senses while learning to operate the new, highly specific physical ones that pinpointed perception in time and place. This pinpointing of perception was of vital importance, for with the full arousal of consciousness in flesh, intersections with space and time [had to be] impeccable.

Dream bodies became physical, and through the use of the senses tuned to physical frequencies—frequencies of such power and allure that they would reach all creatures of every kind, from microbe to elephant, holding them together in a cohesive web of space-and-time alignment.

In the beginning, man's dreams were in certain terms of immediate physical survival. They gave man information—a kind that of necessity the new physical senses could not contain.

Those senses could only perceive the immediate environment, but man's dreams compensated for that lack, and filled out his consciousness by giving it the benefit of that larger generalized information to which it had once had an easy access. When he was asleep man could take advantage of the information banks contained in the units of consciousness that composed his very flesh.

(9:30.) Now (underlined): When he dreamed—when he dreamed (underlined)—man actually returned to a state prior to waking, from which his physical life itself had emerged—only now he was a new creature, a new kind of consciousness, and so were all of the other species. In dreams all of the species familiarized themselves with their old affiliations, and they read their own identities in different fashions. "They remembered how it was." They remembered that they formed each other.

This tale, I admit, is far more difficult to understand than a simple story of God's creation of the world, or its actual production in a meaningless universe through the slippery hands of chance—and yet my story is more magnificent because elements of its truth will find resonance in the minds and hearts of those open enough to listen. For men's minds themselves are alive with the desire to read properly, and they are aware of their own vast heritage. It is not simply that man has a soul that is somehow blessed while the rest of him is not, but that in those terms everything [he knows], regardless of size or degree, is made of "soul stuff." Each portion has its own identity and validity—and no portion is ever annihilated or destroyed. The form may change.

(All with a rolling intensity:) I must of necessity tell this story in serial terms, but the world and all of its creatures actually come together like some spontaneously composed, ever-playing musical composition in which the notes themselves are alive and play themselves, so that the musicians and the notes are one and the same, the purpose and the performance being one, with each note played continuing to strike all of its own probable versions, forming all of its own probable compositions while at the same time taking part in all of the themes, melodies, and notes of the other compositions—so that each note, striking, defines itself, and yet also exists by virtue of its position in the composition as a whole.

The conscious mind cannot handle that kind of multidimensional creativity, yet it can expand into a kind of new recognition when it is carried along, still being itself, by its own theme.

In a way, your world follows its own theme in creativity's composition. You want to know where you came into the musical production, so to speak. *(Pause.)* I use a musical analogy here, if a simple one, to point out that we are also dealing with frequencies of perception. You are tuned into earth's orchestration [you might say], and your perception of time is simply the result of habits—habits of perception that you had to <u>learn</u> in the beginning of the world. And you learned those habits as your physical senses gradually became more alert and specific.

(9:47.) You "timed" yourselves—but greater perceptions always appeared in the background of your consciousnesses and in the dream state. It is the great activity of the dream state that allows you, as psychological and physical creatures, to recognize and inhabit <u>the world that you know</u> *(louder).*

End of dictation.

You did an excellent job of your own dream interpretation, and Ruburt unwittingly added to it with his poetry.[1]

Do you have any questions?

("Have you got anything to say for the beginning of the year, like you did with your resolutions for the start of last year?")

(With considerable humor, staring at me:) I thought I gave you my 1980 speech last time.

("Okay.")

Continue with the resolutions. I expect that sessions like this evening's will themselves help you understand the nature of Frameworks 1 and 2, and the importance of your mental activity in bringing about physical events.

("I was thinking about that.")

I bid you a fond good evening.

("Thank you, Seth. Good night.")

(9:52 P.M. Jane said she'd been pretty far out during the session— then added later while we talked that she was picking up from Seth information on the beginning of our own world, species and civilizations that he intended to give in the next session. Seth, then, was capable of coming through with that material right now. Only Jane's and my own conventions of time and habit, even concerning a phenomenon as unusual as the sessions, stopped him from doing so. Inevitably, the session

Jane delivers for Seth next Monday evening will be somewhat different from the one she could produce tonight. There are many interesting implications here.)

Note: Session 892

1. My dream represented a reaffirmation of a stand I'd taken early in this life—one that perhaps I'd felt since birth. Very simply: I dreamed that I was a youth, and that even though there was snow on the ground I'd been given the task of taking care of a beautiful young tree growing in a large field next to the Butts family home in Sayre, Pennsylvania. (Sayre is only 18 miles from Elmira, New York, where Jane and I live now.) Even though it was wintertime, the tree carried a sparse cover of leaves. Nearby in the dream were old industrial buildings, in which I became lost—but I found my way out of them and returned to the tree. My interpretation is that I saw the tree as the tree of life even then, and that I'd chosen to remain close to the world of nature and art instead of immersing myself in the safer industrial one. Jane was inspired by the dream to write a series of excellent short poems about it today.

CHAPTER 4

THE ANCIENT DREAMERS

(Jane called me early for the session, just to make sure she had one before she became too relaxed. She's been planning on going back to taking breaks between deliveries, so that she can hold longer sessions. By 8:40 she could feel Seth around. "As I say, I'll do the best I can. . . .")

(With a surprising heartiness:) Good evening.

("Good evening, Seth.")

Dictation, to begin: New chapter *(four)*: "The Ancient Dreamers."

Give us a moment. . . . For what would seem to you to be eons, according to your time scale, men were in the dreaming state far more than they were in the waking one. They slept long hours, as did the animals—awakening, so to speak, to exercise their bodies, obtain sustenance, and, later, to mate. It was indeed a dreamlike world, but a highly charming and vital one, in which dreaming imaginations played rambunctiously with all the probabilities entailed in this new venture: imagining the various forms of language and communication possible, spinning great dream tales of future civilizations replete with their own built-in histories—building, because they were now allied with time, mental edifices that automatically created pasts as well as futures.

192

These ancient dreams were shared to some extent by each consciousness that was embarked upon the earthly venture, so that creatures and environment together formed great environmental realities. Valleys and mountains, and their inhabitants, together dreamed themselves into being and coexistence.

The species—from your viewpoint (underlined)—lived at a much slower pace in those terms. The blood, for example, did not need to course so quickly through the veins [and arteries], the heart did not need to beat as fast. And in an important fashion the coordination of the creature in its environment did not need to be as precise, since there was an elastic give-and-take of consciousness between the two.

In ways almost impossible to describe, the ground rules were not as yet firmly established. Gravity itself did not carry its all-pervasive sway, so that the air was more buoyant. Man was aware of its support in a luxurious, intimate fashion. He was aware of himself in a different way, so that, for example, his identification with the self did not stop where his skin stopped: He could follow it outward into the space about his form, and feel it merge with the atmosphere with a primal sense-experience that you have forgotten.

(8:58.) During this period, incidentally, mental activity of the highest, most original variety was the strongest dream characteristic, and the knowledge [man] gained was imprinted upon the physical brain: what is now completely unconscious activity involving the functions of the body, its relationship with the environment, its balance and temperature, its constant inner alterations. All of these highly intricate activities were learned and practiced in the dream state as the CU's translated their inner knowledge through the state of dreaming into the physical form.

Then in your terms man began, with the other species, to waken more fully into the physical world, to develop the exterior senses, to intersect delicately and precisely with space and time. Yet man still sleeps and dreams, and that state is still a firm connective with his own origins, and with the origins of the universe as he knows it as well.

(Pause in a steady, if usually rather subdued, delivery.)

Man dreamed his languages. He dreamed how to use his tongue to form the words. In his dreams he practiced stringing the words together to form their meanings, so that finally he could consciously begin a sentence without actually knowing how it was begun, yet in the faith that he could and would complete it.

All languages have as their basis the language that was spoken in dreams. The need for language arose, however, as man became less a dreamer and more immersed in the specifics of space and time, for in the dream state his communications with his fellows and other species was instantaneous. Language arose to take the place of that inner communication, then. There is a great underlying unity in all of man's so-called early cultures— cave drawings and religions—because they were all fed by that common source, as man tried to transpose inner knowledge into physical actuality.

The body learned to maintain its stability, its strength and agility, to achieve a state of balance in complementary response to the weather and elements, to dream computations that the conscious mind alone could not hold. The body learned to heal itself in sleep in its dreams—and at certain levels in that state even now each portion of consciousness contributes to the health and stability of all other portions. Far from the claw-and-dagger universe, you have one whose very foundation is based upon the loving cooperation of all of its parts. That is given—the gift of life brings along with it the actualization of that cooperation, for the body's parts exist as a unit because of inner relationships of a cooperative nature; and those exist at your birth (most emphatically), when you are innocent of any cultural beliefs that may be to the contrary.

(9:14.) If it were not for this most basic, initial loving cooperation, that is a given quality in life itself, life would not have continued. Each individual of each species takes that initial zest and joy of life as its own yardstick. Each individual of whatever species, and each consciousness, whatever its degree, automatically seeks to enhance the quality of life itself—not only for itself but for all of reality as well.

This is a given characteristic of life, regardless of the beliefs that may lead you to misinterpret the actions of nature, casting some of its creatures in a reprehensible light.

(Pause.) In a fashion those ancient dreamers, through their immense creativity, dreamed all of life's creatures in all of their pasts, presents, and futures—that is, their dreams opened up the doors of space and time to entities that otherwise would not have been released into actualization, even as, for example, the units of consciousness were once released from the mind of All That Is.

All possible entities that can ever be actualized always exist. They [have] always existed and they always will exist. All That Is must, by its characteristics, be all that it can ever be, and so there can be no end to existence—and, in those terms, no beginning. But in terms of your world the units of consciousness, acting both as forces and as psychological entities of massive power, planted the seeds of your world in a dimension of imaginative power that gave birth to physical form. In your terms those entities are your ancestors—and yet [they are] not yours alone, but the ancestors of all the consciousnesses that make up your world.

Take your break.

(9:25. And for the first time in a long while, Jane did take a break during a session. "You did well," I told her.

"Yes, I was really going to town." Even though her delivery had been on the quiet side, still at times Seth had come through with considerable power. "In the winter I like to start sessions earlier," Jane said, "so I can finish sooner and watch TV for half an hour—it's relaxing and cozy, especially when we're alone. . . . I think the rest of the session will be about me."

She was right. Beginning at 9:34, Seth returned with a good amount of material for her,[1] then ended the session at 9:58 P.M.)

NOTE: SESSION 893

1. It's very interesting to see how Seth's information for Jane grew out of his work on *Dreams* tonight. For the most part, I'm presenting only the beginning of the several pages of notes I took from him—just enough to show how even his more personal material can fly in the face of convention (to coin a phrase!):

"Now: It is easy to live—so easy that although you live, rest, create, respond, feel, touch, see, sleep, and wake, you do not really have to try to do any of those things. From your viewpoint they are done for you.

"They are done for you in Framework 2—and further discussions of Framework 2, incidentally, will be interwound throughout our present book. Your beliefs often tell you that life is hard, however, that living is difficult, that the universe, again, is unsafe, and that you must use all of your resources— not to meet [life] with anything like joyful abandon, of course, but to protect yourself against its implied threats; threats that you have been taught to expect.

"But your beliefs do not stop there. Because of both scientific and religious ones, in Western civilization you believe that there are threats from within also. As a result you forget your natural selves, and become involved in a secondary, largely imaginary culture: beliefs that are projected negatively into the future, individually and en masse. People respond with illnesses of one kind or another, or through exaggerated [behavior].

"Living is easy (underlined). It is safe and reliable because it is easy. This is for Ruburt's benefit. . . ."

And later, with much humor: "I am willing to have longer sessions for as long as you put up with me. I will work on one book one night and another one the next, if you prefer, or discuss private material or other questions of a general nature, or work twice a week on our present material—whatever suits your fine fancies."

("Well, for someone who wasn't with it too much, I did okay," Jane said when the session was over. She was rejuvenated to a degree. Both of us were impressed anew by Seth's present and potential creativity. "If it weren't for all that mail we get, I'd try at least three sessions a week," she added. "But you don't have the time to type any more, with all you're doing now."

"I'd make the time. It would be worth it." And I reminded Jane that back in the days of her ESP classes, she'd often given three sessions a week. We held the last class in February 1975, as we prepared to move to the hill house from our downtown apartments.)

SESSION 894, JANUARY 9, 1980
9:08 P.M. WEDNESDAY

(The weather continues to be unseasonably warm for this time of year, with the ground still bare. We've had very little snow this winter. It's hard to believe.

Jane felt tired and harried as we sat for the session at about 8:50. She'd just finished reading the last 25 of the 48 fan letters that had arrived from our publisher this noon; she'd wanted a little time to relax and write a few notes before the session. However, that pile of letters means that people are reading our books, and for that we're grateful indeed. Over the holidays we received more Christmas cards from readers than ever before; in fact, the greetings are still coming in. "I really get pooped, going over the mail," Jane said, "but some of them are great letters." She's answering most of the mail herself these days, since I don't have the time to help her.)

Good evening.

("Good evening, Seth.")

(With many pauses to start:) Dictation: During this period that we have labeled as belonging to the dreamers, certain subjective actions took place as the "structure" of earthly tuned consciousness formed the phenomena of "the self."

What was needed was a highly focused, precisely tuned physical self that could operate efficiently in a space and time scheme that was being formed along with physical creatures—a self, however, that in one way or another must be supported by realms of information and knowledge of a kind that was basically <u>independent</u> of time and space. A knowledge indispensable, and yet a knowledge that could not be allowed to distract the physical focus.

(Long pause.) In one way or another, that inner information had to connect each consciousness on the face of the planet. Earthly creatures must be able to react in a moment, yet the inner mechanisms that made such reactions possible were based upon calculations that could not be consciously kept in mind. In your time scheme, for example, you could never move as quickly as you do if you had to consciously work all the muscles involved in motion—or in speech, or in any such bodily performance. You certainly could not communicate on such a physical level if you first had to be aware of all of speech's mechanisms, working them consciously before a word was uttered. Yet you had to have that kind of knowledge, and you had to have it in a way that did not intrude upon your conscious thoughts.

Basically there are no real divisions to the self, but for the sake of explanation we must speak of them in those terms. First of all you had the inner self, the creative dreaming self—composed, again, of units of consciousness, awareized energy that forms your identity, and that formed the identities of the earliest earth inhabitants. These inner selves formed their own dream bodies about them, as previously explained, but the dream bodies did not have to have physical reactions. They were free of gravity and space, and of time.

(Pause at 9:23.) As the body became physical, however, the inner self formed the body consciousness so that the physical body became more aware of itself, of the environment, and of its relationship within the environment. Before this could happen, though, the body consciousness was taught to become aware of its own inner environment. The body was lovingly formed from EE units through all the stages to atoms, cells, organs, and so forth. The body's pattern came from the inner self, as all of the units of consciousness involved in this venture together formed this fabric of environment and creatures, each suited to the other.

So far in our discussion, then, we have an inner self, dwelling primarily in a mental or psychic dimension, dreaming itself into physical form, and finally forming a body consciousness. To that body consciousness the inner self gives "its own body of physical knowledge," the vast reservoir of physical achievement that it has triumphantly produced. *(Pause.)* The body consciousness is not "unconscious," but for working purposes in your terms, [the body] possesses its own system of consciousness that to some extent, now (underlined), is separated from what you think of as your own normal consciousness. The body's consciousness is hardly to be considered less than your own, or as inferior to that of your inner self, since it represents knowledge from the inner self, and is a part of the inner self's own consciousness—the part delegated to the body.

[Each] cell, then, as I have often said, operates so well in time because it is, in those terms, precognitive. It is aware of the position, health, vitality, of all other cells on the face of the planet. It is aware of the position of each grain of sand on the shores of each ocean, and in those terms it forms a portion of the earth's consciousness.

At that level environment, creatures, and the elements of the natural world are all united—a point we will return to quite often. Your intellect as you think of it operates so clearly and precisely, so logically *(with amusement)*, sometimes so arrogantly, because the intellect rides that great thrust of codified, "ancient," "unconscious" power—the power of instant knowing that is a characteristic of the body consciousness (all very intently).

(Pause, one of many in here.) Thus far in our discussion, we still have only an inner self and a body consciousness. As the body consciousness developed itself, perfected its organization, the inner self and the body consciousness together performed a kind of psychological double-entendre.

(Pause at 9:42.) Give us a moment. . . . The best analogy I can think of is that up to that time the self was like a psychological rubber band, snapping inward and outward with great force and vitality, but without any kind of rigid-enough psychological framework to maintain a physical stance. The inner self still related to dream reality, while the body's orientation and the body consciousness attained, as was intended, a great sense of physical adventure, curiosity, speculation, wonder—and so once again the inner self put a portion of its consciousness in a different parcel, so to speak. As once it had formed the body consciousness, now it formed a physically attuned consciousness, a self whose desires and intents would be oriented in a way that, alone, the inner self could not be.

(All with emphatic rhythm:) The inner self was too aware of its own multidimensionality, so in your terms it gave psychological birth to itself through the body in space and time. It knew itself as a physical creature. That portion of the self is the portion you recognize as your usual conscious self, alive within the scheme of seasons, aware within the designs of time, caught transfixed in moments of brilliant awareness, with civilizations that seem to come and go. That is the self that is alert in the dear preciseness of the moments, whose physical senses are bound to light and darkness, sound and touch. That is the self that lives the life of the body.

It is the self that looks outward. It is the self that you call egotistically aware. The inner self became what I refer to as the inner ego. It looks into that inner reality, that psychic dimension of awareness from which both your own consciousness and your body consciousness emerged.

You are one self, then, but for operating purposes we will say that you have three parts: the inner self or inner ego, the body consciousness, and the consciousness that you know.

These portions, however, are intimately connected. They are like three different systems of consciousness operating together to form the whole. The divisions—the <u>seeming</u> divisions—are not stationary, but change constantly.

(*Long pause at 9:57.*) Give us a moment. . . . To one extent or another, these three systems of consciousness operate in one way or another in all of the species, and in all particles, in the physical universe. In your terms, this means that the proportions of the three systems might vary, but they are always in operation, whether we are speaking of a man or a woman, a rock or a fly, a star or an atom. The inner self represents your prime identity, the self you really are.

(*Very rapidly:*) "Earth is a nice place, but I wouldn't want to live there." A twist on an old quote, I believe—but the fact is, you are physical creatures because you <u>do</u> like to live on earth, you do like the conditions, you <u>do</u> enjoy overall the particular kind of challenge and the particular kind of perception, knowledge and understanding that the earthly environment provides.

(*All very intently:*) That environment, in your terms, certainly includes suffering. If joy has always been one of the characteristics of earth experience, so has suffering, and the subject will be covered in this book. Here, however, I only want to mention one facet, and that is the importance of physical sensation, of whatever kind—for the life of the body provides you, among all things, with a life of sensation, of feeling, a spectrum that must include the experience of all possible sensations within its overall range.

Now as you will see, all creatures, regardless of their degree, can and do choose, within their spheres of reality, those sensations that they will experience—but to one extent or another (underlined) all sensations are felt. We will later discuss the part of the mind and its interpretation, for example, of painful stimuli, but I want to make the point that those attracted to physical life are first and foremost <u>tasters</u> of sensation. Outside of that, basically, there are all kinds of mental distinctions made [among] stimuli. The body is made to react. It is made to feel life and vitality by reacting to an environment that is not itself, by encountering what you <u>might call</u> natural stress. The body maintains its equilibrium by reacting against gravity, by coming in contact with other bodies, by changing its own sensations, by glorifying in the balance between balance and off-balance.

(Long pause at 10:14, then slowly:) Give us a moment. . . . The body consciousness is therefore given a superb sense of its own reality, a sureness of identity, a sense of innate safety and security, that allows it to not only function but to grow in the physical world. It is endowed with a sense of boldness, daring, a sense of natural power. It is perfectly formed to fit into its environment —and the environment is perfectly formed to have such creatures.

The entities, or units of consciousness—those ancient fragments that burst into objectivity from the vast and infinite psychological realms of All That Is—dared all, for they joyfully abandoned themselves in space and time. They created new psychological entities, opened up an area of divine creativity that "until then" had been closed, and therefore to that [degree] extended the experience and immense existence of All That Is. For in so abandoning themselves they were not of course abandoned, since they contained within themselves their inherent relationship with All That Is. In those terms All That Is became physical also, aroused at its divine depth by the thrusting of each grass blade through the soil into the air, aroused by each birth and by each moment of each creature's existence.

All That Is, therefore, is immersed within your world, present in each hypothetical point, and forms the very fabric from which each portion of matter is created.

That will do it.

(10:25.) Now: My cheers to Ruburt. He is making good psychological progress, which means that he is making physical progress as well.

A smaller point I thought I would throw in: My energy is often with you both in ways that you do not expect. End of session, and a fond good evening.

("Good night, Seth.")

(10:26 P.M. "Jesus, I was so exhausted before the session, but I really had the feeling that we were getting some good stuff," Jane said as soon as she was out of trance. She hadn't taken a break during the session, either. "I really enjoy getting up early, because no matter what else happens I know we've got a good morning's work in. . . ."

By "what else," Jane referred to a call she'd received today: Three young members of the ESP class we'd disbanded almost five years ago are in town from New York City, visiting a local friend from the old class. All four are dear friends of ours too, of course, and want to see us.

First, though, they're to visit still another member from class who lives in a nearby town: He has tapes of some early class sessions that Jane had forgotten about; copies of the tapes will be made. "The kids" from the city are to call tomorrow, to learn if Jane will see them. [They did, and she did, for an hour after lunch.])

SESSION 895, JANUARY 14, 1980
9:17 P.M. MONDAY

(Our friend, David Yoder [I'll call him], is 48 years old. He's a bachelor, and a high-school teacher. Jane and I met him in May 1960, when we moved from Sayre into an apartment house close to downtown Elmira. The house had once been a luxurious private home. Jane began the sessions there three years later; indeed, we were to stay there for 15 years. At first David lived across the hall from us on the second floor. Eventually he moved downstairs when a larger apartment right beneath ours became available: Still later, Jane and I rented the apartment he'd had on the second floor, so that we ended up with two apartments, side by side; we needed more room by then, and didn't want to move.

David is one of the kindest people we've ever known. Jane initiated her ESP classes late in 1967—so each Tuesday night for the next seven and a half years, our friend put up with a vast amount of shouting and banging over his head. He knew what Jane was up to, but had only a peripheral interest in "psychic phenomena." David never complained about the racket, though sometimes he secluded himself in a back room down there, or left the house until class was over. It seemed that we were always apologizing for bothering him.

David let Jane use his telephone to call our publisher when we couldn't afford a phone ourselves. He gave us his magazines and newspapers— a practice he continues to this day during his school year. Sometimes we swapped furniture with him; sometimes he sold us at very reasonable cost pieces he'd replaced. He has a passion for neatness and the well-ordered life. He bought a power-driven lawn mower, and for years cut the grass without asking our landlord for any compensation.

In March 1975 Jane and I purchased the hill house just outside Elmira, and within a few weeks David acquired his own place not far from us in the valley below. We didn't see each other as often as we used to, but one morning each week, on his way to school, David left his magazines and newspapers at our back porch door, whether or not we were up, or saw him.

During the last couple of weeks David hadn't made his regular trips up the hill, but Jane and I were so busy that that fact nearly escaped us. Last Thursday morning, then, we were really shocked when Doris, who is also a teacher and a friend from those apartment-house years, called to tell us that David was in the hospital—that he was to undergo triple-bypass heart surgery the next day. Jane and I couldn't believe it. We'd thought David was in excellent health. He'd taken up jogging some time ago and was now running 15 miles at a time, three days a week. As he lay in the hospital, David asked Doris why this was happening to him, when he'd tried to take care of himself, help others, and "do everything right."

Each time someone we know gets in serious trouble, Jane and I start questioning anew our own values, and those of the society we live in, for such challenges seem to come unbidden and unwanted from way out in some far corner of each person's reality. We also had in mind another friend who'd died of cancer last year at the age of 39.

David is recovering well from his surgery now, but cannot have visitors yet. Jane has called the hospital each day to ask about him; she's putting together for him a unique, evocative little book of poetry and paintings. I'm running errands for David, and eventually will be taking him home from the hospital.

Seth talked about illness and suffering in general this evening, and about David in particular. I'm presenting excerpts from the generalized part of his material; but none about David himself. We have no idea of pressing Seth's personal information upon David; doing that would be an invasion of his privacy. Tonight's material, however, adds to our understanding of subjects like free will and choosing, good and evil, sickness and health, and reflects upon many questions people have asked us over the years.

"Well," Jane said as we sat for the session, "I'd almost rather feel that you were the victim of blind chance or accident, rather than that you get sick because of your own dumb ignorance or choice. . . ." When I remarked that I tried not to worry about such things anymore, she replied that she too had better get back to book work and forget the world's troubles: "Come on, Seth, I'm here." But even as she felt him around, she knew that Seth wouldn't be giving book dictation per se.)

(Whispering:) Good evening.

(*Whispering as a joke in return: "Good evening, Seth."*)

For many centuries *(pause)* the structure of the Roman Catholic church held [Western] civilization together, and gave it its meanings and its precepts. Those meanings and precepts flowed through the entire society, and served as the basis for all of the established modes of knowledge, commerce, medicine, science, and so forth.

The church's view of reality was the accepted one. I cannot stress too thoroughly the fact that the beliefs of those times structured individual human living, so that the most private events of personal lives were interpreted to mean thus and so, as were of course the events of nations, plants, and animals. The world's view was a religious one, specified by the church, and its word was truth and fact at the same time.

Illness was suffered, was sent by God to purge the soul, to cleanse the body, to punish the sinner, or simply to teach man his place by keeping him from the sins of pride. Suffering sent by God was considered a fact of life, then, and a religious truth as well.

(Long pause at 9:25.) Some other civilizations have believed that illness was sent by demons or evil spirits, and that the world was full of good and bad spirits, invisible, intermixed with the elements of nature itself, and that man had to walk a careful line lest he upset the more dangerous or mischievous of those entities. In man's history there have been all kinds of incantations, meant to mollify the evil spirits that man believed were real in fact and in religious truth.

It is easy enough to look at those belief structures and shrug your shoulders, wondering at man's distorted views of reality. The entire scientific view of illness, however, is quite as distorted *(with amused emphasis)*. It is as laboriously conceived and interwound with "nonsense." It is about as factual as the "fact" that God sends illness as punishment, or that illness is the unwanted gift of mischievous demons.

Now: Churchmen of the Middle Ages could draw diagrams of various portions of the human body that were afflicted as the result of indulging in particular sins. Logical minds at one time found those diagrams quite convincing, and patients with certain afflictions in certain areas of the body would confess to having committed the various sins that were involved. The entire structure of beliefs made sense within itself. A man might be born deformed or sickly because of the sins of his father.

The scientific framework is basically, now, just as senseless, though within it the facts often seem to prove themselves out, also. There are viruses, for example. Your beliefs become self-evident realities. It would be impossible to discuss human suffering without taking that into consideration. Ideas are transmitted from generation to generation—and those ideas are the carriers of all of your reality, its joys and its agonies. Science, however, is all in all (underlined) a poor healer. The church's concepts at least gave suffering a kind of dignity: It did (underlined) come from God—an unwelcome gift, perhaps—but after all it was punishment handed out from a firm father for a child's own good.

Science disconnected fact from religious truth, of course. In a universe formed by chance, with the survival of the fittest as the main rule of good behavior, illness became a kind of crime against a species itself. It meant you were unfit, and hence brought about all kinds of questions not seriously asked before.

Did those "genetically inferior," for example, have the right to reproduce?[1] Illness was thought to come like a storm, the result of physical forces against which the individual had little recourse. The "new" Freudian ideas of the unsavory unconscious led further to a new dilemma, for it was then—as it is now—widely believed that as the result of experiences in infancy the subconscious, or unconscious, might very well sabotage the best interests of the conscious personality, and trick it into illness and disaster.

In a way, that concept puts a psychological devil in place of the metaphysical one. If life itself is seen scientifically as having no real meaning, then suffering, of course, must also be seen as meaningless. The individual becomes a victim of chance insofar as his birth, the events of his life, and his death are concerned. Illness becomes his most direct encounter with the seeming meaninglessness of personal existence (all quite intently).

You affect the structure of your body through your thoughts. If you believe in heredity, heredity itself becomes a strong suggestive factor in your life, and can help bring about the precise malady in the body that you believed was there all along, until finally your scientific instruments uncover the "faulty mechanism," or whatever, and there is the evidence for all to see.

(Pause at 9:50.) There are obviously some conditions that in your terms <u>are</u> inherited, showing themselves almost instantly after birth, but these are of a very limited number in proportion to those diseases you believe are hereditary—many cancers, heart problems, arthritic or rheumatoid disorders. And in many cases of inherited difficulties, changes could be effected for the better, through the utilization of other mental methods that we will certainly get to someday.

There are as many kinds of suffering as there are kinds of <u>joy</u>, and there is no one simple answer that can be given. As human creatures you accept the conditions of life. You create from those conditions the experiences of your days. You are born into belief systems as you are born into physical centuries, and part of the entire picture is the freedom of interpreting the experiences of life in multitudinous fashions *(all intently)*. The meaning, nature, dignity or shame of suffering will be interpreted according to your systems of belief. I hope to give you along the way a picture of reality that puts suffering in its proper perspective, but it is a most difficult subject to cover because it touches most deeply upon your hopes for yourselves and for mankind, and your fears for yourselves and for mankind.

Give us a moment. . . . You have taught yourselves to be aware of and to follow only certain portions of your own consciousnesses, so that mentally you consider certain subjects taboo. Thoughts of death and suffering are among those. In a species geared above all to the survival of the fittest, and the competition among species, then any touch of suffering or pain, or thoughts of death, become dishonorable, biologically shameful, cowardly, nearly insane. Life is to be pursued at all costs—not because it is innately <u>meaningful</u>, but because it is the only game going, and it is a game of chance at best. One life is all you have, and that one is everywhere beset by the threat of illness, disaster, and war —and if you escape such drastic circumstances, then you are still left with a life that is the result of no more than lifeless elements briefly coming into a consciousness and vitality <u>that is bound to end.</u>

(Pause at 10:05. Jane had delivered all of the above material for Seth with an emphatic mixture of speed, irony, and amusement.)

In that framework, even the emotions of love and exaltation are seen as no more than the erratic activity of neurons firing *(pause)*, or of chemicals reacting to chemicals. Those beliefs alone bring on suffering. All of science, in your time, has been set up to promote beliefs that run in direct contradiction to the knowledge of man's heart. Science has, you have noted, denied emotional truth. It is not simply that science denies the validity of emotional experience, but that it has believed so firmly that knowledge can only be acquired from the outside, from observing the exterior of nature.

I spoke about the quality of life, and it is true to say that in at least many centuries past, if men and women may have died earlier, they also lived lives of fuller, more satisfying quality—and I do not want to be misinterpreted in that direction.

Now, it is also true that in some of its aspects religion has glorified suffering, elevated it to [be] one of the prime virtues—and it has degraded it at other times, seeing the ill as possessed by devils, or seeing the insane as less than human. So there are many issues involved.

Science, however, seeing the body as a mechanism, has promoted the idea that consciousness is trapped within a mechanical model, that man's suffering is mechanically caused in that regard: You simply give the machine some better parts and all will be well *(amused)*. Science also operates as magic, of course, so on some occasions the belief in science itself will seemingly work miracles: The new heart will give a man new heart, for example.

(10:16. After discussing David Yoder's personal situation, Seth returned to his more generalized material at 10:30.)

Illness is used as a part of man's motivations. What I mean is that there is no human motivation that may not at some time be involved with illness, for often it is a means to a desired end—a method of achieving something a person thinks may not be achieved otherwise.

One man might use it to achieve success. One might use it to achieve failure. A person might use it as a means of showing pride or humility, of looking for attention or escaping it. Illness is often another mode of expression, but nowhere does science mention that illness might have its purpose, or its groups of purposes, and I do not mean that the purposes themselves are necessarily derogatory. Illnesses are often misguided attempts to attain something the person thinks important. [Sickness] can be a badge of honor or dishonor—but there can be no question, when you look at the human picture, that to a certain extent, but an important one, suffering not only has its purposes and uses, but is actively sought for one reason or another.

Most people do not seek out suffering's extreme experience, but within those extremes there are multitudinous degrees of stimuli that could be considered painful, that are actively sought. Man's involvement in sports is an instant example, of course, where society's rewards and the promise of spectacular bodily achievement lead athletes into activities that would be considered most painful by the ordinary individual. People climb mountains, willingly undergoing a good bit of suffering in the pursuit of such goals.

(*10:37. Seth came through with some more information concerning David. Then:*)

I do not want any of this to appear too simplistic, but we must begin somewhere in this kind of discussion. . . . This is far from the entire story [of illness], but it is enough for this evening's saga. When you can, encourage your fine wife to follow your example in determining not to worry. It should be the first commandment.

(*"Okay."*)

My heartiest regards, and a fond good evening.

(*"Thank you, Seth, and the same to you."*)

(*10:45 P.M. "My God, your fingers must be ready to fall off!" Jane exclaimed as she quickly came out of her excellent trance state. She moved over to the couch from her rocker. "Why didn't you ask for a break?"*)

"You didn't seem to want to take one." But also, I'd become so interested in the session that I forgot everything else. My right hand was tired now, though.

"I don't remember much of that," Jane said, "but I've got the feeling that Seth meant the material to defuse some of my own thoughts lately— that there isn't any answer for all of the pain and suffering in the world —that the whole thing is so vast that you can't say or do anything that will be of much use to anyone. . . ."

Which might help account, I told Jane, for her response to David's illness, including the book she's making for him. I also said that even though Seth hadn't called this session dictation for Dreams, *he very well could have done so: Large portions of it might at least help answer people's questions.*)

NOTE: SESSION 895

1. Seth certainly touched upon a question that's loaded with ethical and legal dilemmas; many of these have grown out of recent scientific advances in genetics. Some moral philosophers, medical geneticists, physicians, lawyers, and religious leaders believe that those who carry genes for serious genetic diseases do not have the right to reproduce. Others of similar background maintain just the opposite—that the right to recreate one's kind is inalienable. Questions abound involving amniocentesis (examination of the fluid in the womb to detect genetic defects in the fetus); therapeutic abortion; artificial insemination; reproduction by in vitro fertilization; embryo transfer (surrogate motherhood); the responsibilities of the legal, medical and religious communities; whether mentally retarded, genetically defective people should receive life-prolonging medical treatment, and so forth. Years are expected to pass before our legal system alone catches up with the scientific progress in genetics—but, ironically, continuing advances in the field are bound to complicate even further the whole series of questions.

SESSION 896, JANUARY 16, 1980
9:09 P.M. WEDNESDAY

(*Jane has been taking time off from* God of Jane *and* If We Live Again *to work on the Introduction for Sue Watkins's* Conversation With Seth. *Sue took the manuscript for* Conversations *with her when she went to Florida for the month with her son and parents. If those three members of her family are enjoying a vacation, Sue isn't—but at least she's working on her book in warm weather!*

I finished typing Monday evening's session from my notes just in time to get ready for this one. In the meantime Jane called David Yoder at the hospital. To her surprise he sounded weaker than he had the last time she'd spoken to him, and at his request my planned visit tomorrow was put off until Friday afternoon.

Next, Jane quickly went over my recent batch of "Sayre-environment dreams," as Seth called them. I've recorded six of those long and compli-

cated dreams, set in my hometown, since December 22; in them I explored my various, sometimes contradictory beliefs about writing and painting, my relationships with society and the marketplace, and with my [deceased] father as he represented certain other beliefs. I'd recently asked Jane if Seth would comment.

Tonight Seth did comment—and very perceptively put all of the dreams together. "In your heart Sayre stands for your childhood," he said in conclusion, "and to that extent, to you personally, for the childhood of all men. For, again to some extent, each man feels that somehow humanity as a whole was born at his own birth."

We took a break at 9:40. "I'll tell you," Jane said as I congratulated her, "I just glanced at those dreams in your notebook. I didn't take more than five minutes. I'll be damned." She laughed, pleased at Seth's handling of them.

"My memories of those dream events are just as real as the memories of anything else I've done lately," I said. "Going shopping, or working, or whatever. . . ." I've always been intrigued by the simple observation that for me at least, once they begin moving into the past dream events assume an increasingly important place in my life. I think that upon awakening in the present, one is much more likely to call a dream "just a dream," and not assign to it a reality and validity equal to one's "real" experience in the waking state.

Jane wanted to quickly return to the session. Even though the following material isn't book dictation per se, I'm presenting it for obvious reasons. Resume at 9:52.)

A continuation of our discussion *(begun in the last session)* on suffering.

I feel sometimes as if I am expected to justify life's conditions, when of course they do not need any such justification.

Your beliefs close you off from much otherwise quite-available knowledge concerning man's psychology—knowledge that would serve to answer many questions usually asked about the reasons for suffering. Other questions, it is true, are more difficult to answer. Men and women are born, however, with curiosity about all sensations, and about all possible life experiences. They are thirsty for experience of all kinds. Their curiosity is not limited to the pretty or the mundane.

Men and women are born with a desire to push beyond the limits—to, in quotes *(amused and loudly)*: "explore where no man has ever gone before"—a bastard version of the introduction [to a famous television program], I believe. Men and women are born with a sense of drama, a need of excitement. Life itself is excitement. The quietest mood rides the thrust of spectacular molecular activity.

You forget many of your quite natural inclinations, feelings, and inner fantasies as you mature into adults, because they do not fit into the picture of the kind of people, or experience, or species you have been taught to believe you are. As a result, many of the events of your lives that are the natural extensions of those feelings appear alien *(pause)*, against your deepest wishes, or thrust upon you, either by outside agencies or by a mischievous subconscious.

The thoughts of children give excellent clues as to mankind's nature, but many adults do not remember any childhood thoughts except those that fit, or seem to fit, in with their beliefs about childhood.

Children play at getting killed. They try to imagine what death is like. They imagine what it would be like to fall from a wall like Humpty-Dumpty, or to break their necks. They imagine tragic roles with as much creative abandon as they imagine roles of which adults might approve. They are often quite aware of "willing" themselves sick to get out of difficult situations—and of willing themselves well again *(with humor)*.[1]

They quickly learn to forget their parts in such episodes, so that later, when as adults they find themselves ill they not only forget that they caused the illness to begin with, but unfortunately they forget how to will themselves well again.

(10:05.) As I said, there are all ranges of suffering, and I am beginning this discussion, which I will continue now and then in between regular book dictation, in a very general manner. In times past in particular, though the custom is not dead, men purged themselves, wore ashes and beat themselves with chains, or went hungry or otherwise deprived themselves. They suffered, in other words, for religion's sake. It was not just that they believed suffering was good for the soul—a statement which can or cannot be true, incidentally, and I will go into that later—but they understood something else: The body will only take so much suffering when it releases consciousness. So they hoped to achieve religious ecstasy.

Religious ecstasy does not need physical suffering as a stimulus, and such a means in the overall (underlined) will work against religious understanding. Those episodes, however, represent one of the ways in which man can actively seek suffering as a means to another end, and it is beside the point to say that such activity is not natural, since it exists within nature's framework.

(Long pause.) Discipline is a form of applied suffering, as discipline is usually used. People are not taught to understand the great dimensions of their own capacity for experience. It is natural for a child to be curious about suffering, to want to know what it is, to see it—and by doing so he (or she) learns to avoid the suffering he does not want, to help others avoid suffering that they do not want, and to understand, more importantly, the gradations of emotion and sensation that are his heritage. [As an adult] he will not inflict pain upon others if he understands this, for he will allow himself to feel the validity of his own emotions.

If you deny yourself the direct experience of your own emotions, but muffle them, say, through too-strict discipline, then you can hurt others much more easily, for you project your deadened emotional state upon them—as in the Nazi war camps [men] followed orders, torturing other people—and you do that first of all by deadening your own sensitivity to pain, and by repressing your emotions.

(10:25.) Man's vulnerability to pain helps him sympathize with others, and therefore helps him to more actively alleviate whatever unnecessary causes of pain exist in society.

Give us a moment. . . . That will be it for the evening. My heartiest regards to each of you. I have but one more point to make: Each person's experience of a painful nature is also registered on the part of what we will call the world's mind. Each, say, failure, or disappointment, or unresolved problem that results in suffering, becomes a part of the world's experience: This way or that way does not work, or this way or that way has been tried, with poor results. So in that way even weaknesses or failures of suffering are resolved, or rather redeemed as adjustments are made in the light of those data.

In that regard, each person lives his or her life privately, and yet for all of humanity. Each person tries out new challenges, new circumstances, new achievements from a unique viewpoint, for himself or herself, and for the entire mass of humanity as well.

(Heartily:) End of session. A fond good evening.

("Thank you very much, Seth. Good night.")

(10:27 P.M. "Boy, that's excellent stuff," I said to Jane as she came out of a good trance and a good delivery. "I sure hope we can use it somehow, somewhere, instead of letting it just sit on a shelf." So even though I'd inserted the last [nonbook] session into Dreams, *I didn't make any quick decision about doing the same thing with this one.*

"I'm wondering about that too," Jane said. "But the heck with it. Maybe someday we'll be able to use it in a book, but in the meantime I'm not going to worry about it. Maybe he'll keep on with it like this, and it'll end up in a book of its own someday. Who knows?"

I laughed, and told her that with her new resolve not to worry she sounded like me.)

NOTE: SESSION 896

1. Seth's idea that in their play children "try to imagine what death is like" certainly adds an intuitive dimension to my own activities as a child. "Cowboys and Indians" was our gang's favorite game back in Sayre in the late 1920s, and as we roamed the nearby fields all of us made believe we killed our enemies and/or were killed ourselves. We had great fun, and used to play such games to the point of exhaustion.

I'll also endorse Seth's statement that children "are often quite aware of willing themselves sick to get out of difficult situations." I remember very well doing that on certain occasions—usually to avoid some school activity—and that even then I was surprised because my parents didn't catch on to what I was up to. (Getting well after the danger period had passed was no problem!)

Jane said I'd never told her about getting sick on purpose, although I thought I had. I asked her if she'd ever done that. "Sure," she said. "I know that sometimes I made myself sick to get out of stuff like diagramming sentences and doing multiplication tables, in Catholic grade school. I was terrified of those things—I think it was in the fourth grade. I think I gave myself the mumps once, too."

Jane added that her group of playmates hadn't engaged in the same sort of games that mine had. "We might have *played* dead now and then—you know, lain down and closed our eyes, but that would be all." In fifth-grade history class, in the convent she'd been sent to because her mother was hospitalized for treatment of severe rheumatoid arthritis, Jane learned about Marie Antoinette, queen of France, who had been guillotined in Paris in 1793. "I used to play being her all by myself," she said. "I'd be brave and scornful, knowing I was going to be beheaded—that sort of thing."

We were a bit surprised, then, to realize that for both of us at least some of our "willful" experiences had revolved around our early school days.

SESSION 897, JANUARY 21, 1980
9:15 P.M. MONDAY

(The weather is still very warm for this time of year; the temperature is often above freezing in the daytime, and when we do get a dusting of snow it soon melts on the bare ground. This morning I took David Yoder home from the hospital, and this afternoon I took our tiger cat, Billy, to the veterinarian. Billy hasn't acted well since last Saturday, and his beautiful coat has lost its luster. He had a temperature of 105° when the vet gave him a shot and prescribed some pills. Yet the doctor didn't really know why the cat is sick. Jane and I wondered what role Billy's illness might play in our affair with David—surely a way of thinking that would have been quite alien to us before the advent of the Seth material.

We'd also noticed that as soon as Billy lost his appetite his littermate, Mitzi, became "just a little busybody," as Jane put it, playing and running about the house and out on the porches, as if in her own way she was trying to compensate for Billy's unaccustomed lack of activity.

"I wouldn't mind getting something from Seth on why Billy got sick," I said to Jane after supper. She replied that she'd rather wait on the request: She was becoming very relaxed, and didn't want to get involved with "deep questions" that might interfere with her increasingly comfortable state. In fact, my wife just hoped she could hold the session. She'd been "stewing" about David, the state of the world, human frailty, Billy, and herself, and had had to make strong efforts to change her thinking.

Jane knew, however, that provided she held the session Seth's material would be dictation for Dreams. *She'd picked up that from him while doing the dishes tonight.)*

(Whispering:) Good evening.

(Whispering: "Good evening.")

Now: Dictation. Again, your world was not created, then, by some exteriorized, objectified God who created it from the outside, so to speak, and set it into motion. Many [religious] theorists believe, for example, that such a God created the world in such a fashion, and that the process of decay began at almost the same hypothetical moment that the creation ended.

Such an idea is much like some scientific ones, that see the universe running down, [with energy] being dissipated and order gradually disintegrating into chaos. Both versions conceive of a finished creation, though one is a divine production and the other is a result of nothing more than <u>happenstance</u>.

(Pause.) All in all, however, we are speaking of a constant creation, even though I must explain it in serial terms. We are discussing a model of the universe in which creation is continuous, spontaneously occurring everywhere, and everywhere simultaneously, in a kind of spacious present, from which all experiences with time emerge. In this model there is always new energy, and all systems are open, even though they may seem to operate separately. Once again, also, we are considering a model that is based upon the active cooperation <u>of each of its parts</u>, which in one way or another also participate in the experience of the whole.

In this model, changes of form are the result of creative syntheses. This model is seen to have its origin *(long pause, eyes closed)* within a vast, infinite, divine subjectivity—a subjectivity that is within each unit of consciousness, whatever its degree. A subjective divinity, then, that is within creation itself, a multidimensional creativity of such proportions that it is itself the creator and its creations at the same time.

(Long pause at 9:37, one of many.) This divine psychological process—and "process" is not the best word here—this divine psychological <u>state of relatedness</u> forms from its own being worlds within worlds. Your universe is not the only one. Nothing exists isolate in nature, and to that extent the very <u>existence</u> of your universe presupposes the existence of others.

These were, and are, and will be, created in the same fashion as that I have explained—and again, all such systems are open, even though operationally they may appear not to be.

There are literally infinite numbers of sequences, faultlessly activated, that make the existence of your own world possible. I admit that it is sometimes inconceivable to me that a human being can imagine his world to be meaningless, for the very existence of one human body speaks of an almost unbelievable molecular and cellular cooperation that could hardly result through the bounty of the most auspicious works of chance.

(Jane's delivery for Seth hadn't been her fastest by any means, although that "energy personality essence" closed out the paragraph above quite intently and with more than a little amusement. But now her pace slowed down even more; she used many long pauses.)

In a manner of speaking, your universe and all others spring from a dimension that is the creative source for all realities—a basic dream universe, so to speak, a divine psychological bed where subjective being is sparked, illuminated, stimulated, pierced, by its own infinite desire for creativity. The source of its power is so great that its imaginings become worlds, but it is endowed with a creativity of such splendor that it seeks the finest fulfillment, for even the smallest of its thoughts and all of its potentials are directed with a good intent that is literally beyond all imagining.

(9:47.) That good intent is apparent within your world. It is obvious in the cooperative ventures that unite, say, the mineral, plant, and animal kingdoms, the relationship of bee to flower. And your beliefs to the contrary, you have closed your minds to man's own cooperative nature, to his innate desire for fellowship, his natural bent for taking care of others, and *(with elaborate, if gentle emphasis)* for altruistic behavior. But we will discuss those matters later in our book.

Take a brief break.

(9:50. Jane was very relaxed the moment she came out of trance. I didn't mention the frequent long pauses she'd been taking; she'd spent three minutes delivering the last paragraph alone. Her head moved loosely. Her eyelids fluttered. "He shouldn't have given me the break," she said. "This is the worst I've been. . . . I wanted to get back to two-hour sessions. . . ." She sat quietly while I worked on this note. By "worst" she meant relaxed, of course. I told her there was no need to continue the

session. "I don't know if I can go back in, I'm so. . . ." Her head kept
dipping down. She lit a cigarette. "I'm just waiting."
  (See Note 1 for the rest of the session.)

NOTE: SESSION 897

1. *(Seth returned at 9:59.)*
  "End of dictation.
  "Now: Either life has meaning or it does not. It cannot sometimes have meaning, and sometimes not—or man's life cannot
have meaning while the lives of other species do not. But the
meaning may not always be apparent, for of course when we
discuss it, we discuss it from a human viewpoint.
  "Why, for example, did David fall ill? We have discussed that,
dealing with several levels—but meanings often fall into categories that become almost indescribable."
  (10:05.) "Your cat, in a strange fashion, reacted to the weather
—not reacted so much as <u>identified</u> with its interpretation of the
weather's mood—became part of the weather in a fashion,
opened up to it, but became depressed in your terms.
  "To the cat this is an experience. There is some additional
implication, in that he picked up your joint feelings about your
friend David—but that is not the cause, simply an added color-
ation. The give-and-take of weather conditions and animal behavior is little understood. Your other cat, for example, reacted
in an opposite fashion, actively providing herself with additional
stimuli.
  "We will say more at a later date. A fond good evening."
  ("Thank you, Seth.")
  (10:10 P.M. "I thought you didn't want Seth to say anything about
Billy tonight?" I asked Jane as she easily came out of trance.
  She answered the question in her own way. "That was my fault, though
—that was charged material, he would have said more. Stuff about
illness is still pretty charged for me." I thought her own physical difficul-
ties must play a strong role here, although she didn't say so. "It makes me
mad," Jane said quietly. "At break I could feel him getting all ready to
go into Billy's condition, and I began to get all tight inside. I didn't tell
you. Then I said to myself, 'Seth, just go into it, that's all.' So why didn't
he say the cat's going to be all right?"

In reply to another of my questions, she said her emotional charge was also involved with the death of our cat, Billy One, in February 1979. Billy One had been, obviously, the predecessor to the Billy we have now; the present Billy is remarkably similar to him in looks and temperament. "I'm disgusted with myself," Jane said. "I wish we'd called this one Willy, but I know that's all superstitious nonsense."

And even as the session ended, I heard Mitzi out in the kitchen, playing with the wadded-up paper ball I'd made for her. The cellar door was open. Again and again she knocked the ball down the cellar steps, raced down after it, carried it back upstairs and sent it flying down again —just as though, it seemed, she still had to perform for us while a recuperating Billy dozed on a comfortable chair in the living room.

In the 840th session for Chapter 6 of Mass Events, *see my account of Billy One's death.)*

SESSION 898, JANUARY 30, 1980
9:28 P.M. WEDNESDAY

(On January 23 I mailed to our publisher Jane's Introduction for Sue Watkins's Conversations With Seth.

Since holding the last [897th] book session nine days ago, Jane has delivered three remarkable private sessions for Seth.[1] Tonight she was quite at ease, and had been tempted to skip the session and just paint. She's really attracted by strong, bright color. "I love the red couch cover you're sitting on," she said as we waited for the session—and indeed, the corded fabric glowed in the warm light cast by the table lamp on the room divider behind the couch; the divider separates the kitchen from the living room.

I told Jane she needn't have a session if she wanted to paint, but that if she did go into trance I wouldn't mind getting something from Seth on the dream I'd had early this morning. In it I'd been a woman who was the same age as my father. The fact that my father is dead didn't enter into the dream.)

Dictation.

("All right.")

(Long pause.) The waking state as you think of it is a specialized extension of the dream state, and emerges from it to the surface of your awareness, just as your physical locations are specified extensions of locations that exist first within the realm of mind.

The waking state, then, has its source in the dream state, and all of the objects, environment, and experience that are familiar to you in the waking state also originate in that inner dimension.

(Pause.) When you examine the state of dreams, however, you do it as a rule from the framework of waking reality. You try to measure the dimension of dream experience by applying the rules of reality that are your usual criteria for judging events. Therefore, you are not able to perceive the true characteristics of the dreaming state except on those few occasions when you "come awake" within your dreams—a matter we will discuss later on in this book. But in a manner of speaking, it is true to say that the universe was created in the same fashion that your own thoughts and dreams happen: spontaneously and yet with a built-in amazing order, and an inner organization. You think your thoughts and you dream your dreams without any clear knowledge of the incredible processes involved therein, yet those processes are the very ones that are behind the existence of the universe itself.

Also, in a manner of speaking, you are yourselves the ancient dreamers who dreamed your world into being. You must understand that I am not saying that you are passive, fleeting dreamers, lost in some divine mind, but that you are the unique creative manifestations of a divine intelligence whose creativity is responsible for all realities, which are themselves endowed with creative abilities of their own, with the potential and desire for fulfillment—inheritors indeed of the divine processes themselves. Spontaneity knows its own order.

(9:41.) I have said that many times. The world's parts come spontaneously together, with an order that basically defies the smaller laws of cause and effect, or before and afterward. In that regard, again, your dreaming state presents you with many clues about the source of your own lives and that of your world.

Computers, however grand and complicated, cannot dream, and so for all of their incredible banks of information, they must lack the kind of unspoken knowing knowledge that the smallest plant or seed possesses. Nor can any amount of information "possessed" or processed by any computer compare with the unspoken knowing knowledge that is possessed by the atoms and molecules that compose such an instrument. The computer is not equipped to perceive that kind of knowing. It is not equipped for such an endeavor because it cannot dream. In dreams the innate knowledge of the atoms and molecules is combined and translated. It serves as the bed of perceptual information and knowledge from which the dreaming state arises in its physical form.

You are subjectively "alive" before your birth. You will be subjectively alive after your death. Your subjective life is now interpreted through the specialized state of consciousness that you call the waking one, in which you recognize as real only experience that falls within certain space and time coordinates. Your greater reality exists outside those coordinates, and so does the reality of the universe. *(Pause.)* You create lives for yourselves, changing them as you go along, as a writer might change a book, altering the circumstances, changing the plots. The writer only knows that he or she creates without understanding the spontaneous order with which the creativity happens. The processes occur at another level of consciousness (underlined).

In the most basic of ways, the world is formed from the inside out, and from dreaming reality into the physical one—and those processes happen at another level of consciousness *(quietly emphatic).*

Take a break.

(9:55. I thought the break came rather early. Jane's delivery had fluctuated between using many pauses and being rather fast. "I was sort of getting that it would be something like that after supper," she said. She didn't think the session would be a long one. Seth returned at 10:10 —and he did discuss my dream until he said good night at 10:30 P.M.)

NOTE: SESSION 898

1. We called those three very penetrating sessions private, or deleted, because they grew out of our own reactions to David Yoder's challenges, to the illness of our cat Billy, to the playful antics of Billy's littermate Mitzi, and to several other personal matters. All of that material has a general appeal, however, and I wish I could show in a few words the variety and depth of Seth's information.

"Your body consciousness is like the consciousness of any animal," he told us on January 23, for example. "Mitzi, running up and down the [cellar] stairs, is an example of the love of excitement and activity with which man and animals are innately endowed. Animals enjoy being petted, stroked, and loved. They react in their own ways to suggestion, and in that regard your body consciousness responds to your <u>conscious treatment</u> of it. Think of your body, for the purpose of this discussion, as a healthy animal. . . . Animals and your own body consciousnesses <u>have little concept of age.</u> In a fashion almost impossible to describe, [those] consciousnesses—of the body and the animals—are 'young' in each moment of their existences. I am taking it for granted that you understand that I am referring to the 'mental attitude' of animals and of the body consciousness, for they do possess their own mental attributes—psychological colorations—and above all, emotional 'states.' "

Seth's material largely opposes science's mechanistic model of the body wearing down within certain age limits, abetted as that model is by the power of the beliefs that say it will. He had much to say about how the out-of-place stresses we impose upon ourselves through our fearful projections into the future adversely affect our body consciousnesses, which are focused in the present. Telepathy, "molecular mentality," and cellular consciousness are deeply involved in all of this.

SESSION 899, FEBRUARY 6, 1980
8:51 P.M. WEDNESDAY

(We didn't hold the session scheduled for last Monday evening so that we could rest.

I estimate that I'm two-thirds finished with the notes I want to do for Mass Events. *Along with* Dreams, *Jane is back working on* If We Live Again *and* God of Jane. *She's on a "creative high" with the latter.[1] The complicated events surrounding Iran and Three Mile Island continue to develop, as consciousness explores itself in those areas.[2]*

Yesterday and earlier today Jane had scribbled down notes she was picking up from Seth; she'd put them in the session notebook in case I had time to type them. [I didn't.] Then later today she reread all of the material Seth has given on Dreams.*)*

Good evening.

("Good evening, Seth.")

Dictation. *(Pause.)* While men had their dream bodies alone they enjoyed a remarkable freedom, of course, for those bodies did not have to be fed or clothed. They did not have to operate under the law of gravity. Men could wander as they wished about the landscape. They did not yet identify themselves to any great degree (underlined) as being themselves separate from either the environment or other creatures. They knew themselves to be themselves, but their identities were not as closely allied with their forms as is now the case.

The dream world was bound to waken, however, for that was the course it had set itself upon. This awakening, again, happened spontaneously, and yet with its own order. In the terms of this discussion the other creatures of the earth actually awakened before man did, and relatively speaking, their dream bodies formed themselves into physical ones before man's did. The animals became physically effective, therefore, while to some degree man still lingered in that dream reality.

The plants awakened before the animals—and there are reasons for these varying degrees of "wakefulness" that have nothing to do basically with the differentiations of specieshood as defined by science from the outside, but have to do with the inner affiliations of consciousness, and with species or families of consciousness. Those affiliations fell into being as all of the consciousnesses that were embarked upon physical reality divided up *(long pause)* the almost unimaginable creative achievements that would be responsible for the physically effective world.

(9:04.) Again, the environment as you think of it is composed of living consciousness. Ancient religions, for example, speak of nature's spirits, and such terms represent memories dating from prehistory. Part of consciousness, then, transformed itself into what you think of as nature—the vast sweep of the continents, the oceans and the rivers, the mountains and the valleys, the body of the land. The creative thrust of the physical world must rise from that living structure.

(With emphasis:) In a matter of speaking (underlined), the birds and the insects are indeed living portions of the earth flying, even as, again in a matter of speaking (in parentheses) *(with a smile and again with an emphasis upon the word "matter"),* bears and wolves and cows and cats represent the earth turning itself into

creatures that live upon its own surface. And in a matter of speaking, again, man becomes the earth thinking, and thinking his own thoughts, man in his way specializes in the <u>conscious</u> work of the world—a work that is dependent upon the indispensable "unconscious" work of the rest of nature, a nature that sustains him *(all very intently)*. And when he thinks, man thinks for the microbes, for the atoms and the molecules, for the smallest particles within his being, for the insects and for the rocks, for the creatures of the sky and the air and the oceans.

Man thinks as naturally as the birds fly. He looks at physical reality for the <u>rest</u> of physical reality: He is earth coming alive to view itself through conscious eyes—but that consciousness is graced to be because it is so intimately a part of earth's framework.

(Pause.) What was it like when man awakened from the dream world?

End of chapter.

CHAPTER 5

THE "GARDEN OF EDEN."
MAN "LOSES" HIS DREAM BODY
AND GAINS A "SOUL"

(9:15.) Chapter Five: "The 'Garden of Eden.' Man 'Loses' His Dream Body, and Gains a 'Soul.' "

The Garden of Eden legend represents a distorted version of man's awakening as a physical creature. He becomes fully operational in his physical body, and while awake can only sense the dream body that had earlier been so real to him. He now encounters his experience from within a body that must be fed, clothed, protected from the elements—a body that is subject to gravity and to earth's laws. He must use physical muscles to walk from place to place. He sees himself suddenly, in a leap of comprehension, as existing for the first time not only apart from the environment, but apart from all of earth's other creatures.

The sense of separation is, in those terms, initially almost shattering. Yet [man] is to be the portion of nature that views itself with perspective. He is to be the part of nature that will specialize, again, in the self-conscious use of concepts. *(Louder:)* He will grow the flower of the intellect—a flower that must have its deep roots buried securely within the earth, and yet a flower that will

224

send new psychic seeds outward, not only for itself but for the rest of nature, of which it is a part.

But man looked out and felt himself suddenly separate and amazed at the aloneness. Now he must find food, where before his dream body did not need physical nourishment. Before, man had been neither male nor female, combining the characteristics of each, but now the physical bodies also specialized in terms of sexuality. Man has to physically procreate. Some lost ancient legends emphasized in a clearer fashion this sudden sexual division. By the time the Biblical legend came into being, however, historical events and social beliefs were transformed into the Adam and Eve version of events.

On the one hand, man did indeed feel that he had fallen from a high estate, because he remembered that earlier freedom of dream reality—a reality in which the other creatures were still to some degree (underlined) immersed.³ Man's mind, incidentally, at that point had all the abilities that you now assign to it: the great capacity for contrast of imagination and intellect, the drive for objectivity and for subjectivity (softly), the full capacity for the development of language—a keen mind that was as brilliant in any caveman, say, as it is in any man on a modern street.

(9:35.) But if man felt suddenly alone and isolated, he was immediately struck by the grand variety of the world and its creatures. Each creature apart from himself was a new mystery. He was enchanted also by his own subjective reality, the body in which he found himself, and by the differences between himself and others like him, and the other creatures. He instantly began to explore (pause), to categorize, to point out and to name the other creatures of the earth as they came to his attention.

In a fashion (underlined), it was a great creative and yet cosmic game that consciousness played with itself, and it did represent a new kind of awareness, but I want to emphasize that each version of All That Is is unique. Each has its purpose, though that purpose cannot be easily defined in your terms. Many people ask, for example: "What is the purpose of my life?" Meaning: "What am I meant to do?" but the purpose of your life, and each life, is in its being (intently). That being may include certain actions, but the acts themselves are only important in that they spring out of the essence of your life, which simply by being is bound to fulfill its purposes.

(Long pause in a steady, rather fast delivery.) Man's dream body is still with him, of course, but the physical body now obscures it. The dream body cannot be harmed while the physical one can —as man quickly found out as he transformed his experience largely from one to the other. In the dream body man feared nothing. The dream body does not die. It exists before and after physical death. In their dream bodies men had watched the spectacle of animals "killing" other animals, and they saw the animals' dream bodies emerge unscathed.

They saw that the earth was simply changing its forms, but that the identity of each unit of consciousness survived—and so, although they saw the picture of death, they did not recognize it as the death that to many people now seems an inevitable end.

[Men] saw that there must be an exchange of physical energy for the world to continue. They watched the drama of the "hunter" and the "prey," seeing that each animal contributed so that the physical form of the earth could continue—but the rabbit eaten by the wolf survived in a dream body that men knew was its true form. When man "awakened" in his physical body, however, and specialized in the use of its senses, he no longer perceived the released dream body of the slain animal running away, still cavorting on the hillside. He retained memory of his earlier knowledge, and for a considerable period he could now and then recapture that knowledge. He became more and more aware of his physical senses, however: Some things were definitely pleasant and some were not. Some stimuli were to be sought out, and others avoided, and so over a period of time he translated the pleasant and the unpleasant into rough versions of good and evil.

Basically, what made him feel good was good. He was gifted with strong clear instincts that were meant to lead him toward his own greatest development, to his own greatest fulfillment, in such a way that he also helped to bring about the highest potentials of all of the other species of consciousness *(intently)*. His natural impulses were meant to provide inner directives that would guide him in just such a direction, so that he sought what was the best for himself and for others.

(Heartily:) End of dictation.

(9:58. After giving a few notes for Jane and me, Seth ended the

session at 10:13 P.M. "I can't remember the session now, but I think I covered everything I got from him yesterday and today," Jane said.)

NOTES: SESSION 899

1. Yesterday Jane finished typing the final draft of Chapter 2 for *God of Jane*. All of her work on the book is still plastic, however. As she wrote in her journal today: "Great day . . . began typing Chapter Three of *God of Jane* and the book really started taking off; I'm just tickled; I did great, and added lots of on-the-spot stuff as I typed. Did so well I almost forgot to break for afternoon exercises."

That's the way she revels in her creative activities. Yet she has room for even more expression, for she also noted: "Feel like I'd like to do something different again. Small creative writing class? Something with tapes?"

Personally, I like to have all the hard preliminary work done before I start typing a manuscript, so that I can race right through it with few changes.

2. Today is day 95 of the taking of the American hostages in Iran (on November 4, 1979). Any expectations that our country had of the hostages' early release have long since dissipated. I can only hint at the enormously complicated situation involving the whole Middle East these days. The generally explosive predicament in Iran, for example, has been considerably aggravated by Russia's invasion of Afghanistan over the recent Christmas season: Now the unbending revolutionary government of Iran, following its own fanatical interpretation of the Moslem religion, must contend with at least an implied threat on its eastern border as the godless Russians occupy Afghanistan. Jane and I find it fascinating to think about—to attempt to trace—some of the ways by which the overall consciousness of the United States continually becomes involved with—*entwined with*—the consciousnesses of adversaries like Russia and Iran: Such consciousnesses, once created, continue to grow and to complicate themselves in new ways within our concept of "time." Obviously, on an even larger scale of activity, the consciousnesses

of all the nations of our world contribute to the challenges and dilemmas swirling around the Iranian situation.

As for the nuclear power generating plant on Three Mile Island, engineers have not yet been able to enter the contaminated containment building housing the reactor—Unit No. 2— which came so close to a meltdown of its uranium fuel rods on March 28, 1979. Such an entry, to gather radiological data, is now planned for this April (1980). To insure the safety of workers, however, over 55,000 curies of radioactive krypton-85 gas will first be vented from the containment building into the atmosphere.

This prospect has already aroused much opposition—it's another example of the psychological stress placed upon the population of southeastern Pennsylvania. Studies involving the psychology of the fear of nuclear power, irrational and otherwise, are growing, so once again consciousness proliferates and explores itself in new ways: When will a meltdown happen? people ask, even though some of the more than 200 nuclear power plants around the world have operated for more than 20 years now, without a single death caused by radiation. These studies are accompanied by the horde of challenges surrounding the still unresolved, unglamorous disposal of a constantly growing accumulation of nuclear waste products.

(And I wonder: In case of a meltdown, somewhere, sometime, and the release of radiation into the atmosphere, how will the consciousnesses of uranium and plutonium fit into the overall consciousness engendered by that accident? In ordinary terms, synthetic plutonium is probably the most toxic substance on earth. Its 15 known isotopes have radioactive half-lives of from one-fifth of a second to about 88 million years. Pu^{238}, a high-quality isotope consumed in commercial nuclear reactors, has a half-life of about 88 years. [A bomb-quality isotope, Pu^{239}, has a half-life of around 24,400 years.])

3. At first, as I typed this session from my notes a couple of days later, I thought that Seth had contradicted himself here, for earlier in the session he'd stated that "the other creatures of the earth actually awakened before man did, and relatively speaking, their dream bodies formed themselves into physical ones before man's did." Then I came to think that Seth actually meant

that man has consciously separated himself from his dream body to a *greater degree* than other creatures have—that even though those other entities became "physically effective" before man did, they still retain a greater awareness of their dream bodies than man does. I'll try to remember to ask Seth to elaborate upon this point, although I also think he alludes to it later in this session.

SESSION 900, FEBRUARY 11, 1980
8:47 P.M. MONDAY

(At first Jane and I thought of calling this session a deleted one—but its subject matter fits into Dreams *too well for us to do that.*

After supper Jane reread my accounts of my dream of last Saturday morning. February 9, and of my waking experience the next evening.[1] Both events had involved intense perceptions of color and/or light, and I'd told Jane that anything Seth cared to say about them would be most welcome. I'm especially intrigued by any similarities between my two adventures and the near-death experiences we've been reading about lately. In those NDE's, as they're called, people have often reported encounters with intense white light. I hadn't been near death during my own experiences, certainly, but I do feel that through them I'd glimpsed ever so slightly that "light of the universe" that's been so eagerly sought for—and sometimes reported—throughout history.

This morning I tried to rough-in a small oil painting of myself standing before one of those walls of crystal color I'd seen in the dream. I had no trouble with the self-portrait, but still ended up quite frustrated. I'd anticipated the failure to some extent: With mere oil paint I just couldn't match the iridescence of that dream wall of light and color. By session time I was caught. Should I junk the half-finished painting, or try to complete it? I could always make another attempt tomorrow morning, of course, but for some reason I was rebelling at admitting my failure today.

As Seth came through, Mitzi was playing her favorite game—again and again knocking her paper-ball toy down the steps leading into the celler from the kitchen, then racing down after it and carrying it back upstairs.)

(Whispering:) Good evening.

("Good evening, Seth.")

Now: Topic: The light.

There is, as I have told you, an inner *(pause)* "psychological" universe, from which your own emerges, and that inner universe is also the source of Framework 2 as well. It is responsible for all physical effects, and is behind all physical "laws."

It is not just that such an inner universe is different from your own, but that any real or practical explanation of its reality would require the birth of an entirely new physics—and such a development would first of all necessitate the birth of an entirely new philosophy. The physics cannot come first, you see.

It is not [so much] that such developments are beyond man's capacity as it is that they involve manipulations impossible to make for all practical purposes, from his present standpoint. He could theoretically move to a better vantage point in the twinkling of an eye, relatively speaking, but for now we must largely use analogies. Those analogies may lead you or Ruburt, or a few others, to a more advantageous vantage point, so that certain leaps become possible—but those leaps, you see, are not just leaps of intellect but of will and intuition alike, fused and focused.

The light of your questions *(pause)* is, in its way (underlined), an apport from that other inner universe. In your world light has certain properties and limits. It is physically perceived by the eyes, and to a far lesser degree by the skin itself. In your world light comes from the sun. It has been an exterior source, and in your world light and dark certainly appear to be opposites.

Ruburt glimpsed some of the principles involved when you were at [your downtown apartments] on several occasions—once when he tried to write a poem about the comprehensions that simply would not be verbalized.[2] I do not know how to explain some of this, but in your terms there is (underlined) light within (underlined) darkness. Light has more manifestations than its physical version *(intently)*, so that even when it may not be physically manifested there is light everywhere, and that light is the source of your physical version and its physical laws. In a manner of speaking, light itself forms darkness. Each unit of consciousness, whatever its degree, is, again, composed of energy—and that energy manifests itself with a kind of light that is not physically perceived: a light that is basically, now, far more intense than any physical variety, and a light from which all colors emerge.

The colors of which you are aware represent a very small portion of light's entire spectrum, just physically speaking, but the spectrum you recognize represents only one inconceivably small portion of other fuller spectrums—spectrums that exist outside of physical laws.

(Pause at 9:06.) So-called empty spaces, either in your living room between objects, or the seemingly empty spaces between stars, are physical representations—or misrepresentations—for all of space is filled with the units of consciousness, alive with a light from which the very fires of life are lit.

The physical senses have to screen out such perceptions. That light, however, is literally everywhere at once, and it is a "knowing light," as Ruburt's [William] James perceived.[3]

Now: On certain occasions, sometimes near the point of death, but often simply in conscious states outside of the body, man is able to perceive that kind of light. In some out-of-body experiences Ruburt, for example, saw colors more dazzling than any physical ones, and you saw the same kind of colors in your dream. They are a part of your inner senses' larger spectrum of perception, and in the dream state you were not relying upon your physical senses at all.

In that dream your worries were initially reflected—worries that your friend Floyd has also encountered on his own about virility and age,[4] so you saw the two of you in a five-and-ten-cent store, simply representing the world of commerce, where items are sold: Did you still have a value in that world? Were you still virile? You were each to take your test. *(Pause.)* Others saw you but were unconcerned, showing that the concern was your own, but also expressing the feeling that the world might not really care.

Instead of the test, you are greeted with a vision of the shimmering glass with its glowing colors and prisms, rich and intricate, representing the true source of life and sexuality itself—the vast multidimensional mosaic of which sexuality is but one facet. You were viewing your representation of the many-faceted light of your own being.

Now: The lamplight episode. Here you did as you supposed. You viewed that inner light, but the lampshades had two purposes: one, as you surmised, to give you a comforting image, literally to shade your eyes. Ruburt was correct, however, in seeing the connection between the lampshades and the Nazi experiments *(in World War II)* with human skin. The movie *(on television last night)*, about cloning and Nazi atrocities, had made you wonder about the nature of life once again, and man's immortality. The connection with cloning came out in the lampshades made of *(human)* skins, in the old news stories—though your lampshades merely stood for those, and were of fabric. The connection was beneath, however, and also represented your feeling that even those people tortured to death did live again. They were not extinguished. Their consciousnesses were indeed like bulbs, say, turned on in new lamps. The lights connected life and death, then. The lights also represented pure knowing.

(9:26.) When I speak of an inner psychological universe, it is very difficult to explain what I mean. *(Pause.)* In that reality, however, psychological activity is not limited by any of the physical laws that you know. Thought, for example, has properties that you do not perceive—properties that not only affect matter, but that form their own greater patterns outside of your reality. These follow their own, say, laws of physics. You add on to, or build up your own reality, in other dimensions throughout your physical life.

(Long pause.) The paintings that you have envisioned, for example, exist there, and they are every bit as real as the paintings in your studio. I am not speaking symbolically here. There is indeed light that you do not see, sound that you do not hear, sensation that you do not feel. All of these belong to the realm of the inner senses. The inner senses represent your true powers of perception. They represent, say, your native nonphysical perceptive "equipment." The physical senses are relatively easy to distinguish: You know what you see from what you hear. If you close your eyes, you do not see.

The inner senses, though I have in the past described them by separating their functions and characteristics, basically operate together in such a way that in your terms it would be highly difficult to separate one from the others. They function with a perfect spontaneous order, aware of all synchronicities. In that psychological universe, then, it is possible for entities "to be everywhere at once," aware of everything at once. Your world is composed of such "entities"—the units of consciousness that form your body. The kinds of conscious minds that you have cannot hold that kind of information.

(9:44.) Give us a moment. . . . *(A one-minute pause.)* These units of consciousness, however, add themselves up to form psychological beings far greater in number than, say, the number of stars in [your] galaxy *(over 400 billion of them)*, and each of those psychological formations has its own identity—its own soul if you prefer—its own purpose in the entire fabric of being.

That is as far as we can carry that for this evening. We need some new carriers for the concepts. But the light itself represents that inner universe, and the source of all comprehension.

End of session.

("Can I say something?")

You may indeed.

("I didn't get far with my little painting this morning.")

You felt inferior to your own comprehension, for one thing. The colors were more brilliant than any physical ones, and so in a fashion you ended up trying a too-literal translation—too literal because a real translation would require colors and even symbols that you do not have on a physical basis. If you think of those colors as being inside you, even in your own cellular comprehension, then you will not be so careful. Do you follow me?

("Yes.")

You were too careful.

("Yes.")

End of session.

("Thank you.")

(9:59 P.M. Her eyes closed, Jane sat quietly in her rocker for several moments before leaving her trance state. Usually she's "out of it" at once. "I kept waiting there, as though I was at the edge of something, and trying to get over it into something new. As though I was free-sailing. . . . My God, it was short enough," she exclaimed as she looked at the clock for the first time. Actually, the session had lasted 1 hour 12 minutes —slightly longer than her average time of 1 hour 7 minutes for the last five sessions. Jane's sense of time had been elongated while she spoke for Seth: "I feel like I was really far . . . like you were getting more than you could translate, like you were right on the edge of something. . . ."

I told her that Seth's idea of considering the colors in my dream as part of my cellular structure is an excellent one.

A note: I can add that I didn't give up on my dream painting after all. The morning after this session was held I repainted that still-wet wall of colors I'd struggled with the day before. I managed to carry off the painting this time—merely giving impressions of the colors and foregoing their fantastic intensities and patterns. Next, I painted a small oil of the lights emitted by the two table lamps in my waking experience. The practice on the dream painting helped: This time I was able to hint more easily at the great combined radiance of those lights. However, I've learned that contending with the light of the universe can be a humbling task indeed. . . .)

NOTES: SESSION 900

1. I'll report only the portions of the dream that relate to my perceptions of light and color, but will describe in full my waking experience of the next evening. Both accounts are revised from my dream notebook:

"My friend, Floyd Waterman (I'll call him), and I were in a five-and-ten-cent store in Sayre, my old hometown. We were both dressed, but knew that we had to take some sort of tests for sexual potency. We stood near the large plate-glass windows at the front of the store—quite exposed for all to see, in other words, including those eating at nearby tables, yet no one seemed to be paying any attention to us. . . . Floyd had to take the test first, stepping into a little booth such as a cashier might use. As I waited to go next I turned to look out the front windows—and suddenly found myself surrounded on three sides by walls of the most beautiful floor-to-ceiling, intricate and colorful latticework of diamond-shaped glass crystals I could possibly imagine. I cannot describe the intrinsic shimmer and sparkle of those faceted walls, shining and vibrating in warm oranges, browns, yellows, reds, and violets. Each segment of each color was held within a very thin black frame, as on a much cruder scale the pieces of a stained-glass window can be contained by channeled lead strips. I can still 'see' those dream lights and colors as I write this account several hours later, after describing them to Jane. I've thought of trying to do a painting of my best dream images of all time . . . yet wonder how I can do it. . . ."

And for my experience of the next evening:

"Jane and I went to bed at about 1:15 A.M., after watching a movie on television. Subject: World War II. Jane lay quietly on my right, her back to me. As I rested face up in a very pleasant and peaceful state, waiting to enter the sleep state, I became aware of two extremely bright lights shining off to my right, beyond Jane's form but within my peripheral vision. I knew, or saw, that these lights came from ordinary table lamps with columnar shades of white fabric, and that they sat on a round oak table like the one in our living room. The shade of the closest lamp was fatter and taller than its companion's, but this didn't seem to matter: I soon realized that both lights were supernally bright—so strong, indeed, that although I was very tempted to turn my head to look straight at them, I refrained because I wasn't sure I could stand facing them. I understood that the lampshades were both comforting and protective, however, and I felt no fear, or even unease, at this adventure. I knew that I wasn't dreaming, that the experience was most unusual. I also knew that by an act of will I could 'swing' the lights around in front of me if I wanted to, and I tried enough of this to verify that it was possible: As they moved the lights began to grow even more powerful—enough to quickly convince me that I didn't want to confront their glare full blast, even with the shades.

"I'd been at once reminded of my dream of the night before, in which I'd seen many colors. But while these lights were 'only' white, they were both warm and cool, indescribable in their intensity, and really contained all colors.

"I enjoyed the experience for some little time as Jane slept beside me, then let myself drift off to sleep."

The next morning Jane had quite an unexpected insight to add to my own understanding of what those lampshades stood for. I was surprised. Seth discussed her connection later in this session.

2. We moved from our downtown apartments into the hill house almost five years ago (in March 1975), but Jane thinks she tried to write the poem Seth referred to several years before that. (She began speaking for Seth late in 1963.) I have no memory of her struggling with such a poem. I was most curious to see it so that I could quote a bit of it here. Jane has stacks of journals, poetry notebooks, manuscripts, and loose notes of all

kinds, but neither of us could dig out what we wanted. Very frustrating! We hadn't been as careful then about dating our work as we are now. "But I know I didn't throw out whatever I did on that poem," Jane said. One of us will probably find it someday—while looking for something else.

3. See the passages following Jane's entry for March 31, 1977, in Chapter 10 of her *The After Death Journal of an American Philosopher: The World View of William James.*

4. It took me a while to realize that Seth had made a most interesting statement here—implying that somehow I'd picked up Floyd's worries about his age and virility. Floyd, Jane, and I are good friends, and he's well acquainted with our work. He's a few years younger than I am (I'm 60), but as far as I can remember the two of us haven't discussed such matters, even jokingly, Consciously, I enjoy and appreciate my age and virility each day without being concerned about them, yet my dream certainly revealed that on other levels I'm at least speculating about such issues. It's easy to say those cares represent negative beliefs, but I think much more than that is involved—universal questions, actually, that all men and women have chosen to contend with in physical life.

SESSION 901, FEBRUARY 18, 1980
9:20 P.M. MONDAY

(No session, regular or deleted, was held last Wednesday evening, February 13. On that day Tam Mossman of Prentice-Hall called Sue Watkins to ask her permission to publish Conversations With Seth *in two volumes; Sue's account of Jane's ESP classes is now too long for a single book. Actually, then, Sue finished Volume 1 while in Florida last month. Tam plans to have the first volume in the stores this October, and is scheduling Volume 2 for publication in January 1981.*

Jane has been feeling much better in recent days as far as her physical "symptoms" go; she's had some good spontaneous relaxation periods, and her walking has improved considerably. Her creative output also goes well. She's been working on "I Am Alive Again," her longest poem for If We Live Again. *When she lay down for a nap yesterday afternoon she picked up from Seth hints of subjects he's going to discuss in* Dreams: *"man migrations," and "inside and outside cues" as pertaining to man's consciousness. She hopes Seth will go into that material tonight. This afternoon she finished typing her final version of Chapter 5 for* God of Jane.

Today I visited our optometrist—with results that Jane and I find most intriguing.[1])

(Whispering:) Good evening.

("Good evening.")

Dictation. *(Long pause.)* At the time of this awakening man did experience, then, some sense of separation from his dream body, and from his own inner reality—the world of his dreams —but he was still far more aware of that subjective existence than you are now.

The <u>practical</u> nature of his own dreams was also more apparent, for again, his dreams sent him precise visions as to where food might be located, for example, and for some centuries there were human migrations of a kind that now you see the geese make. All of those journeys followed literal paths that were given as information in the dream state. [But] more and more man began to identify himself with his exterior environment. He began to think of his inner ego almost as if it were a <u>stranger</u> to himself. It became his version of the soul, and there seemed to be a duality—a self who acted in the physical universe, and a separate spiritlike soul that acted in an immaterial world.

This early man (and early woman) regarded the snake as the most sacred and basic, most secretive and most knowledgeable of all creatures. In that early experience it seemed, surely, that the snake was a living portion of the earth, rising from the bowels of the earth, rising from the hidden source of all earth gods. Men watched snakes emerge from their holes with wonder. The snake was then—<u>in your terms, now</u> (underlined)—both a feminine and masculine symbol. It seemed to come from the womb of the earth, and to possess the earth's secret wisdom. Yet also, in its extended form particularly, it was the symbol of the penis. It was important also in that it shed its skin, as man innately knew he shed his own bodies.

(Pause at 9:31.) All units of consciousness, whatever their degree, possess purpose and intent. They are endowed with the desire for creativity, and to increase the <u>quality</u> of existence.

They have the capacity to respond to multitudinous cues. There is a great elasticity for action and mobility, so that, for example, in man his conscious experience can actually be put together in an almost limitless number of ways.

The inner and outer egos do not have a cementlike relationship, but can interrelate with each other in almost infinite fashions, still preserving the reality of physical experience, but varying the accents put upon it by the inner areas of subjective life. Even the bare-seeming facts of history are experienced far differently according to the symbolic content within which they are inevitably immersed. A war, in your terms, can be practically experienced as a murderous disaster, a triumph of savagery— or as a sublime victory of the human spirit over evil.

(Long pause, then very intently:) We will return to the subject of war later on. I want to mention here, however, that man is not basically endowed with "warlike characteristics." He does not naturally murder. He does not naturally seek to destroy his own life or [the lives of] others. There is no battle for survival—but while you project such an idea upon natural reality, then you will read nature, and your own experiences with it, in that fashion.

Man does have an instinct and a desire to live, and he has an instinct and a desire to die. The same applies to other creatures. In his life [each] man is embarked upon a cooperative venture with his own species, and with the other species, and dying he also in that regard acts in a cooperative manner, returning his physical substance to the earth. *(Pause.)* Physically speaking, man's "purpose" is to help enrich the quality of existence in all of its dimensions. Spiritually speaking, his "purpose" is to understand the qualities of love and creativity, to intellectually and psychically understand the sources of his being, and to lovingly create other dimensions of reality of which he is presently unaware. *(Pause.)* In his thinking, in the quality of his thoughts, in their motion, he is indeed experimenting with a unique and a new kind of reality, forming other subjective worlds which will in their turn grow into consciousness and song, which will in their turn flower from a dream dimension into other ones. Man is learning to create new worlds. In order to do so he has taken on many challenges.

(Long pause.) You all have physical parents. Some of you have

physical children as well—but you will all "one day" also be the mental parents of dream children who also waken in a new world, and look about them for the first time, feeling isolated and frightened and triumphant all at once. All worlds have an inner beginning. All of your dreams somewhere waken, but when they do they waken with the desire for creativity themselves, and they are born of an innocent new intent. That which is in harmony with the universe, with All That Is, has a natural inborn impetus that will dissolve all impediments. It is easier, therefore, for nature to flourish than not.

Take your break.

(9:56 to 10:09.)

You are aware of such activities now as automatic speaking and automatic writing, and of sleepwalking. These all give signs in modern times of some very important evidence in man's early relationship with the world and with himself.

Sleepwalking was once, in that beginning, a very common experience—far more so than now—in which the inner self actually taught the physical body to walk, and hence presented the newly emerged physically oriented intellect from getting in its own way, asking too many questions that might otherwise impede the body's smooth spontaneous motion.

In the same fashion man is born with an inbuilt propensity for language, and for the communication of symbols through pictures and writing. He spoke first in an automatic fashion that began in his dreams. In a fashion (underlined), you could almost say that he used language before he consciously understood it *(quietly)*. It is not just that he learned by doing, but that the doing did the teaching. Again, lest there be a sharply inquiring intellect, wondering overmuch about how the words were formed or what motions were necessary, his drawing was in the same way automatic. You might almost say—almost—that he used the language *(pause)* "despite himself." Therefore, it possessed an almost magical quality, and the "word" was seen as coming directly from God.

Give us a moment . . . Separately:

(10:19. After giving the material I've excerpted for Note 1, Seth said good night at 10:30 P.M.)

NOTE: SESSION 901

1. In a simplified account: When I was a youngster my mother took me to see our family optometrist. My parents had known him for years. With the best of intentions, that kindly gentleman put bifocals on me. They weren't very strong—but once the habit was set I wore glasses without protest for the next 40 years or so. It wasn't until Jane began coming through with the ideas embodied in the Seth material that I began to question my "need" for glasses. Without being concerned about what I was doing, I began to stop wearing them constantly. The glasses got in the way when I wrote and painted. I had to wear them when driving, though, because my driver's licence bore an "x" opposite "corrective lenses." Other than that, I usually put them on only when I felt tired. At the same time, I avoided giving myself the negative suggestion that my eyes still weren't perfect, even with my improving beliefs.

Last week I received from our current optometrist (whom I'll call John Smith) his standard notice that two years have passed since my glasses were changed. I told myself to ignore it, yet began to feel a sense of strain whether or not I wore the glasses. I thought the power of suggestion was operating. Because of a cancellation I got a quick appointment to see John this afternoon —and received a very pleasant surprise, for his examination revealed that my vision has <u>improved</u> since the last prescription. The glasses I now have are getting to be too strong. Out of habit, I'd thought the opposite was the case. John too was surprised; he double-checked his figures to make sure he was right before ordering the weaker lenses. Once John had assembled his pheropter, or lens unit, the test lenses making up the new prescription, my vision checked out at 20/15—better than the so-called normal 20/20. That score is a considerable improvement over anything I'd ever achieved before, with or without glasses.

Next, when he examined my eyes for glaucoma, John's tonometer gave readings that were midway in the normal range for eye tension, and a point or so better than they had been two years ago. "I'll take those," he exclaimed. "Nice and low." I felt a distinct lift of pleasure as I left his office.

"I must be doing something right," I said to Jane as I explained the situation to her. And Seth addressed some very interesting comments to me in the private portion of tonight's session:

"You wanted some affirmation of your body's vitality, of its resilience and recuperative energies. You also wanted some re-assurance that you could operate as an artist as long as you chose in this life. You used the incident of the optometrist's notice to give yourself a very fine lesson, for in the back of your mind you did indeed worry and wonder that your eyes were becoming tired. Under usual circumstances, those "symptoms" would be interpreted as signs of difficulty. You discovered instead that the so-called symptoms are signs that your glasses have become too strong because your eyesight has not simply held its own, but most remarkably improved, and in a way this is medically de-monstrable.

"They [your eyes] have improved because you are indeed learning to relax about yourself more, and the improvement occurs first of all in that area of your main interest—your work—but it represents what is an overall time of regeneration. Your eyes do not exist alone in your head."

(A note added later: On my last New York State Visual Acuity Report, which he filled out in May 1983, John Smith wrote that I passed the test for driving without wearing glasses [combined Snellen test score 20/30]. However, when the postman delivered my new driver's license—good for four years—that "x" was still there opposite "corrective lenses." I haven't yet taken the time to straighten out that bureaucratic tangle.)

SESSION 902, FEBRUARY 20, 1980
9:08 P.M. WEDNESDAY

(Four months ago I wrote in Note 1 for Session 885 that through a series of misunderstandings the people at Ankh-Hermes, a publishing company in Holland, had violated their contract with Prentice-Hall by issuing a condensed translation of Seth Speaks. *Our editor at Prentice-Hall, Tam Mossman, insisted that Ankh-Hermes publish another, full-length edition of Jane's book in the Dutch language. Now Tam has just forwarded to us correspondence showing that Ankh-Hermes will do this—the new publishing date for* Seth Spreekt *is still uncertain, however.*

Tonight, Seth suggested that "portions of this session can be appended to the book," meaning Dreams, *but I found it easier to offer most of his generalized material verbatim while eliminating his information on one of my dreams.)*

Now: a few remarks on the eye episode.

You were presented—or rather you presented yourself—with a prime example of the abilities of the natural person. I said something once to the effect that so-called miracles were simply the result of nature unimpeded, and certainly that is the case. You are presented now, in the world, with a certain picture of a body and its activities, and that picture seems (underlined) very evidential. It seems to speak for itself.

Instead you are presented, of course, with a picture of man's body as it reflects, and is affected by, man's beliefs. Doctors expect vision to [begin to] fail, for example, after the age of 30, and there are countless patient records that "prove" that such disintegration is indeed a biological fact.

Your beliefs tell you, again, that the body is primarily a mechanism—a most amazing machine, but a machine *(louder)*, without its own purpose, without any intent, a mindless assembly plant of assorted parts that simply happened to grow together in a certain prescribed fashion. Science says that there is no will, yet it assigns to nature the will to survive—or rather, a will-less instinct to survive. To that extent it does admit (underlined) that the machine of the body "intends" to insure its own survival— but a survival which has no meaning beyond itself. And because [the body] is a machine, it is expected to decay after so much usage.

In that picture consciousness has little part to play. In man's very early history, however, and in your terms for centuries after the "awakening," as described in our book, people lived in good health for much longer periods of time—and in certain cases they lived for several centuries.[1] No one had yet told them that this was impossible, for one thing. Their sense of wonder in the world, their sense of curiosity, creativity, and the vast areas of fresh mental and physical exploration, kept them alive and strong. For another thing, however, elders were highly necessary and respected for the information they had acquired about the world. They were needed. They taught the other generations.

In those times great age was a position of honor that brought along with it new responsibility and activity. The senses did not fade in their effectiveness, and it is quite possible biologically for all kinds of regenerations of that nature to occur.

(To me:) You spoke today, or this evening, about some [world] statesmen who are not young at all, and men and women who do not only achieve *(pause)*, but who open new horizons in their later years. They do so because of their private capacities, and also because they are answering the world's needs, and in ways that in many cases a younger person could not.

In your society age has almost been considered a dishonorable state. Beliefs about the dishonor of age often cause people to make the decision—sometimes quite consciously—to bring their own lives to an end before the so-called threshold is reached. Whenever, however, the species needs the accumulated experience of its own older members, that situation is almost instantly reversed and people live longer.

Some in your society feel that the young are kept out of life's mainstream also, denied purposeful work, their adolescence prolonged unnecessarily. As a consequence some young people die for the same reason: They believe that the state of youth is somehow dishonorable. They are cajoled, petted, treated like amusing pets sometimes, diverted with technology's offerings but not allowed to use their energy. There were many unfortunate misuses of the old system of having a son follow in his father's footsteps, yet the son at a young age was given meaningful work to do, and felt a part of life's mainstream. He was needed.

(9:34.) The so-called youth culture, for all of its seeming (underlined) exaggerations of youth's beauty and accomplishments, actually ended up putting down youth, for few could live up to that picture. Often, then, both the young and the old felt left out of your culture. Both share also the possibility of accelerated creative vitality—activity that the elder great artists, or the elder great statesmen, have always picked up and used to magnify their own abilities. There comes a time when the experiences of the person in the world click together and form a new clearer focus, provide a new psychological framework from which his or her greatest capacities can emerge to form a new synthesis. But in your society many people never reach that

point—or those who do are not recognized for their achievements in the proper way, or for the proper reasons. . . .

Man's will to survive includes a sense of meaning and purpose, and a feeling for the quality (underlined) of life. You are indeed presented with an evidential picture that seems to suggest most vividly the "fact" of man's steady deterioration, and yet you are also presented with evidence to the contrary, even in your world, if you look for it.

Your Olympics,[2] on television, present you with evidence of the great capacity of the young human body. The contrast between the activity of those athletes, however, and the activity of the normal young person is drastic. *(Pause.)* You believe that the greatest training and discipline must be used to bring about such activity—but that seemingly extraordinary physical ability simply represents the inherent capacities of the human body. In those cases, the athletes through training are finally able to give a glimpse of the body's spontaneous abilities. The training is necessary because it is believed necessary *(all with emphasis).*

(9:53.) Again, in our material on suffering *(see the 895th session, for instance)*, I mentioned that illness serves purposes—that it has a face-saving quality in your society—so here I am speaking of the body's own abilities. In that light, the senses do not fade. Age alone never brought about any loss of physical agility, or of mental ability, or of desire. Death must come to every living person, yet the time and the means are basically up to each individual. Meaningful work is important at any age. You cannot content the aged entirely with hobbies any more than you can the young, but meaningful work means work that also has the exuberance of play, and it is that playful quality that contains within itself great propensities of a healing and creative nature.

In a fashion, now, your eyes improved their capacities, practically speaking, in a playful manner. The senses want to exceed themselves. They also learn "through experience." You have been painting more lately. Your eyes became more involved to that extent. Your eyes enjoy their part in that activity *(intently)*, as the ears, say, enjoy hearing. It is their purpose. Your own desire to paint joined with and reinforced your eyes' natural desire to see.

When [most of] you think of physical symptoms, of course, you regard your body with a deadly seriousness that to some extent impedes inner spontaneity. You lay your limiting beliefs upon the natural person.

Your dream[3] fits in here in its own fashion, for you see that the ship of life, so to speak, rides very swiftly and beautifully also beneath the conscious surface, traveling through the waters of the psyche. . . . You are progressing very well at under-the-surface levels. There were few impediments. You had clear sailing, so to speak, and the dream was indeed meant as an inner vision of your progress.

(10:02.) Now, portions of this session can be appended to the book.

("I was just going to ask you about doing that."

After discussing another dream of mine, Seth said good night at 10:11 P.M. "I felt so relaxed before the session I was like a dishrag," Jane said with a laugh. I told her the session was excellent, and that I'll be adding relevant parts of it to my dream notebook.)

NOTES: SESSION 902

1. Shades of the great ages given for those patriarchs in the Bible! That was my first thought when Seth told us that in ancient times certain people had "lived for several centuries." My second thought was to cut his statement out of this record entirely, so that Jane and I wouldn't have to contend with it at all. Jane wasn't upset by Seth's remark, and I could appreciate the humorous aspects of my own initial reactions—yet in all of the years he's been giving us material, Seth has never before made a reference to what seems like impossible longevities.

I checked several Bibles, a Biblical almanac, and a Biblical dictionary. But one has only to read Chapter 5 of Genesis to learn what great ages are given to Adam and nine of his descendants up to Noah, or the time of the Flood. Did Adam really live for 930 years, or Seth, the third son of Adam and Eve, for 912? (Why isn't Eve's age given in the Bible?) Enoch, the fifth elder listed after Seth, lived for a mere 365 years, but sired Methuselah, who at 969 years is the oldest individual recorded in the Bible. Methuselah was the father of Lamech (777 years), who was the father of Noah (950 years).

In Genesis 11, the listing of Abraham's ancestors begins after the Flood with the oldest son of Noah, Shem, living some 600 years. Generally, Abraham's forebears didn't live as long as Adam's descendants had, although after Shem their ages still ranged from 148 years to 460. Abraham himself was "only" 175 years old at his death.

During the little time we'd spent thinking about such matters, Jane and I had considered the Biblical accounts of such great ages to be simply wrong, badly distorted, or perhaps epochal— that is, Abraham's ancestors may be listed in the correct genealogical sequence, but with many gaps among the individuals named. Also, a given father-son relationship may have actually been one between a father and a great-great-grandson, for example. There are other epochal lists in the Bible.

Both of us thought that the long-lived individuals postulated by Seth had existed outside of the Biblical framework, however, and in truth far earlier historically. "Seth saying that makes perfect sense to me. It doesn't bother me," Jane said when I asked her what she thought of Seth's material. "You weren't encouraged to read the Bible even in Catholic grade school," she added. "We just didn't deal with it that much to worry about it. I never even read it through. . . ."

My questions about those ancient great ages led Seth to volunteer some more information in a couple of private sessions.

First: "In those early days men and women did live to ages that would amaze you today—many living to be several hundred years old. This was indeed due to the fact that their knowledge was desperately needed, and their experience. They were held in veneration, and they cast their knowledge into songs and stories that were memorized throughout the years. Beside this, however, their energy was utilized in a different fashion than yours is: They alternated between the waking and dream states, and while asleep they did not age as quickly. Their bodily processes slowed. Although this was true, their dreaming mental processes did not slow down. There was a much greater communication in the dream state, so that some lessons were taught during dreams, while others were taught in the waking condition. There was a greater and greater body of knowledge to be transmitted as physical existence continued, for they did not transmit private knowledge only, but the entire body of knowledge that belonged to the group as a whole."

Second: "The Bible is a conglomeration of parables and stories, intermixed with some <u>unclear</u> memories of much earlier times. The Bible that you recognize—or that is recognized—is not the first, however, but was compiled from several earlier ones as man tried to look back, so to speak, recount his past and predict his future. Such Bibles existed, not written down but carried orally, as mentioned some time ago, by the Speakers. It was only much later that this information was written down, and by then of course much had been forgotten. This is apart from the fact of tampering, or downright misinformation, as various factions used the material for their own ends."

Seth first discussed the Speakers, and their oral traditions, in Session 558 for November 5, 1970. See the Appendix of *Seth Speaks*.

2. The 13th Olympic Winter Games are being held at Lake Placid, New York.

3. This account of the dream I had this afternoon (February 20, 1980) is condensed from my dream notebook:

"In brilliant, limpid color: I dreamed that a ship—a freighter colored a warm gray and a rust-red-orange—sank in the ocean. I was underwater, to one side, and viewed everything as an observer. I watched the ship sink on an even keel through the blue-green water to the smooth yellow and tan and brown sandy ocean floor—but instead of settling motionless there the ship began to 'sail' or plow its way across the ocean bottom, almost as though it were a car moving along a road. I saw waves of sand gracefully rise up from the bow of the freighter. I saw no people or fish—just the ship, the ocean, and its floor, which was free of obstacles to the ship's easy passage. The fact that the ship could navigate that way underwater was a revelation to me, and I knew that in some way this boded well for my future. I was very pleased. The colors were beautiful. I'd really like to do a painting of this dream."

SESSION 903, FEBRUARY 25, 1980
9:16 P.M. MONDAY

(*As I type each session from my notes, I file it in one of two series of numbered three-ring binders. We're up to Volume 77 for the "regular" and book sessions, and Volume 22 for the private or "deleted" material. Here's the note Jane wrote this morning and inserted in Volume 77, where I'm keeping a few sheets of paper to record the next session: "Something from Seth over the weekend—only got a little—something about earth's grid of perception being so constructed that. . . . everything had to be created simultaneously or there would be 'holes' in the grid."*

Then as we sat for the session Jane told me that after supper tonight she'd picked up material from Seth "that I wasn't sure of because I didn't understand what he meant. . . ." Involved were her questions about mammals, species, subspecies, and other classifications of living creatures. I thought it obvious that her two latest intuitions from Seth were directly related—and that certain creative portions of her psyche never stopped "working." Quickly I tried to explain that in biology the science of classification is called taxonomy. I had only a little success delineating terms like "phylum" and "genus," since I didn't have a dictionary handy to refresh my own memory; however, I did help her understand that mammals aren't a subspecies of any other group, but are themselves a major class of warm-blooded creatures.

In view of Jane's own limited knowledge of the scientific vocabulary man has devised to classify just the multitude of living forms alone on our planet, it's very interesting that Seth used what I think is the correct popular terminology as he went through the session. Even so, however, he still added meanings of his own to some of those basic categories, or taxa.)

Good evening.

("Good evening, Seth.")

Dictation. *(Pause.)* The world as you know it exists as it does because you are yourself a living portion of a vast "conscious grid" of perception.

Every c-e-l-l *(spelled)*, in those terms, is a sender and a receiver. All of the larger divisions of life—the mammals, fish, birds, and so forth—are an integral part of that living gridwork. The picture of the world is not ony the result of those messages transmitted and received, however, but is also caused by the relationships between those messages. In your terms, then (underlined), all of life's large classifications were present "at the beginning of the world." Otherwise there would have been vast holes in that grid of perception that makes possible the very sensations of physical life.

In a manner of speaking (underlined), the physical universe is "transposed" upon another reality that must be its source. The world was and is created in dimensions outside of time, and outside of space as you understand it *(intently)*.

Other realities quite as legitimate as your own, quite as vital, quite as "real," coexist with your own, and in the terms of your understanding, "in the same space"—but of course in terms of your experience those spaces and realities would appear to be quite separate. No systems are closed, however, so that basically (underlined) the living grid of perception that causes one world or reality is also "wired into" all other such systems. There is a give-and-take between them.

(Pause at 9:30 in an intent delivery.) The grids of perception that compose your world give you the world picture as you (under-lined) experience it because your physical senses put you in a certain position within the entire grid. Animals, for example, while part of your experience, are also "tuned into" that grid at another level. The large classifications of mammals, fish, birds, men, reptiles, plants, and so forth, are [each] an integral part of that larger perceptive pattern—and that pattern (underlined) in those terms had to be complete even in the beginning of your time.

(9:35. As he's taken to doing lately, our cat Billy jumped up on the couch and ensconced himself in a ball tight against my left elbow as I took Jane's dictation.)

In various periods that "gridwork" might "carry more traffic" along certain circuits than at other periods, so that there has been some creative leeway allowed, particularly on the parts of the species that make up your larger classifications. There were always birds, for example, but in the great interplay of "interior" and exterior communication among all portions of this vast liv-ing system, there was a creative interplay that allowed for endless variations within that classification, and each other one.

Your technological communication system is a conscious con-struct—a magnificent one—but one that is based upon your innate knowledge of the inner, cellular communication between all species. Saying that, I am not robbing the intellect of its right to congratulate itself upon that technology.

(9:42.) The large classifications of life give you the patterns into which consciousness forms itself, and because those patterns seem relatively stable it is easy to miss the fact that they are filled

out, so to speak, in each moment with new energy. Man does not in his physical development pass through the stages supposedly followed by the hypothetical creature who left the water for the land to become a mammal—but each species does indeed have written within it the knowledge of "its past." Part of this, again, is most difficult to express, and I must try to fill out old words with new meanings. *(Pause.)* The reincarnational aspects of physical life, however, serve a very important purpose, providing an inner subjective background. Such a background is needed by every species.

Reincarnation exists, then, on the part of all species. Once a consciousness, however, has chosen the larger classification of its physical existences, it stays within that framework in its "reincarnational" existences. Mammals return as mammals, for example, but the species can change within that classification.[1] This provides great genetic strength, and consciousnesses in those classifications have chosen them because of their own propensities and purposes. The animals, for example, seem to have a limited range of physical activity in conscious terms, as you think of them. An animal cannot decide to read a newspaper. Newspapers are outside of its reality. Animals have a much wider range, practically speaking, in certain other areas. They are much more intimately aware of their environment, of themselves as separate from it, but also of themselves as a part of it *(intently)*. In that regard, their experience deals with relationships of another kind.

(Now Jane paused several times in her delivery—and I had the feeling that Seth was groping for the words that would make his meaning as clear to us as possible.)

These grids of perception "do not exist forever" in your dimension of time, for your dimension of time cannot hold anything that is outside it. Once a world exists, however, it becomes imprinted or stamped upon eternity, so that it exists in time and out of it "at once."

When you ask: "When did the world begin?" or "What really happened?" or "Was there a Garden of Eden?", you are referring to the world as you understand it, but in those terms there were earths in the same space before the earth you recognize existed,[2] and they began in the manner that I have given you in the early chapters of this book. The patterns for worlds—the patterns—continue in your time dimension, though in that time dimension those worlds must disappear, again, to continue "their existence outside of time." The patterns are filled out again.

(10:03.) In the case of earth the grid of perception is simply used differently, certain areas becoming prominent in some eras, and less prominent in others. Using your idea of time, I can only say that when the entire gestalt of consciousnesses that formed a particular earth have formed its reality to the best of their abilities, fulfilling their individual and mass capacities as far as possible, then they lovingly turn over that grid to others, and continue to take part in existences that are not physical in your terms. And that has happened many times.

Your tale about the Garden of Eden, then, is a legend about earth's last beginning. Each world is so cunningly constructed, again, that each consciousness, regardless of its degree, plays a vital part. And each of your actions, however inconsequential, becomes connected in one way or another—in one way or another—to each other reality and each other world (all with much emphasis).

Now in a manner of speaking—though I see that little time has passed in this living room where I speak with Ruburt's permission—we have transcended time to some extent this evening, for in what I have said there are indeed hints and illusions—cadences—that can, if you are ready, give you a feeling for existence as it is outside of time's context. Even to try and verbally present such material necessitates alterations involving perception, for while that gridwork appears quite stable to your senses, giving you a reliable picture of reality, this is also because you have trained yourselves to pick up certain signals only. Others at other levels are (underlined) available. You can (underlined) tune into cellular consciousness, for example.

Since this material must be comprehensible, Ruburt and I together form our own pathway of perceptions—he from his end and me from mine, so that we thread back and forth as if (underlined) through the wiring of some vast computer—but a computer that is alive.

(10:18.) End of dictation. End of session, unless you have a question.

("In a session I'm working with now for Mass Events—the 837th, *about the death of our cat, Billy One, a year ago—you said there wasn't any such thing as a cat consciousness, per se."[3] Seth nodded. "Tonight's session reminds me of that one. I see how they fit together.")*

They do indeed. Billy can be as he chooses—reincarnated into any species within his classification—as a mammal.

("That isn't going to run into the idea of transmigration, is it?" I was thinking that man in also a mammal.)

That is something else—that is, men being born as animals. I am including man as his own classification. Remember, however, there are also fragments, which [again] is something else.[4]

("Last Saturday morning I had what seemed to be two dreams that were identical and side by side, or at the same time. But they weren't within the other, as in a double dream—")

You know you can have more than one dream at a time. You can also experience versions of dreams of probable selves, but there will always be some point of contact—that is, there will always be a reason why you pick up such a dream. All of the dreams people have form a mass dream framework. Dreams exist at other levels, and physically of course they affect the body state. In such ways, the world's actions are worked out in mass dream communications that are at the same time public and private.

The country works out national concerns in that fashion. You think when you are asleep as well as when you are awake. But when you are asleep your thoughts have a richer dimensional cast: They are fattened by symbols and images.

End of session, and a fond good evening.

("Thank you very much. Good night.")

(10:25 P.M. "Gee, I have the feeling that we had a fantastic session," Jane enthused once she'd quickly left her trance state. I agreed. "I'm really making an effort to free myself from what science believes about evolution, or anything like that," she said. "That's what I got before the session—about animals reincarnating—and I thought: Oh, no. But it worked out okay." Neither of us could remember Seth stating flat out in any of his material that animals reincarnate, although he may have done so. "After all of this time," Jane mused, "he says that. . . ."

Condensed from my entry in my dream notebook for last Saturday morning, February 23, 1980:

"In color as usual: I can recall hardly any of these, but Jane suggested I write down what I can. I had two dreams, side by side. I believe they

were identical to each other, with the same people in each one and the
same resolution: a decision I reached in a new house on a hillside.
Involved was a male character in a well-known TV program. We saw
the show last night. I'm puzzling over how I could have had the dreams
beside each other, though; it seems they should have been in sequence. I
had no sense of one dream being inside *the other one, as in what I call*
the conventional double dream.")

Notes: Session 903

1. Seth is telling us a great deal here, on a subject Jane and I
have done little to explore with him. We'd like to know much
more. Mammals are animals of the highest class of warm-
blooded vertebrates, the Mammalia. They are usually hairy, and
their young are fed with milk secreted by the female. Dogs, cats,
manatees, lions, dolphins, apes, bats, whales, shrews, sloths, and
deer are mammals, to name just a few. I'm interpreting Seth to
say that a consciousness can choose to range among such forms.
However, for reasons to be hinted at later in the session, the
primate man (who is also a mammal) falls outside of Seth's
meaning here.

I found the scientific, systematic categorization of organisms
to be fascinating. For man alone the arrangement goes in this
descending order from the most inclusive: The kingdom Ani-
malia; phylum Chordata; class Mammalia; order Primates; family Hominidae; genus *Homo*; species name *Homo sapiens*;
common name Man.

2. Seth has told us almost from the beginning of the sessions
that in our terms the earth we know is but the latest in a series
of earths that have existed in the same "space," or "value climate
of psychological reality." According to Seth, however, much
more is involved. From Session 29, for February 26, 1964 (just
16 years ago): "There are endless planes upon your earth, or
rather endless planes occurring simultaneously with your earth.
Your solid earth is not a solid to inhabitants that would seem to
take up the same space as your earth. The idea of taking up the
same space is erroneous to begin with, but I don't see how we
can avoid such terms and still make any sense to you."

Jane and I, and Seth, hadn't cared for the trite term, "plane," even then. "The value climate of psychological reality" is one of Seth's attempts to originate something better. See Appendix 8 for Volume 1 of *"Unknown" Reality*.

3. I'm quoting portions from that 837th session in Note 2 for Session 840, in Chapter 6 of *Mass Events*.

4. Jane and I had always thought of transmigration (or metempsychosis) as meaning the birth of a human soul in just animal form. Actually, however, the term refers to the journey of the soul into *any* form, whether human, animal, or inanimate— thus differing from the ordinary doctrine of reincarnation, or rebirth into the same species. Various interpretations of transmigration are ancient in many cultures. Seth, in Session 705 for June 24, 1975, in Volume 2 of *"Unknown" Reality*: "There is no transmigration of souls, in which the entire personality of a person 'comes back' as an animal. Yet in the physical framework there is a constant intermixing, so that the [molecular components of the] cells of a man or woman may become the cells of a plant or an animal, and of course vice versa." In Note 2 for Session 840, in *Mass Events*, I'm quoting Seth from the 838th session for March 5, 1979: "I want to avoid tales of the transmigration of the souls of men to animals, say—a badly distorted version of something else entirely."

In the 4th session for December 8, 1963, the personality Jane and I had been contacting through the Ouija board, Frank Withers, spelled out with the board's pointer the message that he preferred to be called Seth—and Seth it's been ever since. Shortly before he announced himself as Seth, I'd asked Frank Withers if people were ever "reborn as animals." His answer was as direct as possible: "No." Next I asked him: "Is part of your psyche alive on earth now?" The answer was very strange to us at the time: "Very small part. I hardly miss it. I watch it but I leave it alone. It is a dog fragment." Frank Withers would not give us the location of this dog: "No."

Jane gave her first spoken answer for Seth early in the 8th session for December 15. Although she was by then receiving quick mental answers to many of our questions in the sessions, often she was still cautiously verifying those responses by having at least their beginnings spelled out letter by letter upon the board. (I'd started writing down everything in the very first session.)

In that 8th session Seth gave us more material on fragments: "In some submerged manner all fragments of a personality exist within an entity, with their own individual consciousnesses. They are not aware of the entity itself. . . . The entity operates its fragments in what you would call a subconscious manner, that is, without conscious direction. The entity gives the fragments independent life, then more or less forgets them. . . . Even thoughts, for instance, are fragments, though on a different plane." Then Jane dictated a key sentence: "Fragments of another sort, called personality fragments, operate independently, though under the auspices of the entity."

When I asked him in the same session about his evocative use of "fragment," Seth replied: "That is an original term with me, as far as I know." Within another couple of sessions, however, he began to let "fragment" semantically yield to other terminology as he continued developing his material in ever-deepening discussions of personalities and entities, reincarnation, time, dreams, and other related subjectes. I was surprised when he returned to the word here in *Dreams*. I've designed this note to supplement Jane's writing on fragments in *The Seth Material*, which Prentice-Hall published in 1970.

Some years after the 4th session was held, and without telling us anything else about the subject, Seth volunteered the information that his dog fragment had died. We haven't tried to pursue the matter with him.

SESSION 904, FEBRUARY 27, 1980
8:54 P.M. WEDNESDAY

(Jane called me at 8:15 for the session, but it was 8:50 before we actually sat for it. She wanted to start early because she was so relaxed: "Come on, Seth, if you want a session you'd better bail me out," she laughed. "But I feel him around. . . .")

Good evening.

("Good evening, Seth.")

(With a smile.) Dictation.

("Good.")

Now. *(Pause.)* The emergence of action within a time scheme is actually one of the most important developments connected with the beginning of your world.

The Garden of Eden story in its most basic sense refers to man's sudden realization that now he must <u>act within time</u>. His experiences must be neurologically structured. This immediately brought about the importance of choosing between one action and another, and made acts of decision highly important.

This time reference is perhaps the most important within earth experience, and the one that most influences all creatures. In experience or existence outside of time *(pause)*, there is no necessity to make certain kinds of judgments. In an out-of-time reference, theoretically speaking now, an infinite number of directions can be followed at once. Earth's time reference, however, brought to experience a new brilliant focus—and in the press of time, again, certain activities would be relatively more necessary than others, relatively more pleasant or unpleasant than others. Among a larger variety of possible actions, man was suddenly faced with a need to make choices, that within that context had not been made "before."

(9:02.) Speaking in terms of your time, early man still had a greater neurological leeway. There were alternate neurological pathways that, practically speaking, were more available then than now. They still exist now, but they have become like ghostly signals in the background of neurological activity.

(Jane paused, eyes closed, often seeming to grope for words while in trance.) This is, again, difficult to explain, but free will operates in all units of consciousness, regardless of their degree—but *(whispering)* it operates within the <u>framework</u> of that degree. Man possesses free will, but that free will operates only within man's degree—that is, his free will is somewhat contained by the frameworks of time and space.

He has free will to make any decisions that he is <u>able to make</u> *(intently)*. This means that his free will is contained, given meaning, focused, and framed by his neurological structure. He can only move, and he can only choose therefore to move, physically speaking, in certain directions in space and time. That time reference, however, <u>gives</u> (underlined) his free will meaning and a context in which to operate. We are speaking now of conscious decisions as you think of them.

(Long pause.) You can only make so many conscious decisions, or you would be swamped and caught in a constant dilemma of decision making. Time organizes the available choices that are to be made. The awakening mentioned earlier, then, found man rousing from his initial "dreaming condition," faced suddenly with the need for action in a world of space and time, a world in which choices became inevitable, a world in which he must choose among probable actions—and from an infinite variety of those choose which events he would physically actualize. This would be an almost impossible situation were the species—meaning each species—not given its own avenues of expression and activity, so that it is easier for certain species to behave in certain manners. And each species has its own overall characteristics and propensities that further help it define the sphere of influence in which it will exert its ability to make choices.

(9:17.) Each species is endowed also, by virtue of the units of consciousness that compose it, with an overall inner picture of the condition of each other species *(pause)*, and further characterized by basic impulses so that it is guided toward choices that best fulfill its own potentials for development while adding to the overall good of the entire world consciousness. This does not curtail free will any more than man's free will is curtailed because he must (underlined) grow from a fetus into an adult instead of the other way around.

The differences among all species are caused by this kind of organization, so that areas of choice are clearly drawn, and areas of free activity clearly specified. The entire gestalt of probable actions, therefore, is already focused to some degree in the species' differentiations. In the vast structure of probable activity, however, far more differentiation was still necessary, and this is provided for through the inner passageways of reincarnational existence.

Each person, for example, is born with his or her uniquely individual set of characteristics and abilities, likes and dislikes. Those serve to organize individual action in a world where an infinite number of probable roads are open—and here again, private impulses are basically meant to guide each individual toward avenues of expression and probable activities suited best to his or her development. They are meant, therefore, as aids to help organize action *(pause)*, and to set free will more effectively into motion. Otherwise, free will would be almost inoperble in practical terms: Individuals would be faced by so many choices that any decisions would be nearly impossible. Essentially, the individual would have no particular leaning toward any one action over any other *(all with emphasis)*.

"By the time" that the Garden of Eden tale reached your biblical stories, the entire picture had already been seen in the light of concepts about good and evil that actually appeared, in those terms, a long time later in man's development. The inner reincarnational structure of the human psyche is very important in man's physical survival. Children—change that to "infants"— dream of their past lives, remembering, for example, how to walk and talk. They are born with the knowledge of how to think, with the propensity for language. They are guided by memories that they later forget.

In time's reference, the private purposes of each individual appear also in the larger historical context, so that each person forms his corner of his civilization—and all individuals within a given time period have private and overall purposes, challenges that are set, probable actions that they will try to place within history's context.

(Long pause at 9:37.) Give us a moment. . . .

(Long pause.) End of dictation. Do you have a question?

(My mind seemed to be a blank. I tried to think for a few moments, then shook my head.)

Then I bid you a fond good evening. My heartiest regards to you both.

("Thank you, Seth. Good night.")

(9:39 P.M. "Before the session, I knew he was going to talk about the Garden of Eden, choices, and reincarnation," Jane said. "I felt this great big block of information, and again I felt it was shattering, that he broke through doors once more. I really got the best I could get, or whatever. Do you know what I mean?"

Before I could answer: "Jesus, that was short, though," Jane said as she looked at the clock. The session had lasted 45 minutes. "I feel like I've been gone five centuries' worth. I could have been to the moon. I think I've got psychological jet leg," she said—a great phrase. "That's weird. You can't believe the time when you get back, sometimes, but you couldn't have gotten the information any other way. I feel it's good, anyway. . . .")

CHAPTER 6

GENETIC HERITAGE AND
REINCARNATIONAL PREDILECTIONS

SESSION 905, MARCH 3, 1980
9:27 P.M. MONDAY

(Last Saturday evening Jane and I met here at the hill house with a group of people who used to attend Jane's old ESP class. One of those former students, who now lives out of town, had a rather heavy cold—and now I think that for the first time in many years we too may be developing colds. Or something!

This little session is almost book dictation. I'm also presenting it because it shows how an event on one day of our lives—a television program—influenced Jane's delivery of one session of the Seth material. Other factors are involved, of course, as they always must be, and I refer to one of those at the end of the session.

Jane was very relaxed after supper. When I got out to the living room to wait for the session, I found her watching one of those fascinating, multiple-subject science programs on the educational channel: Various experts were discussing topics like childbirth and sound, Kirlian photography, astronomy, particle physics, and so forth. After the program ended at 9:00 I explained to Jane out of my own limited knowledge how particle accelerators—"atom smashers"—work. She partially grasped what I told her. I suggested quickly showing her an article I'd recently filed on the subject, but she didn't want to see it.

"I don't think I should have watched that program," she said. "It's driven everything else out of my mind. I don't feel Seth around or anything." And: "I don't know whether I can have a session or not." I asked her to go back into her relaxed state. "Well, I vaguely feel him around," she finally said at 9:19.

"Probably he's just getting back from the nearest galaxy," I joked.

"No, it's just that before that program I felt he had a lot of complicated material to give, and I couldn't get it afterward," Jane replied. We continued to wait. At 9:23: "Now I can tell he's got a new chapter heading. . . . I hope he comes through with something. I feel awfully funny. Actually, I feel like I'm in a trance," Jane said with unwitting humor, "but not the right one. . . ." And it developed that she never had had a session quite like this one.)

Good evening.

("Good evening, Seth.")

Now. *(Pause, then quietly:)* We have been trying to form some kind of a neurological bridge in order to convey some particularly pertinent material for our book. This is the cause of Ruburt's sense of disorientation.

He did pick up our next chapter heading *(six)*: "Genetic Heritage and Reincarnational Predilections," and I am trying to give him this other material at different levels. Then later it will indeed be translated into suitable English sentences.

We are also dealing with probabilities, and the information has to do with those data you finally accept as physical experience, why you accept it, where it comes from, and where those events "go" that you do not experience. All of this is connected with the genetic information that any individual receives from the biological bank that belongs to the species at large, and from the inner reincarnational bank.[1] We will see that Ruburt receives the information that he needs at the necessary levels, so that the material can be verbalized. All of this is also intimately connected with those areas in which free will can be utilized, freely, to turn probable events into physically perceived ones.

I am coming through now simply to give you this explanation. On his own levels also, Ruburt is (underlined) undergoing rather accelerated healing processes—you might say at microscopic levels.

One point before I close for this evening: He was quite correct in his interpretation as he watched your expression one evening while you slept—and it was no coincidence that he awakened to see it. You were deeply involved in overall healing processes of your own, in which certain comprehensions on your part were conveyed to the various organs of your body, so that your body came into a far better overall relationship. That relationship was also responsible for [your] eye improvements, and Ruburt was able to perceive differences in you before you were aware of them at all.

Ruburt's sense of disorientation is also partially the result of healing processes within his own body, and altering relationships —again, at intimate microscopic levels—which send their new "healing tremors" upward through the various formations of matter, so tell him to enjoy it.

End of session.

("Thank you, Seth. Good night.")

(9:42 P.M. Seth's references to my facial changes while sleeping touched upon a subject Jane and I had meant to ask him about several times; she'd referred to it again today. My eye improvements had been "officially" verified by our optometrist, John Smith, on February 18. [See Note 1 for Session 901.] A few nights before that, Jane had awakened and turned on her table light, sitting up in bed to have a cigarette as she sometimes does. She'd noticed my expression as I lay sleeping on my back: "One of bliss, almost, though I don't like the word, and it's not the right one anyhow," she told me the next morning. "But I've seen you sleeping before, and I knew the difference.

"It was almost as if you were being reborn," she laughed after tonight's session. "When the Barbers were here the other night with their baby, I saw something like the same thing on the baby's face—only yours was like the adult knowing version of that—you know what I mean?"

I could only reply this evening—as I had at the time—that I was glad she'd had her perception, but that consciously I hadn't been aware of any bodily changes. Neither of us had connected my subsequent eye improvements with her insight, although perhaps we should have. But such associations aren't nearly as easy to foresee as they are to understand in retrospect.

I now reminded Jane that John Smith had knocked on our back door at suppertime tonight. She exclaimed in surprise: She'd consciously forgotten that event, for she hadn't seen John as I briefly talked with him on the back porch. He'd stopped by on his way home to give me my old lenses, since he'd forgotten to do so at his office four days ago, when I'd had them replaced in my favorite old frames by the new, weaker lenses. I told Jane I felt that regardless of John's evocative visit Seth would have mentioned my eye phenomena tonight, given his subject matter for the session. And yet, I added, because of the very nature of the Seth material, I'm also bound to think that beneath that simplified explanation there are "deeper" connections—in which the television program, her reactions to it, John's appearance, and tonight's session are all related. Jane agreed.)

NOTE: SESSION 905

1. Genes are elemental units arranged along the threadlike chromosomes in the nucleus of each cell, and transmit hereditary characteristics to following generations of animals and plants. The gene is primarily made up of protein and a twisted double strand or helix of DNA, or deoxyribonucleic acid. Each gene occurs at a specific location on a chromosome. We humans, for instance, have 46 chromosomes and an estimated 100,000 genes in each cell, and our genes provide the blueprints for the synthesis of some 50,000 proteins. I'm sure that our wonder at the vast organization of nature will continue to grow as our scientists plunge ever deeper into the complexities of genetic research. And what about the philosophical questions involving free will in all of this? Just how much real freedom do we have, if all is programmed by our genetic heritage? (I ask the question aside from the old, still-extant arguments within philosophy, psychology, and religion over whether free will has ever existed —or does—in any context. In addition, now we also have many newer questions about inherited genetic equality and/or inequality!)

For that matter, one can ask the same questions about our supposed reincarnational heritage: Just how much free will does *that* concept leave us? Are we as fated to dance to unknown and unrealized nonphysical reincarnational events, tendencies, and goals, as we are to the physical, genetic ones—that is, do the two operate together? How immutable, or resistant to change, are those two endowments, and what parts of either one can we turn off if we choose to? Will the dissection of a gene, down even to its atomic components, ever yield reincarnational clues? In *Mass Events* Seth told us: "Consciousness forms the genes, and not the other way around, and the about-to-be-born infant is the agency that adds new material through the chromosomal structure." In Chapter 4, see Session 827 for March 13, 1978.

SESSION 906, MARCH 6, 1980
8:52 P.M. THURSDAY

(Jane and I do have colds—full-blown ones, evidently picked up from one of our visitors last Saturday evening. We didn't hold our regularly scheduled session last night because we felt so miserable. Literally, we cannot remember the last time either one of us had a cold.

This afternoon Jane said she'd learned from Seth that we'd come down with those indispositions because we wanted to use our bodies' immune systems; those structures needed the workouts, in other words. I'd had a vaguely similar thought this morning, and it had reminded me of my feelings on Saturday night—that our friend's continual sneezing amid the group was actually a prolonged act of aggression.

"I've been getting some fascinating stuff," Jane said as she did the supper dishes. "It comes and goes. I suppose I'll try to have a session tonight, if my voice holds out. Besides, I'm bored, sitting around watching TV all night. A couple of nights of that are enough. . . ."

Tonight's session isn't book dictation, but the large portions of it I'm presenting convey useful insights into our social behavior and social health—and as I show in Note 1, those states can include our interactions with animals.

When Jane began the session her voice was a bit rough and very quiet, but by listening closely I could understand Seth well enough.)

Now.

("Good evening, Seth.")

Subject: Viruses as part of the body's overall health system, and viruses as biological statements.

Viruses serve many purposes, as I have said before.[1] The body contains all kinds of viruses, including those considered deadly, but those are usually not only harmless, or inactive, but beneficial to the body's overall balance.

The body maintains its vitality not only through the physical motion and agility that you perceive, but by microscopic agility, and actions within microseconds, that you do not perceive. There is as much motion, stimulation, and reaction in the interior bodily environment as the body meets through its encounters with the exterior environment. The body must now and then "flush its systems out," run through its repertoire, raise its temperature *(pause)*, activate its hormonal actions more strongly. In such ways it keeps its system of immunities clear. That system operates always. To some extent, it is a way that the body distinguishes between self and nonself.

(9:01.) In certain fashions (underlined), that system also keeps the body from squandering its energies, preserving biological integrity. Otherwise it would be as if you did not know where your own house began or ended, and so tried to heat the entire neighborhood. So some indispositions "caused by viruses" are accepted by the body as welcome triggers, to clean out that system, and this applies to your present indispositions.

More is always involved, however, for those viruses that you consider communicable do indeed in one way or another represent communications on a biological level. They are biological statements, literally social communications, biologically made, and they can be of many kinds.

(Still quietly, but at a good pace:) When a skunk is frightened, it throws off a foul odor indeed, and when people are frightened they react in somewhat the same fashion at times, biologically reacting to stimuli in the environment that they consider alarming. They throw off a barrage of "foul viruses"—that is, they actually collect and mobilize from within their own bodies viruses that are potentially harmful, biologically trigger these, or activate them, and send them out into the environment in self-protection, to ward off the enemy *(more vigorously)*.

In a fashion this is a kind of biological aggression. The viruses, however, also represent tensions that the person involved is getting rid of. That is one kind of statement. It is often used in a very strong manner in times of war, or great social upheaval, when people feel frightened.

Now, your friend had been to the Olympics *(last month, at Lake Placid, New York)*, and he was charged by the great physical vitality that he felt watching that athletic panorama. [Because of that, and for other personal reasons], he could find no release for the intense energy he felt, so he got rid of it, protected himself, and threw out his threatening biological posture: the viruses.

(With a smile:) Your bodies had not received any such goodies in some time, so they exuberantly used them as triggers to re-generate the immune systems.

Many people had such reactions as your friend's, coming from the Olympics, in that they did not know how to use and release their own energies—as if they themselves felt put in an inferior position in comparison to such achievements.

(Pause at 9:17.) There are all kinds of biological reactions be-tween bodies that go unnoticed, and they are all basically of a social nature, dealing with biological communications. In a fash-ion viruses—in a fashion—again, are a way of dealing with or controlling the environment. These are natural interactions, and since you live in a world where, overall, people are healthy enough to contribute through labor, energy, and ideas, health is the dominating ingredient—but there are biological interactions between all physical bodies that are the basis for that health, and the mechanisms include the interactions of viruses, and even the periods of indisposition, that are not understood.

All of this has to do with man's intent and his understanding. The same relationships, however, do not only exist between human bodies, of course, but between man and the animals and the plants in the environment, and is part of the unending bio-logical communication that overall produces the vitality of phys-ical experience.

One note to Ruburt on vitamins: They are most effectively used for periods of two or three weeks, where they act as stimuli and reminders to the body. Then drop their use for two or three weeks, so that the body then produces by itself those elements you have reminded it you want. Any steady use of vitamins is not to your overall benefit, for you give the body what it needs too easily, and its ability to produce such material on its own becomes sluggish. Do you follow me?

("Yes.")

(9:27.) Give us a moment. . . . Certain "diseases" are protec-tions against other diseases, and the body on its own is its own excellent regulator.

Obviously those abilities operate best when you trust them. The body's systems know what diseases are in the air, so to speak, and will often set up countermeasures ahead of time, giving you what you experience as an indisposition of one kind or another—but an indisposition that is actually a statement of prevention against another condition.

There is great traffic flow in a city: A body knows how to leap out of the way in a moment's time from an approaching car. In the interior physical environment there is far greater traffic flow. There are decisions made in periods of time so brief you cannot imagine them—reactions that are almost over before they begin, reactions so fast you cannot perceive them as the body responds to its inner reality, and to all the stimuli from the exterior environment. The body is an open system. As solid as it seems to you, there are constant chemical reactions between it and the world, electromagnetic adjustments, alterations of balance, changes of relationships—alterations that occur between the body and its relationship with every other physical event, from the position of the planets and moon and the sun, to the position of the smallest grain of sand, to the tiniest microbe in anyone's intestine (intently).

All of those adjustments are made without your conscious notice, and yet fit in with your overall purposes and intents.

End of session.

("Thank you, Seth. That was very good. Good night.")

My fondest regards to each of you.

(9:35 P.M. "Jesus, I didn't know whether I could do it or not," Jane said, "but I felt all that stuff there in a great big block, and I just had to get it out. I like it when I do that. I also like it when I don't have to." So once again I'd seen it happen: Jane had done very well with a session when she'd felt poorly beforehand. Although her voice had remained muted, her delivery had increased in vigor and emphasis as the session progressed. It was as though she'd acquired an infusion of energy from Seth—yet once the session was over she announced that she wanted to go to bed.)

NOTE: SESSION 906

1. Seth first mentioned viruses in the 17th session for January 26, 1964, when I asked him to comment upon the recent deaths of our dog, Mischa, at the age of 11, and of a pair of kittens Jane

had obtained from the janitor of the art gallery where she worked part time. (The kittens had the same mother, but had come from successive litters.) I was 44 and Jane was 34, and in conventional terms both of us were still struggling—not only to learn about ourselves and the world, but to find our creative ways in that world. Seth's answer to my question was more than a little surprising and saddening to us, and opened up a number of insights:

"The particular atmosphere surrounding your personalities just prior to the animals' deaths was destructive, short-circuited, and filled with inner panics. I do not want to hurt your feelings. That is, I am sorry to say, a natural occurrence on your plane. The fact is that the animals caught your emotional contagion, and according to their lesser abilities translated it for themselves.

"The viruses and infections were of course present. They always are. They are themselves fragments, struggling small fragments without intention of harm. You have general immunity, believe it or not, to all such viruses and infections. Ideally, you can inhabit a plane with them without fear. It is only when you give tacit agreement that harm is inflicted upon you by these fragments. To some degree, lesser, dependent lives such as household pets are dependent upon your psychic strength. They have their own, it is true, but unknowingly you reinforce their energy and health.

"When your own personalities are more or less in balance, you have no trouble at all in looking out for these creatures, and actually reinforcing their own existence with residues of your creative and sympathetic powers. In times of psychological stress or crisis, quite unwittingly you withhold this strong reinforcement.

"In the cats' deaths, both cats inherited the peculiar illness, which was a virus, that killed them. In the case of the first cat, you were able to reinforce its strength and maintain its health for quite a while, and then you needed your energies for yourselves. The second cat barely enjoyed such reinforcement at all, and quickly succumbed.

"Your dog's illness was incipient. You could not have maintained his health for many long years in any case. I would like to make clear, of course, that animals certainly do have energy to maintain their own health, but this is strongly reinforced as a rule by the vitality of human beings to whom the animals are emotionally attached. The fact is, you were not able to give your dog that added emotional vitality at a time when he needed it most. There is no need to blame yourselves. It was beyond your control.

"Animals, like people, sense when they are a burden, and the dog sensed that he was a burden, and also something of a nuisance. I would have preferred that you did not ask me this question, but since you did, and since you both loved the dog, it deserves an answer."

Mischa, who was part shelty, or Shetland collie, was the last dog we've had. He certainly was a true companion to us. Even now, as I write about him over 16 years later, I feel a strong emotional pull toward him.

SESSION 907, APRIL 14, 1980
8:47 P.M. MONDAY

(It's hard for us to believe that five and a half weeks have passed following Jane's last regularly scheduled session, the 906th for March 6. She's held but one private session, on April 9, since.

Session 906, in which Seth discussed viruses and the social aspects of many diseases, turned on Jane so much that the next day she wrote several additional pages on those subjects. The material came from both Seth and "herself," and I added it to the notes for that session. It's quite frustrating that we have no room in Dreams *for such interesting information. Perhaps Seth will develop it in another work. In putting together the Seth books most of my decisions concern what to* leave out, *rather than what to include.*

I had the same feelings of limitation concerning the session for April 9. In it Seth dealt with the creation of art: not only by "natural man," but by other creatures—and yes, also the flora—of the earth.[1]

While Jane has been enjoying many periods of ease and relaxation, she's also had bouts of blueness over her general stiffness and walking difficulties [her "symptoms"]. But she's finally dispensed with the last stages of her cold, which had turned out to be much heavier than mine, and is feeling a resurgence of energy for the sessions. Her own work has been going well for the most part, however—she expects to finish Chapter

12 of God of Jane *tomorrow. Because of her concentration on that book she hasn't done much on her book of poetry,* If We Live Again, *since late February; and as I mentioned in the Preface for* Dreams, *she laid aside her third Seven novel,* Oversoul Seven and the Museum of Time, *in May 1979 when she began* God of Jane. *As for myself, I've progressed to working with Session 860 [for June 13, 1979], which bridges chapters 8 and 9 in* Mass Events.

Today Jane reread her recent sessions for Dreams; *she wanted to resume work on the book tonight, and picked up on it from Seth throughout the day. She told me bits of the material at times, but I didn't retain them. [She also relayed to me Seth's comments about an article on bird migration that I read to her while we were having lunch, but I lost those too.] Jane called me early for the session—at 8:20, while I was still busy with* Mass Events. *She wanted to get started: "I still feel nervous about going back to the book. . . ."*

As soon as she delivered the first phrase of the first full sentence for Chapter 6, I recalled that she'd accurately quoted it to me this afternoon, saying that that was the way Seth would start the session.)

(Whispering:) Good evening.

("Good evening, Seth.")

Dictation.

(With humor: "Hooray.")

(Slowly:) Chapter Six. Now: Any real discussion of genetic heritage must also bring up questions involving free will and determinism,[2] and to some extent those issues must also lead to questions concerning the nature of the reasoning mind itself.

Reasoning, as you are <u>familiar</u> with it, is the result of mental or psychic processes functioning in a space-time context, and in a particular fashion. To some extent, then, reasoning—again, as you are <u>familiar with it</u> (underlined)—is the result of a lack of available knowledge. You try to "reason things out," because the answer is <u>not</u> in front of you. If it were, you would "know," and hence have <u>no</u> need to question.

The reasoning mind is a uniquely human and physical phenomenon. *(Long pause.)* It depends upon conscious thinking, problem-solving methods, and it is a natural human blossoming, a spectacular mental development in its own framework of activity.

Your technology is one of the results of that reasoning mind. That "reasoning" is necessary, however, because of the lack of a larger, immediate field of knowledge. Thoughts are mental activity, scaled to time and space terms so that they are like mental edifices built to certain dimensions only. Your thoughts make you human (underlined).

(Still slowly at 8:59:) Other creatures have their own kinds of mental activity, however. They also have different kinds of immediate perceptions of reality. All species are united by their participation in emotional states, however. It is not just that all species of life have feeling, but that all participate in dimensions of emotional reality. It has been said that only men have a moral sense, that only men have free will—if indeed free will is possible at all. The word "moral" has endless connotations, of course. Yet animals have their own "morality," their own codes of honor, their own impeccable senses of balance with all other creatures. (Pause.) They have loving emotional relationships, complicated societies,[3] and in a certain sense at least—an important one— they also have their arts and sciences. But those "arts and sciences" are not based upon reasoning, as you understand it.

Animals also possess independent volition, and while I am emphasizing animals here, the same applies to any creature, large or small: insect, bird, fish, or worm; to plant life; to cells, atoms, or electrons. They possess free will in relationship to the conditions of their existence (underlined).

The conditions of existence are largely determined by genetic structure. Free will must then of course function in accordance with genetic integrity. Genetic structure makes possible physical organisms through which life is to be experienced, and to a large extent that structure must determine the kind of action possible in the world, and the way or ways in which volition can be effectively expressed.

The beaver is not free to make a spider web. (Long pause.) In human beings the genetic structure largely determines physical characteristics such as height, color of eyes, color of hair, color of skin—and, of course, more importantly, the number of fingers and toes, and the other specific physical attributes of your specieshood. So physically, and on his physical attributes alone, a man cannot use his free will to fly like a bird, or to perform physical acts for which the human body is not equipped.

The body is equipped to perform far better, in a variety of ways, than you give it credit for, however—but the fact remains

that the genetic structure focuses volition. The genetic appara-
tus and the chromosomal messages actually contain far more
information than is ever used. That genetic information can, for
example, be put together in an infinite number of ways. (*Long
pause.*) The species cares for itself in the event of any possible
circumstance, so that the genetic messages also carry an endless
number of triggers that will change genetic combinations if this
becomes necessary.

Beyond that, however, genetic messages are coded in such a
way that there is a constant give-and-take between those messages and the present experience of any given individual. That
is, no genetic event is inevitable.

Now besides this physical genetic structure, there is an inner
bank of psychic information that in your terms would contain
the "past" history—the reincarnational history—of the individual. This provides an overall reservoir of psychic characteristics,
leanings, abilities, knowledge, that is as much a part of the individual's heritage as the genetic structure is a part of the physical
heritage.

A person of great intelligence may be born from a family of
idiots, for example, because of that reincarnational structure.
Musical ability may thus appear complete—

(*9:27. We were startled by the sudden ringing of the telephone.*)

Take your break.

(*A close friend, one who used to attend Jane's ESP class, had called
our unlisted number to ask one of us some psychic questions. Jane had
been jolted out of trance, of course. After I hung up we wondered why
our friend, who knows our usual routine so well, hadn't realized that
we'd probably be having a session at this time on a Monday evening.*

*Yet, at 9:30 Jane resumed the session just as though there hadn't been
any interruption.*)

—with great technical facility, regardless of family background, genetically speaking, and again, the reincarnational
bank of characteristics accounts for such events. That inner reincarnational psychic structure is also responsible for triggering
certain genetic messages while ignoring others, or for triggering
certain combinations of genetic messages. In actuality, of course
—say that I smiled—all time is simultaneous, and so all reincarnational lives occur at once.

(*Pause.*) Perhaps an analogy will help. An actor throwing himself or herself into a role, even momentarily lost in the part, is still alive and functioning as himself or herself in a context that is larger than the play. The character in the play is seemingly alive (creatively) for the play's duration, perception being limited to that framework, yet to play that role the actor draws upon the experience of his own life. He brings to bear his own understanding, compassion, artistry, and if he is a good actor, or if she is, then when the play is over the actor is a better person for having played the role.

Now in the greater framework of reincarnational existences you choose your roles, or your lives, but the lines that you speak, the situations that you meet, are not predetermined. "You" live or exist in a larger framework of activity even while you live your life, and there is a rambunctious interplay between the yous in time and the you outside of time.

(Long pause.) The you inside of time adopts a reasoning mind. It is a kind of <u>creative</u> (underlined) psychological face that you use for the purposes of your life's drama. This psychological face of our analogy has certain formal, ceremonial features, so that you mentally and psychologically tend to perceive only those data that are available within the play's formal structure. You cannot see into the future, for example, or into the past.

You reason out your position. Otherwise your free will would have no meaning in a physical framework, for the number of choices available would be so multitudinous that you could not make up your mind to act within time: With all the opportunities of creativity, and with your own greater knowledge instantly available, you would be swamped by so many stimuli that you literally could not physically respond, and so your particular kinds of civilization and science and art could not have been accomplished—and regardless of their flaws they are magnificent accomplishments, unique products of the reasoning mind.

Without the reasoning mind the artist would have no need to paint, for the immediacy of his mental vision would be so instant and blinding, so <u>mentally accomplished</u>, that there would be no need to try any physical rendition of it. So nowhere do I ever mean to demean the qualities or excellence of the reasoning mind as you understand it.

You have, however, become so specialized in its use, so prejudiced in its favor, that your tendency is to examine all other kinds of consciousness using the reasoning mind as the only yardstick by which to judge intelligent life. You are surrounded everywhere by other kinds of consciousness whose validity you have largely ignored, whose psychic brotherhood you have dismissed—kinds of consciousness in the animal kingdom particularly, that deal with a different kind of knowing, but who share with you the reality of keen emotional experience, and who are innately aware of biological and psychic values, but in ways that have escaped your prejudiced examination.

To some extent that emotional reality is also expressed at other levels—as your own is—in periods of dreaming, in which animals, like men, participate in a vast cooperative venture that helps to form the psychological atmosphere in which your lives must first of all exist.

End of dictation. End of session, unless you have a question. Ruburt can relax now (*with amusement*).

(*"Okay, Seth. No questions. That was very good."*)

I bid you a fond good evening.

(*"Thank you. Good night."*)

(*10:01 P.M. "Gee, I thought some of that was great while I was giving it, but now I can't remember what it was," Jane said as soon as Seth had gone. "But I feel better. . . . I think I got all kinds of goodies out of all proportion to time."*

Once the session was over, Billy and Mitzi came out to play.)

NOTES: SESSION 907

1. These excerpts from the session for April 9 (which we hadn't requested, by the way) indicate Seth's response to discussions Jane and I had been having about our personal functions as artists, as well as the use of art generally in our chosen probable reality. As usual, Seth had added his own wider, penetrating views:

"All creatures of whatever degree have their own appreciation of esthetics. Many such creatures merge their arts so perfectly into their lives that it is impossible to separate the two: the spider's web, for example, or the beaver's dam—and there are endless other examples. This is not 'blind instinctive behavior' at all, but the result of well-ordered spontaneous artistry.

"Art is not a specifically human endeavor, though man likes to believe that this is so. Art is above all a natural characteristic. I try to straddle your definitions—but flowers, for example, in a fashion see themselves as their own artistic creations. They have an esthetic appreciation of their own colors—a different kind, of course, than your perception of color. But nature seeks to outdo itself in terms that are most basically artistic, even while those terms may also include quite utilitarian purposes. The natural man, then, is a natural artist. In a sense, painting is man's natural attempt to create an original but coherent, mental yet physical interpretation of his own reality—and by extension to create a new version of reality for his species."

(To me, loudly:) "You are still learning. Your work is still developing. How truly unfortunate you would be if that were not the case! There is always a kind of artistic dissatisfaction that any true artist feels with work that is completed, for he is always aware of the tug and pull, and the tension, between the sensed ideal and its manifestation. In a certain fashion the artist is looking for a creative solution to a sensed but never clearly stated problem or challenge, and it is an adventure that is literally unending. It must be one that has no clearly stated destination, in usual terms. In the most basic of ways, the artist cannot say where he is going, for if he knows ahead of time he is not creating but copying.

"The true artist is involved with the inner workings of himself with the universe—a choice, I remind you, that he or she has made, and so often the artist does indeed forsake the recognized roads of recognition. And more, seeing that, he often does not know how to assess his own progress, since his journey has no recognizable creative destination. By its nature art basically is meant to put each artist of whatever kind into harmony with the universe, for the artist draws upon the same creative energy from which birth emerges."

2. Free will is the philosophical doctrine that the individual has the freedom to choose, without coercion, some actions consistent with his or her particular morals and ideals. Determinism is the opposing doctrine that everything, even the individual's course of action, is determined by conditions outside one's will.

Through the centuries philosophical and religious thinkers

have created numerous complicated variations of ideas involving free will and determinism, so that neither thesis is as simple as it first appears to be. Man related the concept of free will long ago to the question of whether he could deliberately choose evil, for example. He still does. And he still struggles with questions about his freedom before God's omnipotence and foreknowledge, and whether those qualities cause events, or can cause them, and whether they involve predestination. Opposing determinism is the idea that man has always fought for his personal responsibility—that instead of being controlled entirely by his heritage, he's capable of forming new syntheses of thought and action based upon the complicated patterns of his own history.

In a strange way, determinism has always seemed lacking as a concept to Jane and me—for if it means what it's supposed to mean, then surely human beings set up the parameters within which determinism is said to operate. I see this as a contradiction of the notion that the individual is entirely at the mercy of his or her history and of nature. How can we be, if through the ages we've created that history and nature against which we react? In other words, on joint and individual scales, vast though they may be, we do create our joint and individual realities.

I want to add that even with ideas of religious determinism— that man cannot know God's will, for instance, or is quite dependent upon that divine grace—we're still creating our conscious ideas of what God is, in those terms. So once again we have a determinism that operates within our sensual and intellectual boundaries: another framework within which we ceaselessly attempt to understand "the meaning of life."

Even in modern terms, our psychological and medical knowledge of mind and brain have added more complications to the doctrine of free will, yet it survives and grows. And all the while I worked on this note, I felt strong connections involving free will, determinism, and probable realities—connections largely unexpressed and unexplored in our world's societies.

3. See the Preface for *Dreams*. In the notes immediately preceding the private session for September 13, 1979, I quoted some of the very evocative material on animal cultures and civilizations that Seth had given in Chapter 5 of *Mass Events*.

SESSION 908, APRIL 16, 1980
8:49 P.M. WEDNESDAY

(This morning I showed Jane the portrait in oils that I'm working on. It's of one of my imaginary male heads, and I began it a week ago, following Seth's material on art for me in the private session for April 9. [See Note 1 for the last session.] I explained to Jane that even while it's incomplete, the painting contains improvements that I can already tell will be developed further in the next one. Once I start a work in a certain mode, it becomes somewhat set in that expression; this is inevitable if one is to ever complete the physical painting. Those sensed, additional improvements have to wait for the next effort: A creative tension between the present and the future is set up, then—one that I've often felt, an impatience to leap ahead to the next step even while I'm still working out the current one. I asked that Seth comment upon the painting tonight if he cared to.

Without being specific before the session, Jane said she felt "lots of stuff from Seth churning around." Even though Monday's session had been for Dreams, *she was still nervous about going back to the book after being away from it for well over a month before that—yet she was ready to go.)*

(Whispering:) Good evening.

(With a laugh: "Good evening, Seth.")

Now: The reasoning mind represents human mental activity in a space and time context, as mentioned earlier.

Again, it is involved with the trial-and-error method. It sets up hypotheses *(pause)*, and its very existence is dependent upon a lack of available knowledge—knowledge that it seeks to discover.

In the dreaming state the characteristics of the reasoning mind become altered, and from a waking viewpoint it might seem distorted in its activity. What actually happens, however, is that in the dreaming state you are presented with certain kinds of immediate knowledge. It often appears out of context in usual terms. It is not organized according to the frameworks understood by the reasoning portions of your mind, and so to some extent in dreams you encounter large amounts of information that you cannot categorize.

The information may not fit into your recognizable time or

space slots. There are, in fact, many important issues connected with the dreaming state that can involve genetic activation of certain kinds: information processing on the part of the species, the insertion or reinsertion of civilizing elements—and all of these are also connected with the reincarnational aspects of dreaming.

I have not touched upon some of these subjects before, since I wanted to present them in that larger context of man's origins and historic appearance as a species. I also wanted to make certain points, stressing the importance of dreams as they impinge upon and help form cultural environments. Dreams also sometimes help in showing the pathways that can be taken to advantage by an individual, or by a group of individuals, and therefore help clarify the ways in which free will might most advantageously be directed. So I hope to cover all of these subjects.

(Long pause.) Let us first of all return momentarily to the subject of the reasoning mind, its uses and characteristics. It seems to the reasoning mind that it must look outside of itself for information, for it operates in concert with the physical senses, which present it with only a limited amount of information about the environment at any given time. The physical eyes cannot see today the dawn that will come in the morning. The legs today cannot walk down tomorrow's street, so if the mind wants to know what is going to happen tomorrow, or what is happening now, outside of the physical senses' domain, then it must try through reason to deduce the information that it wants from the available information that it has. It must rely upon observation to make its deductions accordingly. In a fashion, it must divide to conquer. It must try to deduce the nature of the whole it cannot perceive from the portions that are physically available.

(9:10.) Children begin to count by counting on their fingers. Later, fingers are dispensed with but the idea of counting remains. There have been people throughout history who mentally performed mathematical feats that appear most astounding, and almost in a matter of moments. Some, had they lived in your century, would have been able to outperform computers *(just as some* are *outperforming computers these days!).* In most cases where such accomplishments show themselves, they do so in a child far too young to have learned scientific mathematical procedures to begin with, and often such feats are displayed by

people who are otherwise classified as idiots *(idiot savants)*, and who are incapable of intellectual reasoning.

Indeed, when a child is involved, the keener his use of the reasoning mind becomes the dimmer his mathematical abilities grow. Others, children [or adults] who would be classified as mentally deficient, can tell, or have been able to tell, the day of the week that any given date, past or present, would fall upon. Others have been able, while performing various tasks, to keep a precise count of the moments from any given point in time. There have been children, again, with highly accomplished musical abilities, and great facility with music's technical aspects— all such accomplishments before the assistance of any kind of advanced education.

Now, some of those children went on to become great musicians, while others lost their abilities along the way, so what are we dealing with in such cases? We are dealing with direct knowing. We are dealing with the natural perceptions of the psyche, at least when we are speaking in human terms. We are dealing with natural, direct cognition as it exists before and after *(pause)* man's experience with the reasoning mind.

Some of those abilities show themselves in those classified as mentally deficient simply because all of the powers of the reasoning mind are not activated. In children under such conditions, the reasoning mind has not yet developed in all of its aspects sufficiently, so that in a certain area direct cognition shines through with its brilliant capacity.

Direct cognition is an inner sense. In physical terms you might call it remote sensing. Your physical body, and your physical existence, are based upon certain kinds of direct cognition, and it is responsible for the very functioning of the reasoning mind itself. Scientists like to say that animals operate through simple instinctive behavior, without will or volition: It is no accomplishment for a spider to make its web, a beaver its dam, a bird its nest, because according to such reasoning, such creatures cannot perform otherwise. The spider must spin his web. If he chooses not to, he will not survive. But by that same reasoning—to which, of course, I do not subscribe—you should also add that man can take no credit either for his intellect, since man must think, and cannot help doing so.

Some pessimistic scientists would say: "Of course," for man

and animal alike are driven by their instincts, and man's claim to free will is no more than an illusion.

(9:33.) Man's reasoning mind, however, with its fascinating capacity for logic and deduction, and for observation, rests upon *(pause)* a direct cognition—a direct cognition that <u>powers</u> his thoughts, that makes thinking itself possible. <u>He thinks because he knows how to think by thinking</u> *(intently)*, even though the true processes of thought are enigmas to the reasoning mind.[1]

(Long pause.) In dreams the reasoning mind loosens its hold upon perception. From your standpoint you are almost faced with too much data. The reasoning mind attempts to catch what it can as it reassembles its abilities toward waking, but the net of its reasoning simply cannot hold that assemblage of information. Instead it is processed at other levels of the psyche. Dreams also involve a kind of psychological perspective with which you have no physical equivalent—and therefore such issues are most difficult to discuss.

The reasoning mind is highly necessary, effective, and suitable for physical existence, and for the utilization of free will, which is very dependent upon perception of clearly distinguishable actions. In the larger framework of existence, however, it is simply one of innumerable methods of organizing data. A psychological filing system, if you prefer.

Your dreaming self possesses pyschological dimensions that escape you, and they serve to connect genetic and reincarnational systems. You must, again, realize that the self that you know is only a part of your larger identity—an identity that is [also] historically actualized in other times than your own. You must also understand that mental activity is of the utmost potency. You experience your dreams from your own perspective, as a rule. *(Long pause.)* I am simply trying to give you a picture of <u>one kind</u> of dream occurrence, or to show you one picture of dream activity of which you are not usually aware.

If you are having a dream as yourself from your own perspective, another reincarnational self may be having the same dream from <u>its</u> perspective—in which, of course, <u>you</u> play a minor role. In your dream, that reincarnational self may appear as a minor character, quite on the periphery of your attention, and if the dream were to include an idea, say, for a play or an invention, then that play or invention might appear as a physical event in both historic times, to whatever degree it would be possible for the two individuals living in time to interpret that information. But culture throughout the ages was spread by more than physical means. Abilities and inventions were not dependent upon human migrations, but those migrations themselves were the result of information given in dreams, telling tribes of men the directions in which better homelands could be found.

(Louder:) End of dictation.

("Okay.")

(9:55.) Give us a moment. . . . Direct cognition: You know what you know.

(To me:) Your knowledge knows how to flow through the techniques you have learned, to use them and become part of them, so that a painting emerges with a spontaneous wisdom. That is what you are learning. That is what the painting shows. That is where you are.

To some extent each vision, each subject matter, will itself make minute alterations in technique if you allow it to. Your impulses have shadings as your colors do. They should mix and merge with your brushstrokes, so that the idea of your subject matter is almost magically contained in each spot of paint, and that is what you are learning. Or rather, you are learning to take advantage of your direct cognition.

End of session.

("Thank you.")

A hearty good evening—and tell our friend *(Jane)* to be more playful—work at it, I said *(with much humor)*.

("Good night, Seth.")

(10:01 P.M. "Boy," Jane said, "I sensed a whole bunch of stuff on dreams, and when I reached that part on reincarnation and dreams, I knew that's where I was supposed to get. I felt like it was great." She'd begun to tune into Seth's material on idiots savants just before the session. "In certain parts of the book, like in the beginning and tonight, I feel like I've gone at an accelerated rate, outside time somehow," she said. "And at a few other times in between, too. . . .")

NOTE: SESSION 908

1. With a little reflection it become obvious, but I think it important to note that Jane's expression of the Seth material is cer-

tainly the result of her direct cognition. Because she has to deliver it linearly in words, which take "time," she cannot produce her material almost at once, as the mathematical prodigy can his or her answers, but in their own way her communications with Seth are as psychologically clear and direct as the calculator's objective products are with numbers, or the musician's are with notes. From the very beginning of the sessions, in late 1963, I appreciated the speed with which Jane delivered the Seth material, and began recording the times involved throughout each session. I now think that spontaneously starting to do that reflected my own intuitive understanding of her direct cognition, long before either one of us knew how to describe it. And when Jane speaks extemporaneously for Seth, her delivery is even more rapid. It was most definitely faster—sometimes spectacularly so—during all of those years she gave sessions in ESP class.

More is involved, of course. I've read that mathematical prodigies are in love with their numbers, and rely upon their dependability in an often unsure world. Jane has a deep love for words. Words, however, can be very elusive tools, and vary from language to language, although intrinsically through the Seth material Jane conveys depths of meaning that continue to develop within whatever language others may cast it. This psychological growth, and the many challenges involved, set her work apart from the mental calculator's numbers or the musician's notes, which are ever the same: Those friendly columns of figures, for instance, add up to identical sums in any language. In her own direct cognition Jane deals with feelings and ideas that are often quite divorced from any such reliability and acceptance.

Regardless of who or what he is, then, with Jane's permission Seth adds his material to the information possessed by her reasoning mind—and thus offers it to the reasoning minds of others.

SESSION 909, APRIL 21, 1980
9:05 P.M. MONDAY

(*Just before she took a nap this noon, Jane received a letter from a man who explained that he'd married a woman with genetic deformities of her hands. A daughter just born to the couple carries the same "flaws." The writer has obviously learned much from reading the Seth material, and revealed insight as to why he and his lady had chosen to marry to begin with. Yet he still expressed sorrow, and asked: "Why?" He's troubled by the challenges of one who has to live with a so-called deformed wife— and now a child—each day. Jane plans to inform him that he and his family are doing much better than they know.*

During her nap, Jane had a little out-of-body experience that she described to me as soon as she got up. Then this afternoon she picked up from Seth that in a new chapter he'd explain how physical deformities are, among other things, manifestations of the great range of abilities encompassed within our species' genetic pool, and that we retain such flexibility in case wide changes are ever needed. She added that our genetic requirements are also linked to our reincarnational patterns. The attributes that can result in the supposedly handicapped, then, are needed to keep our species adaptable in many, and often unexpected, ways. Jane had more to say, but I didn't write it down at the time. She thought Seth might comment tonight upon the correspondent's situation.

We held the session in the living room, as usual. Jane was very relaxed as she sat in her rocker. "I'm having it just because I want to," she said, "But I don't know how far I'll get. I'm really out of it. . . ." In back of her and off to her right, our cats, Billy and Mitzi, were crouching in the light cast on the rug by one of our homemade lamps from its position on a low bookcase: An insect, seemingly mesmerized by the illumination, was flying round and round inside the bright cone of the lampshade. The cats had been fascinated by this phenomenon for several minutes; just as Jane went into trance they lost patience and started to leap up at the insect. And although she began the session slowly, Jane proceeded right along with it.)

(Whispering:) Good evening.

("Good evening, Seth.")

Dictation. Now: Man's first encounter with physical reality in life is his experience with the state of his own consciousness.

(I had to spoil the cats' fun: I had to get up and turn off the lamp before they pulled it off the bookcase. Jane waited in trance.)

He is aware of a different kind of being. He encounters his consciousness first, and then he encounters the world—so I am saying, of course, that each person has an identity that is larger than the framework of consciousness with which you are usually familiar in life.

When you are born, you understand that you have a new consciousness. You explore its ramifications. It is your primary evidence that you exist in flesh. Basically, each person must confront the experience of reality through a direct encounter with it. This encounter takes place through the use of the physical senses, of course, as they are used to perceive and interpret physical data. The very utilization of those senses, however, is dependent upon the nature of your consciousness itself, and that consciousness is aware of its power and action through the exercise of its own properties.

Those "properties" are the faculties of the imagination, creativity, telepathy, clairvoyance, and dreaming, as well as the functions of logic and reason. You know that you dream. You know that you think. Those are direct experiences. *(Pause.)* Anytime you use instruments to probe into the nature of reality, you are looking at a kind of secondary evidence, no matter how excellent the instruments may be. The subjective evidence of dreaming, for example, is far more "convincing" and irrefutable than is the evidence for an expanding universe, black holes, or even atoms and molecules themselves. Although instruments can indeed be most advantageous in many ways, they still present you with secondary rather than primary tools of investigation—and they distort the nature of reality far more than the subjective attributes of thoughts, feelings, and intuitions do.

(9:21.) The human consciousness has not, therefore, developed the best and most proper "tool" with which to examine the nature of reality. It is because you have used other methods that much evidence escapes you—evidence that would show that the physical universe exists in quite different terms than is supposed.

You are taught not to trust your subjective experience, which means that you are told not to trust <u>your initial and primary connection</u> with reality.

Evidence for reincarnation is quite available. There are enough instances of it, known and tabulated, to make an excellent case; and beside this there is evidence that remains psychologically invisible in your private lives, because you have been taught not to concentrate in that direction.

There is enough evidence to build an excellent case for life after death. All of this involves direct experience—episodes, encountered by individuals, [that are] highly suggestive of the afterdeath hypothesis; but the hypothesis is never taken seriously by your established sciences. There is far more evidence for reincarnation and life after death than there is, for example, for the existence of black holes. *(With amusement:)* Few people have seen a black hole, to make the most generous statement possible, while countless people have had private reincarnational experiences, or encounters that suggest the survival of the personality beyond death.

Those experiences are usual. They have been reported by peoples of all kinds and in all ages, and they represent a common-sense kind of knowledge that is frowned upon by the men of learned universities. Throughout this book we will often be talking about experiences that are encountered in one way or another by most people, but are not given credence to on the part of the established fields of knowledge. Therefore, dreams will be considered throughout the book in various capacities as they are related through genetics, reincarnation, culture, and private life. We will also be considering the matter of free will and its role in invidual value fulfillment.

(A closing note, added following Seth's completion of his sessions for Dreams *on February 8, 1982:*

After we had published Seth's "Unknown" *Reality in two volumes back in 1977 and 1979, Jane and I decided that we wanted to keep his books shorter, and to issue them more frequently. Never again would we go the way of two volumes, we thought—yet here we are, doing it once more!*

When I began putting together Seth's dictation for Dreams, *and adding Jane's and my own notes, plus excerpts from other relevant sessions, it soon became obvious that the entire work was going to be too long for one volume. There would be publishing difficulties having to do with sheer bulk—with the cost of typesetting, with binding such a thick book, with marketing and price, and so forth. So with the help of our editor, Tam Mossman, and others at Prentice-Hall, the decision was made to publish* Dreams *in two volumes. At first I was sorry for the reader's sake to think of* Dreams *being interrupted, yet glad for myself, for in addition to presenting Seth's book dictation I was given the space in which to develop those other personal and secular themes of Seth's, Jane's, and my own that I think add even more dimensions of meaning to* Dreams.

This time, however, unlike the case with "Unknown" Reality, there won't be any two-year wait between the production of the two volumes for Dreams—*only a few months at the most. In the meantime, here are Seth's chapter headings for the second volume, to show the direction his material takes:)*

Chapter 7   Genetics and Reincarnation. Gifts and "Liabilities."
             The Vast Sweep of the Genetic and Reincarna-
             tional Scales. The Gifted and the Handicapped
Chapter 8   When You Are Who You Are. The Worlds of
             Imagination and Reason, and the Implied Uni-
             verse
Chapter 9   Master Events and Reality Overlays
Chapter 10   The Pleasure Principle. Group Dreams and Value
             Fulfillment
Chapter 11   The Magical Approach, and the Relationships Be-
             tween "Conservation" and Spontaneous Develop-
             ments
Chapter 12   Life Clouds

(Seth used Session 909 as a bridge between chapters 6 and 7 in Dreams. *This means that now the session also serves as a connective— a very effective lure, say—between volumes 1 and 2. Indeed, in retro- spect it also seems as though Seth, that "energy personality essence," planned it that way! And Jane and I look forward with intense interest to the final version of* Dreams, *for as always this work will be as reveal- ing and educational for us as it will be for anybody else. I thank each reader for his or her patience in accepting the publication of* Dreams *in two volumes. Robert F. Butts.)*

INDEX

THE SETH AUDIO COLLECTION
AND NEW SETH BOOKS

RARE RECORDINGS OF SETH SPEAKING through Jane Roberts are now available on audio cassette. *The Seth Audio Collection* consists of Seth sessions recorded by Jane's student, Rick Stack, during Jane's classes in Elmira, New York in the 1970s.

Volume I of *The Seth Audio Collection* consists of six (1-hour) cassettes plus a 34-page booklet of Seth transcripts. The majority of selections in Volume I have never been published in any form and represent the best of Seth's comments gleaned from over 120 Seth Class sessions.

Topics covered in Volume I include: creating your own reality — how to free yourself from limiting beliefs and create the life you want; dreams and out-of-body experiences; reincarnation and simultaneous time; connecting with your inner self; spontaneity — letting yourself go with your being; creating abundance; parallel (probable) universes and exploring other dimensions; spiritual healing, handling emotions, overcoming depression, and much more.

NEW SETH BOOKS — "THE EARLY SESSIONS" — BY JANE ROBERTS VOLUME I AND VOLUME II NOW AVAILABLE

The Early Sessions is the material given by Seth in the first 6 years of his relationship with Jane Roberts and her husband Robert Butts. It consists of the first 510 sessions dictated by Seth and it is anticipated that it will be published in 8 – 10 volumes. The majority of *The Early Sessions* material has never been published in any form. It contains great new material and insights from Seth on a vast array of topics.

FOR A FREE CATALOGUE including the most recent releases and a detailed description of *The Seth Audio Collection* and *The Early Sessions*, please send your request to the address below.

ORDER INFORMATION:

If you would like to order a copy of *The Seth Audio Collection* Volume I (Price $49.95), and/or a copy of the set of *The Early Sessions* Volumes I and II (Price $39.90 for a set of two books), please send your name and address, with a check or money order payable to New Awareness Network, Inc., plus shipping charges. New York residents add appropriate sales tax. Allow 2–3 weeks for delivery.

Shipping charges: US - $3.75 first item/$2.00 more for 2nd item
Canada - $6.00 first item/$2.00 more for 2nd item
Foreign orders - $14.00 first item/$8.00 for 2nd item

Mail to: NEW AWARENESS NETWORK, INC.
P.O. Box 192
Manhasset, New York 11030
(516) 869-9108 between 9:00–5:00 P.M. EST
http://www.Sethcenter.com

SETH NETWORK
INTERNATIONAL

Seth Network International (SNI) is a network of Seth/Jane Roberts readers from over 30 countries who meet to explore the ideas and share the excitement of the Seth material. SNI, a non-profit company, was established in 1992 to provide Seth readers with a meeting place, or forum, for gathering. Its primary purpose is to offer Seth readers a platform for expression and discussion.

SNI publishes a quarterly magazine, *Reality Change: The Global Seth Journal,* holds conferences and workshops each year, and offers a mail-order store filled with Seth/Jane Roberts books, tapes, art, and other products directly related to the Seth material.

You can find SNI on CompuServe (GONEWAGE), where an on-line conference is held weekly, and where you can peruse a library of Seth-related articles and follow ongoing discussions on the message board. On our World Wide Web home page you can peruse almost 100 screens of information on the latest happenings around the Seth material and SNI (http://www.efn.org/~sethweb).

For further information, please contact:

Seth Network International
Post Office Box 1620
Eugene, Oregon   97440 USA
Phone: (541) 683-0803   Fax: (541) 683-1084

The "Unknown" Reality. A Seth book in two volumes. In Volume One of *The "Unknown" Reality,* Seth initiates a journey in which it seems that the familiar is left behind. Where do the events of our lives begin or end? Where do we fit into them, individually and as members of the species? These questions, with Seth's explanations, are the heart of Volume One. In Volume Two of *The "Unknown" Reality,* Seth invites us to join in and discover the unknown reality for ourselves through a series of exercises geared to illuminate the inner structures upon which our exterior ones depend. Volume One provides the general background and information upon which the exercises and methods in Volume Two are based.

Dreams, "Evolution," and Value Fulfillment. A Seth book in two volumes. In Volume One of *Dreams, "Evolution," and Value Fulfillment,* Seth charts a conscious, self-aware universe that is constantly recreated by our own thoughts, dreams, and desires. He explains that humans are alive not only for the continuation of the species, but to add to the very quality of life itself. In Volume Two, Seth explains the links between reincarnation and genetics, showing how the human species keeps within its genetic bank millions of characteristics that might be needed in various contingencies, and expands upon his vision of a thoroughly animate universe.

The Way Toward Health. This was the last book ever dictated by Seth, and has never before been published. It is an in-depth examination of the miracle of life in a human body, woven through the poignant story of Jane's courageous attempt to understand why she had contracted the crippling condition that ultimately led to her death. Seth speaks about the mechanics of self-healing and the influence of the mind upon our physical health.

Amber-Allen Publishing is dedicated to bringing a message of love and inspiration to all who seek a higher purpose and meaning in life.

AMBER-ALLEN PUBLISHING
Post Office Box 6657
San Rafael, California 94903